In the
Company
of Actors

CAROLE ZUCKER

In the Company of Actors

REFLECTIONS ON THE
CRAFT OF ACTING

Foreword by Sir Richard Eyre

Theatre Arts Books/Routledge · New York

To the imagination, devotion and courage of actors,

'We can telegraph and telephone and wire pictures across the ocean; we can fly over it. But the way to the human being next to us is still as far away as the stars. The actor takes us on this way.'

MAX REINHARDT

Paperback edition published in North America in 2001 by
Routledge
29 West 35th Street
New York, NY 10001
www.routledge-ny.com

By arrangement with A&C Black

First edition originally published in 1999 by
A & C Black (Publishers) Limited
35 Bedford Row, London WC1R 4JH

ISBN 0–87830–109–7 (hb)
ISBN 0–87830–139–9 (pb)

CIP catalog data is available from the Library of Congress.

Typeset in 9.75pt on 12pt Photina by Florence Production Ltd, Stoodleigh, Devon
Printed and bound in the United Kingdom by Biddles Ltd, Guildford and Kings Lynn

Contents

Acknowledgements

There are many thanks to be given for a project as extensive as this. On the financial side, my gratitude to the Social Sciences and Humanities Research Council of Canada, the British Council (and specially Sarah Dawbarn), Christopher Jackson, Dean of the Faculty of Fine Arts at Concordia University, Jack Lightstone and the Office of Research Services, and the Concordia Aid to Scholarly Activities for their assistance during the four year duration of this project.

Much gratitude is owed to many people. First and foremost, to the actors who participated in this project, for the gift of their time, energy, emotional and intellectual generosity. I would especially like to thank Alan Bates, who spoke to me after a long day of shooting in Rome; Simon Callow, for providing not only intellectual but nutritional sustenance; Sir Nigel Hawthorne, Simon Callow, Ian Richardson and David Suchet for the donation of personal photos. Particular thanks to Janet Suzman for providing photos, and much more – a connection that was both comforting and stimulating. I would also like to thank the actors who participated in the project in a spirit of great benevolence, but whose interviews could not be included. Many thanks to the agents and their assistants who made this project move along. Appreciation to the staff of the British Film Institute, with special kudos to Ros Cranston. To Pippa Ailion, who I first met at Central School, for her gracious support in so many ways, as well as her enduring friendship. To Sir Richard Eyre for kindly writing the foreword to this book. To Eugenie Shinkle, my research assistant of ten years, who has used her miraculous powers to facilitate the genesis of two books, which could not have been completed without her resourcefulness and devotion. To Doreen Montgomery, my agent at Rupert Crew, for her incredible warmth, patience, sense of humour and hard work, and most of all for her never-ending encouragement. Finally, to my husband, Mario Falsetto, I quote Stanley Spencer's words to his wife, Hilda, 'My union with you is my union with the world'.

Foreword

Most actors are as reluctant to theorise about acting as cows are to theorise about veterinary science. As Robert Stephens said once: 'I have no great views about acting except this. Number One: if you are going to act be serious about it. Number Two: for God's sake speak properly.'

Actors are lucky – the talented ones that is – they get paid for doing what they enjoy. It's offstage and offscreen that they have a hard time: they're always being asked to account for themselves. Finding it difficult – if not impossible – to talk about how they approach their work, they find themselves talking about their lovers, their family, their holidays, their possessions and their pets, when all the time they want to imitate the dancer Pavlova when she was asked what she meant when she was dancing: 'If I could tell you,' she said, 'I wouldn't dance it.'

I don't know a good actor who is not intelligent, but an actor's intelligence is like a musician's, to do with timing, rhythm, hearing, sensibility, physical co-ordination rather than with cleverness and the ability to express ideas. Actors have more in common with spiritualist mediums than with dons, and the world of their work occupies a different universe to the articles of intellectual faith which underwrite university life.

Which makes it all the more surprising that Carole Zucker – a native New Yorker, who is a Professor of Cinema at a Canadian university – has compiled a book of interviews which is illuminating, informative and entertaining. She's a sympathetic and informed ear and a deft editor.

Acting is a mystery: in the medieval sense, it's a handicraft, and it's also something that's hard to understand. 'How do you learn your lines?' – actors are often asked by people eager to unlock the magic of how another human being transforms themselves into another. But, as Penelope Wilton says in this book, 'acting is a much more down-to-earth thing than people make out.' It's a pragmatic craft: the actor imitates other people, and has to retain a child's appetite for mimicry, for demanding attention, and above all for pretending to be someone else. And an actor has to see with a child's heart, innocent of judgement.

As adults we're all actors in that we simulate feelings we don't feel, we lie, we pretend to be what we aren't. It lures a lot of people to believe that they can do for their living what they've practised so much in life, but it's a tantalising paradox that what seems so familiar and attainable to us in life, should be so exasperatingly difficult to do onstage or screen; without talent, will, and character, it's impossible.

Acting embraces a number of paradoxes: you must be conscious of yourself, but not be self-conscious; you must know yourself, but also forget yourself; you must be selfless, but will undeniably be selfish; you must communicate but in somebody else's voice, and you must find the balance between the heart and the head, reason and instinct. Courage is essential to the good actor; in the bad it is mere folly. As Eileen Atkins says:

'you shouldn't be an actor unless you're willing to show everything that's in you – everything. I've been on stage stark naked and covered in shit, so I'm not somebody who's holding back . . . .'

To express anything an actor must have a technique. It may be latent, but it must be trained. The training will always be empirical, learning by doing, and adding to that by watching other actors, listening to them, copying them, stealing their tricks, and re-inventing them for yourself. 'You've got to find your own way', says Alan Bates, 'you've got to take from what makes sense to you, what's real to you, what applies to you, what works for you, and apply it to who you are.'

I really admire what actors do, not least because I can't do it myself. I particularly admire the actors in this book: I've worked with many of them and some of them are my friends. I was surprised, and occasionally ashamed, to find out how little I knew about some of them. I wasn't surprised – but saddened – to be reminded of the low esteem in which directors are held: most actors regard them as warily as they do their dentist. But it can't hurt for a director to be reminded that however much of themselves they invest in their work, for the actor and the audience there is only one question worth asking – as Judi Dench says:

'It all has to come down to the same thing: does it make you believe in that person; do you believe in that person?'

Sir Richard Eyre
London, 1999

Introduction

The desire for hearing and telling stories is universal and timeless. At base, all forms of art are a fulfilment of that need for storytelling. The theatre and cinema are equipped to convey stories in a magical and unique way because of their potential to synthesise the visual, literary and plastic arts. And it is mainly through the actor's participation that we gain access to the rite of storytelling. This is not to deny the achievements of playwrights, screenwriters, directors, designers and other members of the creative team engaged in crafting a play or film. But this book is born of a desire to focus our attention on the actor as a dynamic, imaginative and essential part of the creative process. The energies and accomplishments of actors are all too often regarded as non-creative. Actors are viewed, not least by themselves, as mere vessels or interpreters. There is someone – a writer, director or designer – with a more complete vision of the words and concepts they enact. Yet, who is better positioned than the actor to communicate the story of a play or film? And what better place to call upon actors to speak about their profession than in Britain and Ireland, where language has an unequalled splendour and pre-eminence. As Penelope Wilton says, 'The magic of the theatre is in the words, and the stories we tell. That is a living thing, and it has to be kept alive.'

What makes someone want to become an actor? Particularly a stage actor, who, in the words of Fiona Shaw has an 'incredible throw-away relationship to eternity'. Who would 'choose a way of life where you give your life's blood to concentrating and perfecting events that pass in a second, and only live in the memories of those people who are watching it?' How do we understand the actor's creativity, passion and devotion to a profession that is at least as difficult and demanding as it is rewarding? The primary impulse of this book is the desire to hear the actor's own story. It is my experience that their stories are as compelling and original, in their own particular way, as those of any fictional character.

This process began long ago for me, as a theatre-loving Anglophile raised in New York. My adolescent obsessions centred on Peter Brook's production of *Marat/Sade* and *A Midsummer Night's Dream*, Eileen Atkins, Beryl Reid and Coral Browne in *The Killing of Sister George*, Alan Bates in *Poor Richard*, Ian Holm and Paul Rogers in *The Homecoming*, Vivien Leigh and John Gielgud in *Ivanov*, Irene Worth in *Tiny Alice* – in short, anything that was British and came to Broadway. Most of the plays, I'm certain, surpassed my youthful understanding, but nonetheless, there was something about those performances that stirred me in an unforgettable way. Those feelings were consolidated on my first trip abroad at the age of 19, when I discovered theatre in London, and most memorably, saw Judi Dench in back-to-back performances of *The Winter's Tale* and *Twelfth Night* at the Aldwych. I was seized by the immediacy and inspiration that is generated by a profoundly gifted and masterful actor. This volume is a declaration that my youthful enthusiasm has not diminished but ripened with time, hopefully with the more seasoned and observant eye of experience.

My preparation for this book took several directions. First, to cultivate a first-hand knowledge about the various impulses that inform acting in the UK, I sat in on classes at a number of drama schools. I audited different types of classes – voice production, movement, scene study, characterisation – at LAMDA, the Central School, East 15, the Bristol Old Vic Theatre School, Guildhall and Manchester Metropolitan University. I spoke extensively with students, instructors and the director of each school about their experience and philosophy, as well as attending rehearsals and public student performances. Policy at RADA and the Drama Centre prohibits 'interlopers' in the classroom. However, Nicolas Barton, principal of RADA kindly lent me several tapes of scene-study classes, and I was able to audit classes at Central taught by former students of the Drama Centre. For me, as an educator and former acting student, this part of the research was edifying and exhilarating. I often found myself amazed by the talent and quality of the students' work. I would not have been surprised to see any of them the next evening in a professional production on the London stage. But it became equally clear that, as Janet Suzman says, '. . . with acting at its best . . . there's a kind of inner burn which can't be taught, and which a talented performer will have – where the detail with which you illuminate your character's life seems preordained and infinitely natural.' There is a consensus amongst the actors interviewed for this book that talent is an innate, unlearn-able commodity, and that it is technique – a crucial component of every good actor's ability to communicate – that is acquired through training.

   The next stage of my research was a somewhat delicate one. Which actors to include out of a seemingly limitless fund of superb performers? Sometimes I was guided by my long-time respect and allegiance to a particular performer. At other times, my choice was entirely spon-taneous and instinctual – I was enraptured by a performance in a play or a film, and felt compelled by my enthusiasm to learn more about a particular actor. This strategy came into play when I saw *A Doll's House* with Janet McTeer. It was what I call one of my 'great evenings of theatre' where one truly feels one has witnessed something important, fresh and even heroic; I felt I must meet this extraordinary woman. I spoke with many more actors than I was able to include in this volume. But in the end, it is my feeling that the actors represent a solid cross-section of backgrounds, techniques and styles.

   In order to prepare to speak with each actor, I viewed hundreds of hours of film, televi-sion series, mini-series, t.v. dramas, and filmed plays at the British Film Institute. In addition to the many, many live theatre performances I attended in London, Stratford, Bristol, Richmond, Dublin, Montreal and New York (when a performer opened a show or toured abroad) over a period of years, the B.F.I. experience gave me the opportunity to see a range of performances in a variety of media. I felt that in order to speak with an actor about his or her work with a modicum of authority and sensitivity, it was crucial to understand the breadth and scope of their career. The task was an entirely pleasurable one, leading to the discovery of many little gems, and a comprehension of hitherto unsuspected dimensions of a performer's capabilities.

   In conversation with actors, there was a consistent pattern to the questions, to focus and structure the book's content. The range of responses, however, is diverse, and provides a lively dialogue amongst the very different personalities of the participants. My talks with the actors – because of the highly individualised sensibilities of the participants – often diverged from the scripted text. The questions posed were divided into several main areas:

the social and cultural background of each actor; their training and early acting experience; their preparation for particular roles; ways to cope with 'actors' problems such as
difficulty in understanding a role, or 'creative differences' with other actors or directors; the
modulation of one's work for different media; issues of national character, i.e. what makes
British or Irish acting different to performance in other countries; classical acting vs. the
'method'; and the contemporary fissure between acting that is text-based and more spectacular forms of theatre. I found that my questions evolved as I was exposed not only to
different personalities, but as I experienced different types of theatre, film and television,
read more, and spent more time in England and Ireland. As Stephen Rea says, 'I believe
that you're only playing one part, and you're moving towards the ideal statement of that
part. You're finding out more and more about yourself, and you're finding out more and
more about everybody else while you're doing it.' That assertion could very well describe
my experience of meeting and talking with the vital, thoughtful and often charismatic people
represented in this book. My role as an author, while always connected to a personal sense
of identity and purpose, continually shifted as I was exposed to an assortment of beliefs,
temperaments and experiences. I feel extraordinarily privileged to have had access to the
stimulating and imaginative world of these actors; I hope the reader shares my feelings of
wonder and excitement in this adventure.

Carole Zucker
Montreal, Canada

Eileen Atkins

'... I never understood why people get into such a state about nudity. For God's sake, it's much, much more difficult and revealing, and incredible, to show your soul, and that's what you've got to be willing to do. Why anyone should want to be an actor, without being prepared to do that, I have no idea.'

Eileen Atkins was born in London in 1934. She debuted in London as Jacquenetta in *Love's Labour's Lost*, followed by repertory seasons, including several years with the RSC. Subsequently Atkins played the Queen in *Richard II*, Miranda in *The Tempest*, and Viola in *Twelfth Night* at the Old Vic. Her contemporary roles include *Semi-Detached* with Laurence Olivier, *Exit the King* with Alec Guinness, *The Cocktail Party* and *The Killing of Sister George* for which she won her first Evening Standard Best Actress Award, and which also marked her debut on the New York stage. Atkins won a Variety Club Award for her performance in *Vivat! Vivat! Regina*. Other London credits include *St. Joan* at the Old Vic and *Medea* at the Young Vic, and Nell in *Passion Play* for the RSC at the Aldwych. For the National Theatre, Atkins played Hesione in John Scheslinger's production of *Heartbreak House*, and leading roles in *Cymbeline* and Pinter's *Mountain Language* and Richard Eyre's productions of *The Night of the Iguana* and *John Gabriel Borkman*. She received an Olivier Award for Best Supporting Actress in Peter Hall's production of *The Winter's Tale*.

Atkins' one woman show *A Room of One's Own*, in which she appeared as Virginia Woolf, won the Drama Desk Award for Best Solo Performance and a special Citation from the New York Drama Critics Circle. The production played on tour in America, and the West End before it was recorded for Thames television. Atkins wrote *Vita and Virginia*, in which she once again portrayed Woolf. Atkins has appeared numerous times on the American stage, in *As You Like It*, *The Duchess of Malfi*, *Mary Barnes*, the title role in *Prin* and *Indiscretions* (*Les Parents Terribles*). She starred in the London production of *A Delicate Balance*, for which she won her second Evening Standard Best Actress Award. Atkins also won the Olivier Best Actress Award for her work in *The Unexpected Man*, which is due to transfer to Broadway.

Amongst numerous television credits, Atkins has played leading roles in *The Three Sisters*, *The Heiress*, *Sons and Lovers*, *Titus Andronicus*, *Smiley's People*, *The Lost Language of Cranes*, *The Maitlands* and *Cold Comfort Farm*. She acted the title roles in *Major Barbara*, *The Duchess of Malfi*, *Electra*, *The Lady from the Sea*, and *The Jean Rhys Woman*. Her film work includes: *The Dresser*, *Equus*, *Let Him Have It*, *Wolf*, *Jack and Sarah*, *The Avengers* and *Women Talking Dirty*. Atkins co-wrote *Upstairs, Downstairs* and *House of Elliot* with Jean Marsh, and the script for the film, *Mrs Dalloway*. She is a CBE.

I spoke with Eileen Atkins at her home in Chiswick in October, 1997.

East End beginnings

I was born in the East End, in the Clapton Salvation Army Home. We then moved to Tottenham, something called the White Hart Lane Estate, which is now one of the worst estates going for crime. It's pretty well the lowest form of living. Because I was the third child born in my family, we qualified for a council house. My father had been in service – hence, my writing *Upstairs, Downstairs* – and my mother didn't like the idea of marrying someone who was in service, so he got a job as a gas meter reader.

I went through a period of saying that I was treated badly as a child. I think that was because I got to know people from drama school later on, who had such different lives. But while it was happening – I have to say at this great age I am now – it probably wasn't that bad. We didn't have much money, and it did tend to run out towards the end of the week; there was endless worry about that. My mother was an extremely domineering woman and so am I, and I suppose that's why we clashed tremendously. But she was also the person who pushed us through. My mother and father couldn't have been more different. My father was Jack the lad; he wanted a good time, he loved the old-time music hall, and he used to get up at parties, and sing funny songs. Until I was about 8, I thought he was the funniest man in the world, and I adored him.

My mother didn't send me to school for ages; she wanted me around her. I was her darling. She was 46 when she had me, and she was just so thrilled to have a girl, she wouldn't let me go. I learned, very early on, to cry every time anything went wrong. The Blitz started and my mother thought it would do me good and take my mind off the bombs, to take dancing classes. So she sent me to a simply terrible dancing school. I kept crying every time I went, and finally she found another one where I used to lie about all the terrible things the girls did to me, because I didn't want to dance. Then I became sort of the star of the dancing school; I was a very good tap dancer. The woman who ran the dancing school couldn't have children, and tried to adopt me, my mother let her have me for a couple of weeks, I cried again, and was sent home. This woman did one wonderful thing for me, she said 'Well, if I can't have her, will you make sure that she's decently educated?' She found a little private school in Tottenham which was a simply divine place, with the most wonderful teachers; my life has been saved by school teachers. So my childhood was a very strange mixture.

From the age of 7, I tap danced in working men's clubs. Ordinary working men had clubs, where they'd drink and play cards, and have cabarets. People like Morecambe and Wise, a lot of our best comedians started out in those clubs. I find it slightly pornographic now, when I think about it, because clearly what they liked was seeing a little girl show her bum, and I used to sing incredibly sexy songs. I didn't know what they were about – I used to do the full thing (points and turns bum toward imaginary audience, points at face); I disliked doing it. And I used to fall asleep in school. I got fifteen shillings, which I was happy to see, and that was what Morecambe and Wise got, too. This was a huge help, of course, with family budgeting, and for my dancing classes – by then I was going to dance class four or five times a week. Everyone thought I would be a dancer; my father wanted me to be something called a 'Tiller Girl' which was a long chorus of girls who used to kick all the same. That's what my family's hope for me was.

This woman, who had taken an interest in me, paid two guineas a term for me to go to Latymer's in Edmonton, which was considered frightfully posh. It was one of the largest and most advanced ordinary schools in England. It was pretty frightening to go from a small school to such a big one – but again, wonderful teachers. By the time I got to 12, 13, I'd also been a professional in panto at Clapham and Kilburn, and I'd even spoken a few lines. My mother realised, when I got the lines in panto, that maybe I had a cockney accent. She would never have said that in so many words, but she did say, 'It would be better if you spoke really nicely'. Because none of my family would have admitted that they had accents – and they all had broad cockney accents. She sent me to the speech-training mistress, asking for private lessons, but it was too expensive for my family, so the idea was dropped.

Then this very bizarre man who used to take us for religious instruction, stopped me one day in the corridor, and said 'I hear you want to learn to speak properly', and I said 'Yes, but my mother can't afford it'. He said 'You come to me whenever I say, and do everything I say. And I will teach you.' I'd read the bible a couple of times in his class, and he'd got very interested in me. He taught me everything. Without him, I could never have moved out of what I came from. Slowly, I began to speak better. He introduced me to Shakespeare so painlessly that I've never had a worry about Shakespeare. He gave me a speech of Helena's he'd typed out, and said 'What do you think that's about?' And I said (cockney accent)'It's about some girl who can't get a boyfriend, in' it? And she thinks she's ugly, and things like that.' He said 'Anything else about it?', and I said, 'Well, it's funny, in' it? It's sort of poetry, but it isn't really poetry'. He said 'It's Shakespeare'.

We used to do terribly advanced work; Lee Strasberg's classes were nothing on this man's classes at my grammar school; he was way out advanced. Rather than do a play, twice a year he used to do something called a 'drama demonstration', where we used to improvise. There were two of us who were very naughty, we used to improvise terrible things. But I heard this teacher at one of those demonstrations say, to Aubrey Woods, who came back to the school as a grand actor, 'I don't know what to do about that kid; I think she's really talented but I know how hard it is in the theatre. She's not pretty, and I know that you need that if you're going to go in the theatre. It's terribly important'. And this actor said – I was about 14, 15 – 'No, she's not pretty, but she's sexy. I'd take a chance'. I thought 'Oh, I'm not pretty, but I'm sexy . . .' I used to be down at the chip shop every night trying to get boys; I was obsessed by boys, so it was no surprise to me, that I was sexy. It was strange, because even though I wasn't pretty, I never had a question about my looks, because I could get what I wanted most of the time. I had a lot of confidence like that. And then this teacher put me in for little competitions, and I started to win. My mother thought 'Oh, that's good, she's going to have a nice voice and be able to get parts in musicals.' And then he said to my parents 'She really should go to drama school'.

Now, they were pretty fed up that I was staying in school until I was 16, because my sister had left at 14, my brother at 15, and they were just about biting the bullet about me staying to 16 before earning money. The thought of going on for any further education was appalling to them, because I wouldn't be bringing any money in, and they certainly couldn't pay any money out! So this teacher came to an agreement with them that he would put me in for scholarships for one drama school, and if I didn't get the scholarship, he would arrange for me to do a teaching course at one of the other drama schools. I just missed the scholarship to RADA; the telegram to say I hadn't got it came on my sister's wedding day, and I ruined the wedding by sitting and howling throughout.

Drama school

He got me to Guildhall, on a teaching course. The minute I got there, I realised that nobody would question it if I went into the drama classes, so I enrolled for every drama class, and it wasn't until my third year there, when I was teaching one day a week, that they realised I should not have been doing all these drama classes. I was in three plays that year, and the principal had me in, and said 'Eileen, I'm terribly confused. You're down on the teaching course, you're gradually getting your teaching diploma, but you're in the plays.' And I said 'Well, yes, I've been doing both courses', and he said 'Good luck to you'. It's that kind of cheating you can't do now, which is a shame.

I doubt whether I learned anything much there. We had two hours a week when we had private lessons, one-to-one, with what we called professors. That's where I learnt anything. The last one I had was mad keen on T. S. Eliot, and I think I did practically the whole of T. S. Eliot with him. We learnt from just doing plays. The Guildhall School of Music and Drama was so to do with opera; opera came top, music was next, and we were the poor end of it. It's much better now, especially since they've moved to the Barbican. I learnt a bit of confidence there, though I was very taken aback by the other pupils at first. There was one chap there who was from my area, but everybody else was so rich! I had some terribly embarrassing, awful, humiliating things happen. I only had one set of clothes, I hadn't got the money to do things. All the same, I'm lucky to have the kind of personality that gets on, that isn't crushed by things on the whole, and lets a lot slide off my back. But it was hard. Guildhall was down in the basement of John Carpenter Street. I'm one of those people who's never looked very healthy, but I was grey by the time I left Guildhall, because I was doing two courses. I was utterly exhausted. The last year I had to teach one day a week, and I hated it. So I kept it quiet from my parents that there was no way I was going to be a teacher.

I taught something called 'Free Drama', it was a nightmare. It was the days when everybody thought that everything had to be frightfully free. It was the early '50s, and they were saying 'No desks', so you couldn't get the children sitting at desks. I remember endlessly saying to the children 'We're playing going to sleep now; I want you all to imagine you're asleep'. I don't believe in all that unstructured teaching. I only ever learned anything by people being pretty strict with me.

In those days you had something called matriculation when you were sixteen, and I'd come bottom in my form every year in the grammar school, because I was doing drama, and out with boys. It was only because this wonderful teacher said to me, 'I know you're intelligent, and you keep coming bottom. What's the matter with you?' I said 'Well, I find it so hard to concentrate. I look out the window, and my brain thinks of other things. I can't be bothered.' He said 'You come with me, and I'll show you what'll happen if you go on not bothering.' He took me to an absolutely huge typing pool, with all these girls, and he said 'This is where you'll be if you don't concentrate'. That's the only reason I did well, in the end. I shut up, and by the time I left, I was third or fourth in the class. But I would never have done it if people hadn't been strict, and said, 'Look, there are some things you just have to sit and learn! You can't expect to get everything in a lovely way'. I loved acting, so I worked my socks off at drama school.

I remember thinking a few years after I left drama school 'What did I learn there?', because people would say, 'Do you think it's worth going?' and I thought 'Well, I learned how to make up . . .' It was the private lessons that gave me a lot of confidence, and where you could express yourself. Whereas if you're always in classes, some people get pushed down. In mixed classes, the males tend to dominate. I know in rehearsals, still, men dominate. Not with somebody like me, now, because I'm old and I've got a bit of clout, but I can see the younger girls being pushed down. The one-to-one business was good, but I didn't learn anything about the theatre. I learned a lot about poetry, and I did a lot of plays, but I don't remember anything in the class that really struck home, nothing. And I didn't have any money to see things. The only theatre I saw was when they put on the notice board 'Drama students will be welcome at a dress rehearsal' or 'This show is now coming off, you can have a seat', so I remember seeing Paul Scofield in *Ring Round the Moon*, and *Waters of the Moon*, with Edith Evans. I only went to Saturday afternoon pictures as a kid. My only interest in cinema, which I still love, were old American musicals.

Starting out

I had a terrible time. Nobody got an agent. They used to say 'If you're a woman, give yourself eight years, and if after eight years you are not working steadily, give it up. Men, give yourself five years, and if you're not working steadily, give it up.' Well, I went nine years before I was working steadily. It took me so long to get going, hanging around for two seasons at Stratford. When I first went there, they wouldn't even allow me to understudy, I just went as the wife of my then-husband, Julian Glover. I really started to learn about acting at Stratford. I'd done a few seasons of weekly rep in dreadful places, and then I married Julian. We'd been in rep together in a holiday camp in Skegness, and we were both 21. Then he'd got a walk-on job at Stratford. I was always very sharp; I said to him 'Michael Redgrave's going to be the leading actor in Stratford this year. They'll want tall people so that he doesn't look too tall. You're tall; make sure you get an audition.' I think a lot of cockneys are canny, I just used to know where it was at. So he got into Stratford, and I'd given up by then; I'd had two terrible years, with only a few weeks of rep here and there, and I thought 'Well, I'll just go up and be a wife'. I gradually went up the scale at Stratford; I worked as an usherette, and then they asked me if I'd like to work on the postcard stand in the foyer, and I sold postcards of all the old actors, and answered questions about the theatre. I was so miserable, I so wanted to be backstage with the actors.

That season, suddenly, they'd lost about five people, and they were thinning in the ranks of the walk-ons because everybody had moved up. My husband heard they were going to take on some more extras for a crowd scene, and he went to Glen Byam Shaw and said 'Look, my wife's here with me, and she's dying to be in it', and he said 'Listen old chap, we just don't take people's wives, because you want', and my husband said 'I think she did an audition for you once'. He looked up my audition, and he said 'All right, she can come into the company, but she will not even be allowed to understudy. Okay?' I was allowed in the company. The thrill! I went in halfway through the season. And I'd only been there six weeks, and the girl who was playing Audrey in *As You Like It* – Dame Peggy Ashcroft was playing Rosalind – was taken to hospital for six weeks. Then *her* understudy was taken to hospital in the night with some kind of chest thing, she couldn't breathe. And I thought 'She's the understudy, who is going to play Audrey tomorrow night? What if she's not better?' So I stayed up all night and learned Audrey, and made sure I was in the theatre the next day, and they were all saying 'Oh my God, is there anyone who knows Audrey?' and I said 'Yes, I know it, I've played it'. I lied, and I went on as Audrey, and from then on they accepted me at Stratford. But you see, I was cunning.

The 'kitchen sink' period

We were going to sweep away the old thinking, the Binkie Beaumont, the tea-party, nicely dressed theatre; it was the beginning of 'kitchen sink drama'. The people who started to be famous when I left drama school were Albert Finney, Tom Courtenay, that was the group. It was very much the first of the new wave of *real*. I did a play at the time with Larry Olivier called *Semi-detached*. Oddly enough, it was one of his few failures, and I had a big success in it. He was just so generous to me. I know people say awful things about Larry, but I adored him. To me, he was the absolutely typical actor: wicked, two-faced, and a lot of other things, but he'd always give you a show. The first time I worked with him, I nearly fainted, I could hardly get through the morning's rehearsal. There was one point in that play with Larry where I had to go off-stage, run upstairs and come down, and make an entrance again. There were actual stairs, so that people could hear me running up the stairs and back. I had this moment, and I was always a tiny fraction of a second late on my entrance, and he said to me, 'Darling, why are you always late on that thing?' and I said 'Well, I'm running like mad, to get to the top and down'. He said 'Why are you going to the top of the stairs?' and I said 'Because that's what supposed to do, go to the top of the stairs.' He said 'Darling, you're off-stage. It's magic on stage, not reality, magic.' He said 'You just go halfway up the stairs.' That sounds a silly lesson, but I learned that total reality isn't necessarily what's total reality on stage. That's the art of acting half the time, making people think it's reality.

But if you do total reality on stage, mostly it doesn't work. A perfect example of that: when we were at Stratford, Albert Finney was in *Lear*. Everybody else – because they couldn't afford it – were in felt costumes. But because Albert Finney was Albert Finney, they gave him real leather. When I sat in the audience, his costume looked lousy and all the felt ones looked great. The felt ones looked like leather, and his looked like plastic. I get awfully bored, if someone says 'We're going to cook real sausages on stage'. That was very much my early plays; very much what I started to make a name doing, was in utterly realistic stuff.

I pretended to be from the Midlands for years, because that was the vogue, but again, that was just cunning of me. All the plays were coming from Midland and Northern writers. My husband was watching me in *The Duchess of Malfi* (for the BBC), because someone wanted to make a movie of it. I wandered in, looked at it, and said 'My God, I was gorgeous, why wasn't I a film star?' and left the room. I happened to say this to a friend, and she said 'Well, you know why you didn't get to be a film star, Eileen, it's because you played those endless washed-out Midlands and Northern women. That was your main diet when you were in your late 20s and early 30s, and that stopped you from being accepted. You didn't do the looks thing.' Anyway, I think I've had a far more interesting life than if I'd done movies. I mean, I've had a charmed life, so what the hell.

I still don't understand actors who want to be famous or make a lot of money. To me, the whole joy and plea-sure of acting – and it is a great joy and pleasure, with all its hard work – is to become, or to persuade people, that you are someone else. That is the pleasure, to enter someone else's persona, someone else's whole being, and persuade a lot of people that you are not who you are, you are someone else! That process is wildly exciting. Last night, I had the thrill of my life; Alec Guinness, who is an old friend, and who has been very good to me in my career indeed, came to see the play (*A Delicate Balance*) and he said 'Eileen, you were

Eileen Atkins in *The Duchess of Malfi* (1972)

marvellous. I could not see *you* at all'. That, to me, is it. I know that's not stardom, because stardom is people wanting to go and see what they expect, and getting it. That's a different thing; and some stars manage to be stars and still sink into their roles. There will always be wonderful actors . . .

When I was very young – I never know whether it's envy or jealousy – but I immediately could scout out who was going to be the opposition. Maggie Smith and I were both sacked when we were 20, from Assistant Stage Managing at Oxford rep. But I was aware, even then, from the tiny bits that I saw her do in university shows, that she was terribly talented, we were the same age, we looked rather alike, and I thought 'If ever you get going, that's going to be someone who's going to be very, very strong competition'. And let's face it, she's beaten me! Glenda Jackson and Maggie Smith and I were all after the same parts. Luckily, I thought that they were all wonderful, and I never minded giving in to someone I thought was terrific. I used to get very angry if I thought someone wasn't talented, and I didn't get the part. I used to say so, which wasn't very good. I was not very nice about some of the older ones. It took me ages to appreciate Peggy Ashcroft.

Acting lessons

The biggest things I've learned have always been from other actors. Not directors, but other actors. Peter O'Toole said to me very early on – I don't think it's quite true, but it had a big effect on me: 'You're either an actor who goes on the stage and says 'Love me', or you go on the stage and say 'Fuck you, this is what I'm playing, like it or not!' And I thought, 'Ooh, that's me. Fuck you. This is what I'm playing.'

The nearest I came to not doing a part – it was Ian McKellen who told me off about it – was when I was asked to do *Sons and Lovers* on the television, playing the mother. Now, that mother was so like my own mother, and I know that I'm so like my own mother – and there was a huge percentage of me that didn't like my mother. A huge percentage of me hates what's in me that is like my mother, and I knew I was going to have to pull out everything I knew about my mother and me. And I said no to it three times. Finally, Stewart Burge, the director, said, 'I just don't know why you keep saying no to this, Eileen. They all want you to do it.' And Ian McKellen said to me 'You're not doing it because you don't want to be your mother,' and I thought 'He's right. I'll do it.' But then I never wanted to play Saint Joan, because I thought 'Oh, God, I'm not even religious, I don't want to play her'. I'd seen it and always thought 'All that sickly praying and going on', but I was forced into that accidentally to help a dear friend who was opening a theatre. And that made me very religious for a while! It was weird, but I got in touch with something in me. By then I'd played Celia Copplestone in *The Cocktail Party*, and that had a terrific effect on me. I very nearly became a Catholic while that was going on, because I was working with Alec Guinness, who is a Catholic. He wasn't pushing me in any way, but he would lead me through, and he'd give me stuff to read while I was playing it that helped towards those feelings.

My now-husband – who's been married to me twenty years, and who's not an actor – says to me very early on when I do a play, 'I'd like to read the part so I can know who I'm going to be living with for a few months'. I find it irritating when people say 'Oh, you live the part'. You don't, it's not that you live the part, but certainly in rehearsals, you're having to endlessly go back inside: 'If I use that bit of me, I'm thinking like that, therefore, how will I react, or say that line?' I do one of the few exercises that people told me they learned in another drama school, which was to do your lines while doing very menial tasks, like cooking. It's a very useful thing to do, and so often when I'm cooking I go through lines. Then my husband will say something to me, and I'll answer him as the character, because that's what I'm fishing up at that moment. Once you're playing, the pressure isn't on quite so much; you probably aren't still thinking all day. By the time you've opened you've got your performance in some way, so you're not as bugged by it. But certainly, while I'm doing rehearsals, I am very effected.

All parts have some effect on me, all of them. Because of course – every actor will say this – you have everything in you. Each human being has every possibility in them, I would hope. And you mustn't accept a part if you really don't think you've got that in you. Any part you go into, you're going to fiddle about and pull out things that may be things you don't like very much. You've got a killer in you – everyone has somewhere; you've got a sexual being somewhere in you, and it depends, as an actor, on what you are willing to show. I think you've got to be willing to show everything, and that to me is what makes one actor better than the other. I've seen good actors actually stop themselves by not being willing to be ugly, or plain, or vicious. I've seen actors want to be nice. It's the worst thing about America. It's not an accident that for the nasty parts, on the whole, they use British actors! I don't know what that is; I suppose American actors want people to love them.

I often think that actors really shouldn't need psychoanalysts, or any kind of analysts; I think we're terribly lucky because we get to go through things legitimately, and get paid for it! We get to release things. Oddly enough, I think the most difficult thing to play, and I hardly ever attempt it, is farce, because you're not going through anything. It's technical. And if the other actors aren't all giving you what you want, it's the most miserable thing to play in the world. You're often happier playing something quite miserable, because it's cathartic. You feel great at the end of the evening, and people come round backstage and say 'Oh, God, what a terrible thing, what you've been through'. But you're released by having let something out.

But, strangely, I've never made a deliberate decision, I've always done the work, and the plays I like. It's very bizarre, because I'm not an intellectual in any way, shape, or form, and it took me long time – because I always felt lacking in brain – to know that I was even intelligent. But I have always had a very good nose for what is a good play. The only bad play that I've been in – which was a Jeffrey Archer – was the only deliberate choice I've made, and that was so I could work with Paul Scofield. We thought we'd all do it for a bit of fun.

Rehearsals

I will do almost anything if someone thinks that's the way to get the part. As you get older, it does get a little more difficult with directors. I had a lot of difficulty with the director for *Indiscretions*, in New York, Sean Matthias. I've known him a long time, really charming man. I talked to him before we started, and he said 'Look, Eileen, everyone wants you for this part, and I think you'd be terrific, but I have a method of working that I think you'll buck against'. I said 'Oh, God, are we going to play games?' He calls them exercises, I call them games. And I said 'Look, all right. If that's the way you work, that's the way you work. I think they're absolute rubbish, and do no good whatsoever, but if that's the way you work, and we've got six weeks, I will do it so that no other member of that cast will know that I think they're rubbish. I will do them full tilt, because you've been honest, and that's what we're going to do.' And I did! Those games do one thing, they make sure that everyone talks to everybody, that everybody knows each other's name, and that you all know that you're a group, and you should be pretty relaxed with each other by the time you act. But for my money, that should be a given before you start, that you always talk to everybody! The same thing would have been done getting there a quarter of an hour before rehearsal, and all having coffee together. To me, it was a thorough waste of time. It meant that I learned my part before I went into rehearsal, because I thought 'I'm not going to get enough rehearsal to learn it in rehearsal'. I think it's rubbish.

I watched Tony Sher on *Omnibus* with a highly regarded voice teacher, Cis Berry. But he did a speech where she made him keep changing chairs. It would be like 'To be (moves) or not to be (moves); that is the question'. I thought 'You're an intelligent man, Tony Sher. Why can't you look at the speech, know you need variation, work out where it is, and just think it through?' I don't understand why they need some of these exercises. Sometimes in Shakespeare, if it's all got bogged down and everybody's getting a bit speechy-speechy, and you don't quite know what they're saying, okay then, let's stop and say 'What's this scene really about?' Often, by the side of the classics, I write little modern things like 'Well, fuck you', as if that's what that means, really. But to me, that's homework! Or that's just a chat in rehearsal, like 'Here, though we've got all these words, I'm saying da-da-da-dum, and you're saying to me da-da-da-dum. Isn't that so? Or do you think something else?', and then you discuss it with the director.

Edward Albee said at one point, 'Oh, English actors can't feel any emotion until they've moved, and American actors can't move until they've felt an emotion.' It isn't true. There are many ways to skin a cat, and everybody has their own method of getting somewhere. There is no absolute, fail-safe method. I've seen people use all kinds of things and end up good or bad. The best actors for my money have been the ones that are pretty straightforward. Give me the blocking, work it out. You don't throw beanbags; you discuss a scene, but not endlessly go on and on. Some discussion, but every part and every play is different, and almost any method will work if you've got good actors. You will not get a good performance from bad actors. You can take them all through different methods, but finally, were the actors any good or not? That's what it's about. It won't make any difference to an actor who is really good what method you use to get him there. It just means that sometimes you do more work at home.

On the Method

Acting is about you being real to that character, in that situation, in that play. This is where Method acting goes wrong. The weird thing is, I've never come across it in America. The difference between American and British, is a barrier often put up that is not actually there. It's played up by both lots, but having done a lot of work in both countries, I find very little difference. I've done so many plays there, but I've only found extreme professionalism. And text acting. The reason I wanted to work in America was that I did feel that English actors were too head-based, and not gut-based, and they worked everything out; everything was beautifully done in the head. I often thought they didn't have the rest of the body, and I thought 'I'd like to learn to feel more of the whole'. We had a spill of some coffee on the stage the other night, and in character, I hope, I immediately said 'Claire, that was your fault, you made me do that', and Maggie (Smith) said 'Oh yeah, I would be blamed, wouldn't I?' And it was off and over, and we went back to the text, because we were being extremely professional. We knew we couldn't lean on the coffee, we wanted to make it look as if nobody knew it was out of text. It was an accident that we used and got rid of, because there's a brain telling you that you've got to get on with the play. Anthony Page kept on saying that Janet McTeer did different moves every night, and I said 'That was fine, she was the lead, everybody had to work around her. If you're going to have six of us doing what moves we want every night, you're going to have traffic jams, and the audience won't hear half the play'. There is a technique to acting as well. The best actors have the technique, and have massive feeling, which they are able to show, and the emotion is bound within that evening's play, and not about their own wanking! And it is wanking, a lot of the time: 'Oh, how do I feel, this will be terribly interesting'. It's nonsense.

People who are real Method actors don't do theatre much. You can do that in film. Wonderful on films, it gives some marvellous, offbeat things. Vanessa Redgrave does things off the top of her head, and I've worked for six months with her. Oddly enough, it's very easy to act with her, because she doesn't indulge. She doesn't affect you by what she does. If she's going to mess herself up – and I've seen her mess herself up on-stage – that's her own problem. What I can't forgive, is when they mess you, and the story, and the author up, because you should be serving the author, that's your first priority, to do what the author wrote. Not what you want to do. That's the interest: what did he mean, how did he want it? Most of them – Edward Albee's still alive – can't tell you half the time. They've written it down, but they can't tell you, so you've got to find it. I would be hard pressed to give you sensational stage actors that are totally bound up with what I call absolute Method acting. I loved it when somebody told me a story about Helen Mirren, and I believe I've heard the same story told about Marlon Brando – somebody said to them 'The understudy's on tonight', and they both said 'Oh, good, that'll be interesting'. That is different; I'm with that: 'Oh, I'm going to get something different thrown at me tonight, that I'll react to.'

One of the worst things I find about the few so-called Method actors – and I think most people get the Method wrong; I know there's Stanislavsky's Method, and there's Lee Strasberg's Method, and it's all very different – is that one of the things they do is hesitate a lot: 'Well, um, I think . . . uh . . . it would be a good idea, uh, if . . . we went out'. Certainly no British person would ever speak like that, and I don't know any Americans who speak like that. It's not real. You think, just occasionally, maybe some Mafia boss might speak like that, but my American friends speak, sometimes stop, sometimes hesitate because they don't know what they're going to say next, but they don't have all these grunts, and oohs and aahs. I think being real is much harder work than that, much deeper work, much less easy than 'Mmm aahh mmm rrrr'.

But to make out that there are two forms, and that some people go on and their priority is reacting, and somebody else's is text, I don't see that. They're both the same thing. You've got to react, whoever you are. Reacting is why one only wants to work with good actors; it's tennis, and you have to react to that ball coming back! And your eye's always got to be on what's coming back to you, and you have to react to that. It's unfortunate to do too much work at home, because the wardrobe doesn't react the same way as your fellow actor. That's the only reason for not learning too much at home. But all the same, a lot of time is wasted in rehearsal. The ideas of the Method, should be used by every actor. But it's natural, I don't see why you have to do all these exercises to get there. I can do improvisation – the 'airy-fairy nonsense' of imagined situations – I'm not very good at it, but I'll do it. But I don't see the use of it at all.

Whether it's classical or the latest, wildly modern, it all needs the same kind of acting. What I get very depressed about is all the kids coming out who can do one or the other – classical or modern. All it needs is that you can act. It connects with something else I get very upset about, which is, that they don't get rid of the accent now. It's considered not PC to get rid of your accent. If somebody had done that to me, all I would ever have played would be scrubbers. It seems to me utterly sensible, if you're going to act, to learn received pronunciation first, and make that your basic voice, because that's the one you're most likely to be asked to use. Now, if you go in only with a cockney accent, only with a northern accent, you might say to whoever is casting you (cockney accent): 'Oh, yer, I can do posh, yer, I do upper class . . .' It won't work! In their heads, you are as you present yourself. So what's happening is there are class distinctions again, and they've done it to themselves by being PC! It seems to me absolutely stupid. And you are getting two sets of actors now. There are some actors who are turns, they're not actors, they're revue artists, and that is a different kind of acting. You should be able to do anything! I played the most way-out stuff at the Royal Court when I was young, but swapped over to the classics as well.

On the necessity for imagination

You shouldn't be an actor unless you have a huge imagination; you shouldn't be an actor unless you're willing to show everything that's in you – everything. I've been on stage stark naked covered with shit, (in *Mary Barnes*) so I'm not somebody who's holding back, here. Much more important, I never understood why people get into such a state about nudity. For God's sake, it's much, much more difficult and revealing, and incredible, to show your soul, and that's what you've got to be willing to do. Why anyone should want to be an actor, without being prepared to do that, I have no idea. I don't understand the necessity to do exercises to stir the imagination. My imagination is so big I can't sleep at night anyway, I have to take a sleeping pill every night, and I have done for thirty-five years. When I was a child, my mother took me to a doctor and said 'This child doesn't sleep, she's driving us crazy'. He said 'She has too big an imagination'. Nowadays, I would be sent to a psychiatrist, I suppose.

People can never understand why I wouldn't be in *Upstairs, Downstairs*. They think it's snobbish of me. It's quite simple: it would have meant I was one character for four or five years. And once you get the character, the interest, as far as I'm concerned, starts to wane. I'd like to only ever do anything for three months, and then the interest is in trying someone else again. To play one character, not even to be famous, but a household name, seems to me utterly depressing. I can see when you're very young, if you get a series, then yes, take it, if that's going to pay the rent, and it makes everybody look at you and start casting you. But then the minute they start casting you, for goodness sake, try and get away from that, and say 'No! That isn't me, let me do something very different'.

I get bored quickly, although I have various outlets to stop me being bored. When I was very sick two years ago, I wouldn't let myself be bored. I immediately rang up the BBC and said 'Can I do Virginia Woolf's diaries on radio? I think I can manage that', and I had huge fun trawling through them. It's only through boredom that you're forced to use your imagination. I think we're killing off kids' imaginations, because they sit there pressing buttons. John Standing, who comes from a very posh family, was talking to me last night, 'Oh yes, I used to go down in the kitchen to practise circuses with the cook. We used to spin plates on things'. I said 'Oh, did you? I had circuses in my bedroom; I used to put poles between the beds, and of course I was the tightrope walker.' He said 'My kids would think I was mad if

I said to them to play games like that.' The minute boredom comes to me – and it does come – I fish around in the mind for something to do. I'm making myself sound rather goody-goody, but I suppose I find it boring if things are too easy. They sure haven't been easy the last few years! (laughs) It's not too bad to have a stick at your back, too, for work.

The Lost Language of Cranes

I was very intrigued by *The Lost Language of Cranes*. Sean Matthias had done the adaptation; he rang me up and asked if I would do it. And he said 'Eileen, I don't think you're going to want to play the woman,' and I said 'It's a wonderful part, I'd love to play it.' He said 'But Eileen, everybody's going to hate you,' and I said 'No they're not, Sean,' and then I got onto the set, and I think everyone who worked on it was gay, except me and Brian Cox, and the boy who played my son, and of course in the film, both of them were gay too. Every gay man there said 'You're going to be so disliked,' and I thought 'I simply don't understand what they're thinking. This woman is a rather marvellous woman; I don't often get to play someone as nice as this.' But it was because she had the scene with the boy when she got angry. That seemed to me the most natural and ordinary thing. It wasn't a very hard part to play, because I just thought of most women I knew, and what their first reaction would be. It might not be PC, but I know that any woman will have a shock when she first realises that her son is gay. She will. That might change, it'll be different in 15 or 20 years, because what people think changes all the time, and that'll be great, but you can't dislike the woman for living in her time. That was such a genuine and real script. The most difficult thing is to do something you feel is not real. So it came naturally to me. And then to find out your husband is gay as well, I think that's a natural feeling of terrible betrayal. Indeed, she accepts her son at the end, and her love for him comes through, which is also very real and natural. The reason you choose things is because they seem incredibly real to you, your mind immediately says 'This is real. This is how they would speak, this is how they would react, this isn't being done for any other reason'. I look as much as possible, in every single script for humour, and I'm happy to say I pulled it off even in *John Gabriel Borkman*! I only accepted that play to work with Vanessa Redgrave, Paul Scofield and Richard Eyre; all of whom I like very much. I hated the part when I first read it; I thought 'Oh, God, this is a nightmare of a bore of a woman, she's monstrous'. I said to Richard Eyre 'Can't I find any laughs?' and he said 'If you can find them . . .', and one did. But there is humour, even of a black kind, in nearly everything. I'm told *Lost Language of Cranes* – I only saw it at a private showing – collects laughs at some points. And that's fine too, because in the most terrible situations, things are funny. If you don't see the humour in human beings, then you're lost, you're going to have a very hard life.

Agnes in *A Delicate Balance*

A quick rundown of how I work on a part – I read it, decide whether I've got in me what I think that part has, and if I can pull it out. I say 'yes' or 'no', and don't look at it again until the first rehearsal, because I don't like doing a lot of work by myself. I want to hear what the director has to say, what the other actors are going to be doing, and I don't want to have too many set ideas, because I want to be able to move.

I memorised Agnes, because I was so frightened of letting Maggie Smith down. It was so difficult to learn, that I'm glad I did. But if you do learn before – Peter O'Toole learns everything before, and tried to persuade me to do that years ago – you are a bit more set in railway lines. You have come to some conclusions, because you've had to learn it. I'm glad I did it for Agnes, otherwise I honestly don't think I could have played the part. As it was, I dried in Edinburgh on the first night. It was much harder to learn than my one-woman show, *A Room of One's Own*. It's a little more difficult to undo when it's fixed in your head; you might have some rivetted, wrong ideas from learning it first. But even when you start learning in rehearsal, with others, you still, in the process of learning, rivet yourself into ideas you're going to have to undo anyway. That's Peter O'Toole's argument; he says you have to undo it anyway; you endlessly do something and undo it, do something and undo it. The thing that always annoys me most in a rehearsal is when an actor says to a director 'But, I'm doing what you told me to do yesterday and you've changed your mind'. Well, of course you change your mind; it's an endless form of change; it always becomes something else. You think 'Oh, I've got that, I see, now. I know I said that yesterday, but today it's changed.' So what you're doing has to be extremely malleable, and it becomes a little harder to undo, if you go in the first day with everything learned. Especially as we get older.

Albee is a nightmare to learn, I mean, just a nightmare! He doesn't speak in the way I'm sure most Americans speak! It is totally convoluted, and every word he uses is exactly the word you wouldn't normally use. One has to talk about the cat who's been killed. I have to say 'Well, what else could you have done, there was no meeting between you'. Now, that's a very bizarre word to choose. There was no 'meeting' between you? Albee's rhythm is very strange. You must pick up the author's rhythm, and any playwright who's any good has a very strong rhythm. So you have to work on text. I don't only work in rehearsals during the day. I get what's come up from the day, I go home at night, I do nothing else when I'm rehearsing. I don't go out, all I do is cook for myself or the two of us if my husband's in, and go over what I've done in a day. Have a break and do something silly, just to release the mind. Then I go over the text, what's happened in the day, and look back at the text. You endlessly go back to the text, because, in the end, that is what you're doing. You're doing the text, and you've got to make it live. It's a sort of tortuous but interesting process. Then you go back the next day, and try and do it, and by then the other actors have changed too, and you see what happens again. It's such a weird process. I personally think it's unteachable, I really do. I always think you can act or you can't act, and you will only learn from doing it, and you will only learn from doing it with the best.

You shouldn't have trouble with modern stuff, it should be natural to you. You should be taught to observe people. Most drama students are so in their own little world; I think it makes them more 'me-me-me' than they should be. You should be out with your eye on people: 'Ohh . . . an old woman in a bus by herself, upstairs smoking a fag. Oh, how interesting she did that.'

I always remember going to see Robert Stephens when he was married to Maggie Smith, and this is the kind of mind that an actor has. I'd gone to see Robert about something; Maggie said 'I'll go and make us some coffee'. She pulled the door, and she caught all four fingers

in it, it was very bad. And she stood at the door (mimes action of excruciating pain with no sounds coming out of her mouth). And Robert and I both sat and looked at her, and then we both got up and said 'My God', and rushed into the kitchen and put her hand under the tap. She had very swollen fingers, but she hadn't broken anything. Afterwards, Robert and I went back to talk, and we had both immediately thought 'How interesting. When you really hurt yourself like that, you're not screaming, you just open your mouth without making any sound. I must remember that.' That is the first thought of an actor; you should be observing all the time.

Agnes is very difficult because she's not a totally real character. How many women do you know who can start off with that long monologue? It's silly to call it anything else but a monologue, because Tobias, her husband, has hardly any lines at all. Normally, I would break down what he said. I didn't even do that this time. Most of my scripts are

Eileen Atkins in *A Delicate Balance* (1997)

marked with things, I'm always putting it into my own language, which is appalling, a lot of swear words. A lot of my script is marked: 'Come on, let's talk about Claire!' 'So what?' Things like that. So the thought is there, but then you have to make your voice say that language. I just find it interesting to try and make it work.

What drove me potty was that the director and everybody kept saying when we were on tour, that the play was failing, because I started it off so badly, and that was very hard for me. They would all come in to my dressing room, very pleased with themselves – I had four or five of them in there; two producers, a director, writer – and they'd all say 'Everything's fine, except it's on the ground when you start, Eileen, at the beginning'. In the end I was crying and saying 'Will you please stop telling me that I'm the one letting everybody down. I can't bear it any more'. I said to Albee one night 'You've written a boring opening. You tell me how to do it'. 'But it's just light', that's all Anthony (Page) would keep saying. I kept thinking, 'How can I be light with this dialogue?' It was very sweet, the other night, I had two drama students who had seen it on the second night, and they'd come back again to see it again the night before last. They didn't want autographs or anything, they said 'We've just come round to say it's been absolutely fascinating to see how your performance has already changed in two and a half weeks.' And of course the more I do it, the more I see, yes, you can be light. Anthony would say to me 'It should be like Noël Coward'. Well, of course it's not like Noël Coward, because Noël Coward has got very little underneath it, whereas this has got all this going on underneath it. It's just difficult to do, but I can't describe how one does it, except keep trying. On the whole you learn from repetition more than anything. When you know something inside, backside, outside, every which way, you can let your mind loose, and then you can fly on it, and you can just feel. Then you just speak. You don't get much help from directors on the whole. I mean, one or two have been wonderful. Richard Eyre was wonderful with me in *Night of the Iguana*, just wonderful.

The most difficult thing in the world is to speak as if you're doing it for the first time, as if you don't know what's around the corner. It's only possible if you know the text. One actor said they were doing their lines while swinging round a gym. Well, very few of us have got a gym, but I do things so that I can say the lines whatever's happening. But text first! Once you've got the text so that you're never worrying 'Oh, what do I say next?', you can begin to be real. Then, you can just say to yourself, and indeed the director, on the first night said, 'Right now, we all know it, we all know what we're doing. Now just listen to each other'. But you can't listen until you know it so well that whatever happens – coffee spilling – won't matter. Because I don't care what anybody says, if people are thinking 'Oh, what do I say next?', it comes out wrong because they're not feeling properly. You can't feel until you know. So the text has to come first; the text has to be a priority.

Somebody said the other day 'Oh, the play is dated, because it was written when people were frightened of the Bomb. Is that what he means?' Certainly at my age, and at the age all these people are, death is a pretty big terror. I doubt whether there's more than two days go by that I don't think about it. That is quite a big terror, but even for young people, there is 'the terror'. If you really think about it, what is this where we are? What the hell is this existence that we're in? I can terrorise myself; I can look up at night sometimes, at the stars, and look at infinity, and be terrorised. I can see that someone like Agnes knows that if you think like that every day, madness is upon you. So you've got to drive away madness. And to have her best friend come in the house – and say they've come to stay because they've suddenly become frightened – she starts to know that there is a terror, it exists. Of course, we're in Virginia Woolf-land now. So Agnes, quite rightly, is trying to keep the equilibrium. Even Virginia Woolf, who did go mad, said 'The doctor told me to have a mutton chop, and my goodness, it worked. I felt better after I'd eaten a mutton chop'. Now Agnes knows that you must eat the mutton chop, and then maybe you won't think about the terror, and the terror's not going to do you any good anyway, so she is trying to keep everybody calm. That's because I'm playing her at the moment. If I was playing one of the other cast, I'd be feeling differently. I think Agnes is rather sensible, and doing the right thing. When people say 'I don't understand what the terror and plague are that make her want to get everybody out of the house.' Well, I think, to have two people in the house who are looking into the abyss every day, would affect anybody, and I think she's quite right to get them out. But that's me. I know when I first saw it, I thought it was pretentious. But it's always the same, when you're in it, and you think about it, it's a very brilliant play. It's like T.S. Eliot and Beckett. It doesn't only speak to the '60s and to Americans. It's universal, and that's why it's a classic, and why it's so brilliant.

Alan Bates

'You just have to keep yourself very free, very loose so that something can happen, even if it's not what happened the night before, even if it's not what you thought would happen. Something must remain alive and flexible . . ..'

Alan Bates was born in Derbyshire in 1934. He was amongst the first actors to perform with the English Stage Company at the Royal Court Theatre, creating the role of Cliff in John Osborne's *Look Back in Anger*. Bates starred in Pinter's *The Caretaker* on stage in London and New York, and duplicated his role in the film version. He received the Clarence Derwent Award for his performance as Edmund in *Long Day's Journey Into Night* by Eugene O'Neill. The actor has appeared in Arnold Wesker's *Four Seasons*, Lindsay Anderson's productions of David Storey's *In Celebration* (which was also filmed) and *Life Class*. Bates played the title role in *Hamlet*, first in Nottingham, then in London. He starred in *The Taming of the Shrew* at Stratford, and Pinter's production of Simon Gray's *Butley* in both London and New York. For this performance, Bates received the Evening Standard Award as Best Actor, and the Tony Award on Broadway. The actor's association with Gray continued with starring roles in *Otherwise Engaged, Melon* and *Life Support*. Other key performances have been in *The Seagull*, Osborne's *A Patriot For Me, The Dance of Death, Ivanov, Much Ado About Nothing, The Master Builder* and Turgenev's *Fortune's Fool*. Bates also performed in a one-man show at the Edinburgh Festival entitled *A Muse of Fire*.

His film career started with *The Entertainer*, and includes *Whistle Down the Wind, A Kind of Loving, Nothing But The Best, The Caretaker, Zorba The Greek, Georgie Girl, King of Hearts, Far From The Madding Crowd, The Fixer, Women in Love, The Go Between, A Day in the Death of Joe Egg* and *The Three Sisters*. Bates has also appeared in *An Unmarried Woman, The Rose, Nijinsky, Quartet, Duet for One, Prayer for the Dying, Pack of Lies, We Think the World of You, Mr. Frost, Dr. M., Hamlet, Secret Friends* by Dennis Potter, Sam Shepard's *Silent Tongue, The Grotesque, Nicholas' Gift* and *Varya*.

Alan Bates has had a varied television career as well, including Pinter's *The Collection*, Arthur Miller's *A Memory of Two Mondays*, Simon Gray's *Plaintiffs and Defendants* and *Unnatural Pursuits, The Mayor of Casterbridge*, John Mortimer's *Voyage Round My Father, Separate Tables*, Alan Bennett's *An Englishman Abroad* (for which he won a BAFTA Best Actor Award) and *102 Boulevard Haussmann*, Dickens' *Hard Times* and *Oliver's Travels*, Alan Bates was awarded an O.B.E. in 1995.

I spoke with Alan Bates in Rome, where he was filming *Nicholas' Gift*, in December, 1997.

Derbyshire

What would I call myself? Middle class, I suppose. I don't quite know what all these denominations and categorisations mean. I was a child in the war years, so I just remember the strictness, the rations. It was a very simple life, really, that I lived. My father was a cellist and my mother was a pianist, and they were both very fine players, and had a huge love of music, so I grew up in a house where music was played and heard a great deal. That was a subtle influence of some kind, I'm sure. My brothers and I all resisted – as children wilfully and sometimes wrongly do – to follow them into it, but then my brothers were both rather gifted artistically. One is a painter now, and an art lecturer. My other brother began in art direction but gave it up, and I became an actor. We almost deliberately did something else, which sounds a bit perverse. I suppose it's not; if that's what we wanted to do. Hopefully, people in life do what they either want to do, or are good at.

As a child, I listened to the radio. My mother, when I was 9 or 10, started taking me to the local theatre, and I started going to the local cinema. I became infatuated; I *had* to go every week. I realised, about the age of 11, that the reason I was going was that I'd found out what I wanted to do, and what I thought I could do. I admired certain films, and certain actors. I wanted to be *me*, I didn't want to be them, but I think actors do influence you. I will always remember James Mason, from the day I started going to see films, as absolutely, one of the finest movie actors perhaps who's ever been. He somehow resonated with me. And I think, later, in my teens, I was influenced by all sorts of people: Gerard Phillipe, and then a bit later on, Mastroianni, and Swedish actors, and American actors like Spencer Tracy and Montgomery Clift, and others. You don't want to be like them, but you like what they do, so therefore they are, to some extent, influencing you.

My parents supported my decision to become an actor. They filled me with all the warnings, you know. They said 'If you haven't done it by the time you're 26, then think about stopping', but they were basically very encouraging. My father got me into a class with a marvellous voice teacher, and my mother got me into the local Shakespeare society, so they both took a very positive stand towards me doing what I wanted to do.

RADA

I applied for RADA, just that one place, and got it. I don't think I knew about the others. And I got it because of a brilliant teacher in Derbyshire, called Claude Gibson, who was absolutely terrific. He really knew how to get hold of somebody with talent, and draw something out of you, he knew that you had to learn how to speak first. He got you to really articulate, to breathe properly. I went really quite prepared for RADA, from this great teacher.

I was there in the last years of a wonderful character called Sir Kenneth Barnes, who was really at the end of his powers. He was running the place, and he was the brother of two famous actresses – Irene and Violet Vanbrugh, which is why the theatre at RADA is called the Vanbrugh Theatre. It was very technically based; it was based on diction, on movement. The teachers were varying degrees of good and not so good. Clifford Turner was a wonderful teacher. He wrote a great book on voice, which is a classic. So we did have some very good people. There was a highly competitive feeling to it, which was quite good training, although not really what drama schools are meant to be about. For the wrong reasons, perhaps, it got you quite used to the rat race. I mean, there was a rat race right there, or the beginnings of one, anyway: trying to get into the public show, trying to get jobs. You were a little bit aware of the favourites. I wasn't one to start, but I became one of them. I really knew both sides of that; I knew what it was like to be just a student, and then suddenly I was chosen for something and did it well. And you could just feel the change in the attention of the teachers if that spotlight suddenly falls on you a bit. When you've got a hundred people there, training, some are bound to stand out. Perhaps it's inevitable.

It was a terrifically good year; I don't think they've really had a year like it. I don't quite know how it happened, but you will know a lot of these names: Richard Briers, John Vernon, Brian Bedford, John Stride, Albert Finney, Peter Bowles, Peter O'Toole, Roy Kinnear, myself, Keith Baxter, Rosemary Leach, James Booth; it was really quite astonishing. And we were always competing with each other perhaps without knowing it. It was a real great clutch of people.

The outside world: talent and luck

But of course the world outside was waiting, was ready, and we fell into the theatre just as it was coming into a very powerful time with a lot of astonishing young writers – Wesker, Osborne and Pinter. People like Joan Littlewood at Stratford East and George Devine at the Royal Court Theatre. So they were there to grab us, you know. It was a very lucky time, quite apart from however good we all were, or not, or whatever has happened to all of us. Whatever we actually were, we were also lucky. Of course you've got to be able to do it, you can't just be lucky.

At the beginning of my career, I took what job I could get, which was with the Midland Theatre Company, and it happened to be Frank Dunlop who was running it. I went into a company that he was directing in Coventry, which was a very, very strong and well-thought-of company. In a way, I was slightly better off, because if you went to Stratford, you walked on, you were the crowd, you might have a line or two, then you would graduate. It could take years, if Stratford got hold of you in those days. They would keep you for a very long time before they let you begin to emerge. In the other companies, like Liverpool, Birmingham, Coventry, Bristol, Nottingham or Dundee, all these places, you went and played big parts, or at least parts with substance, if not big ones. But friends who got into Stratford weren't learning anything by experience. They were learning by apprentising, but they weren't actually *functioning* as well as you were if you were in one of the other regional theatres. Even at the National, in much later days, it took you a long time to get what Olivier once said to somebody, was his 'turn', which is an awful phrase, really: your 'turn'. I suppose, practically speaking, that's what it amounts to.

Another pure bit of luck was the Royal Court. For me, that was better than going to Stratford and waiting five years to get a speaking part. At the Midland Theatre Company, in the middle of my contract, I heard about the Royal Court from a wonderful actress called Sheila Ballantyne. She said 'You really ought to go and audition for it', which I did, and got in. I didn't really know what I was going into. It was London, it was a step further on; I'd not heard of this new theatre which was to be a writers' theatre. I went in to it quite innocently, but I got in. And then three or four of us auditioned for this part in *Look Back in Anger*, quite soon after getting there. I think it was the third or fourth production, and I got the part of Cliff, so the luck really followed me through the end of RADA, into Frank Dunlop's season, and then into the Royal Court, with *Look Back in Anger.* That's the sort of thing where people say, 'I should be so lucky'. I was following a path. I can't describe it to you; it was intuition, and I suppose, being aware of opportunities and taking them, and it was very much to do with me, the actor. I became aware of where I was when I got there, what it was all about, and considered myself very fortunate.

The American actors – like Brando and Montgomery Clift – were a huge influence; they were very much admired. I would think that the individuals that came out of the Method, what James Dean and Julie Harris, and others were doing, were all powerful images, beautiful work to go and watch. European films were very much admired, too, in those days. And also, of course, our own older actors; the whole range of people such as Olivier, and Ralph Richardson, Michael Redgrave. We had various pools of influence to respond to. And of course it was all discussed, everything was always discussed.

Inspiration and technique: crawling up to a role

It's very hard to explain. Acting is inexplicable, so we're having a very weird conversation to start with, because I cannot really tell you what it's all about. You've got to find your own way, you've got to take from what makes sense to you, what's real to you, what applies to you, what works for you, and apply it to who you are. You can't just suddenly be a Method actor, except that I think all good actors are. It's such a personal thing; if you're good you're good, you know. You work through these things, you're not made by these things. You fall down as an actor, if you're not good. We all take a part, or a moment, or a time in our lives where it all comes together and we go beyond our average accomplishments. When you're lucky, you go beyond yourself; you get a bit of inspiration, or a meeting of yourself and the part. I don't think it's got anything to do with any particular training. It has to do with what you've drawn from everybody; it's hanging onto your own instincts, rather than being too influenced by someone else.

I once went as an observer to the Actors Studio, and I watched a girl get up and do a piece – it was the first time she'd done anything there – and it was marvellous. And Lee Strasberg said 'That was absolutely terrific; do you know what you were doing?' And she said 'No', and I thought 'Please, Mr Strasberg, don't say anything else. She mustn't know. She must find out; don't tell her what she's doing, she must find out herself. Give her a lot more class work, give her a lot more space, give her a lot more stuff to do, but don't tell her what she's doing, especially if she doesn't know, because that would spoil it.' I'm afraid I get very nervous when people move in on people who are doing something good. You trust your instincts, you trust your responses, you trust your imagination. I mean, you have to be free. There are actors who are not, who haven't found a way to be free and daring, to follow their instincts fully. For that you need what in the old days would be called technique.

I always think: how do you do a performance eight nights a week? You can't really get to the same depth of feeling every night, so you have to have a way of doing it, and I think you have to trust the fact that once you have found something, even if you don't feel it the next time, you have *been* there, and you will be convincing to an audience. Representing someone else is convincing yourself sufficiently that you are in someone else's shoes, to convince people watching you that you're in that person's shoes.

I do believe in going into a part. I think in a lot of older traditions of English acting, there's a style of acting where people go straight for it; they have an image of the part, and they never change it. They come in at the first reading with the part, and that's it, and then they get stuck and they can't change it even if they want to. I mean, for some people, that works. But I like to let the part creep up on me, just take it on slowly with thought. I've fallen into that trap a couple of times in my life, because sometimes you can see a part so clearly that you go straight for it, you know *exactly* how it should be, and you go for it, and what you haven't done is you haven't crawled up to it. You've taken a shot at it, and you've probably landed on target, but it's not as interesting as it would have been if you'd really allowed yourself to creep up to it. Maybe that's my version of Method. I don't know. I'm not trying to hit it too soon, or to convince the director that he's cast it well, or whatever is motivating it. It's usually because you can see it; you know how it should be. I rather like parts where you crawl around them for a bit, and you start selecting. Sometimes you don't feel the change in yourself, but it's happening, because you're doing it so slowly. Whereas if you shoot straight for a part, you feel the change, but it might not be as deep as it could be.

There really are no rules. I remember Celia Johnson, when I did *Hamlet*, she played Gertrude, and the director suddenly said, which wasn't the cleverest remark, 'I don't think it's moving enough'. She looked rather annoyed, and said 'Oh, really?' and she said 'Shall we do it again?' and he said 'Yes, I think I'd like to do it again'. So she started the scene and everyone fell silent, and just became hypnotised by what she was doing, and completely moved and involved with her. She came to the end of the scene, and she said suddenly, 'Do you mean like that?' She was really saying 'If you want me to, I could do it, and I will do it, and I can do it any way you want.' There aren't any rules about this thing. You can do it like that, or you can do it like Celia Johnson, you can do it like Gerard Depardieu, you know.

You should give of yourself as much as you can every time you do something. I think eight performances a week are killers, really. Singers don't do that, violinists don't do that, pianists don't do that, dancers don't do that; only we do it, I don't know why. I don't know why we think we can. I know we always have, for probably hundreds of years, but it's odd, isn't it? It is madness, really. You should do an evening, but not a matinée on the same day. It's part of an actor's psychology, five o'clock comes, and you start preparing for the evening performance, even if you've been doing it for six months. You start preparing for it, and it's often exciting. You give yourself a whole day, you conserve your energy, you make sure you have some food, or not, depending on what your metabolism happens to be. You just give yourself to the thing. You just have to keep yourself very free, very loose so that something can happen, even if it's not what happened the night before, even if it's not what you thought would happen. Something must remain alive and flexible; and you have to develop technique for that. You have to have a way of speaking and moving, and you have to be able to rely on what you've decided to do with a certain scene, and at the same time, keep it fresh.

Staying open: 'no decisions'

I do my own version of improvisation, to myself. I think most actors do these things. I've always liked acting, but I certainly haven't been good in everything I've done. You can always go further, I think, there's always more to find out, there's always more to give a part, you can't ever rest with it, and say 'Oh well, that's it'. I don't think I've ever hit a moment where I've ever been over satisfied. I've been pleased with some of my work, and disappointed, at times, when I haven't taken it as far, where two years later you think 'Oh, I wish I could do that again, because I can see something now that I couldn't see then'.

Sometimes you know you've met the part, you know that you're right, you know you're in tune, and really onto the centre of the part. You know it sometimes – unfortunately not all that often. You have to work quite hard, even when you're excited about it, and can see how it should be, to find your own way to it. You don't always succeed. But I don't ever feel I've dried up, and if I have wanted to rest, I've rested. I don't think you should go staggering out of the theatre.

When you read a script that you want to do, then you understand what the main emotions are that you've got to follow. I think that's part of knowing you want to do it. I worked with a director called Richard Wilson, who directed a Simon Gray play, which I did quite recently in Chichester, and he was terrific. He used to say 'Right, no decisions. I want no decisions from anyone for days'. And he would suddenly stop in the middle of a rehearsal, and say 'Sorry, you've made a decision, and we're not ready for it. Stay open, stay open'. And suddenly it all begins to come together; if you stay like that for ten days, suddenly it all begins, suddenly it becomes very clear where you have to go. It takes a lot of nerve to do that. More and more it bothers me not to have enough rehearsal. You've really got to have time to come to grips with something, and to get on top of it. There's nothing worse than chasing yourself.

Don't learn a script for the stage, unless you've only got five days or something before you go. Occasionally I've learned half of it, or chunks of it, because there's just so much dialogue, and so little rehearsal time. It's always fatal when you know it all, because you're absolutely stuck in it. But you know the Noël Coward thing: he wanted everybody word perfect on the first day. Maybe that suited him. I don't know, I haven't done a Noël Coward play directed by Noël Coward – in fact, I haven't done a Noël Coward play. But I would say, make sure you have enough rehearsal, and learn as you go.

On directors

I think the best gift a director has is what the actor brings to a part. But I think it is up to the director to control the part, and to understand it, and to be able to tell him where to go and where to withdraw. Sometimes an actor touches something, and doesn't know he's touched it, and he has to know that he has. I have taken a couple of parts where I haven't quite seen where they ought to go, because I've liked the project, or the script, or the director or something, and I haven't felt right about the part. I think you should know where you want to go with a part. You should have a fairly clear vision of it before you take it on. And of course, if you find yourself floundering, you've got to go to your director.

But you can ask only some for help. Certainly not all. There are some directors you meet – Robert Markowitz (*Nicholas' Gift*, 1997) is one of them – and you just feel a complete sympathy; he's got an understanding of each separate actor, and each actor's way of working. He can see when someone's nervous or whether they're confident; he's brilliant with the children. Lindsay Anderson was a wonderful director with actors, because he liked them. I think a lot of directors don't like actors. A lot of directors assume that because they're the director, they've got to be the one that knows everything, whereas they haven't. They've got to be the leader, yes, but they have to be open. I love a director who will actually pick up an idea from a cameraman or an actor and say, 'Hey, I hadn't thought of that, that's wonderful'. That's a director, not someone who ignores everyone else's ideas.

It's very hard sometimes when there's conflict, because I don't think you can act unless you've shared it with your colleagues. Unless you look at them and listen to them, you're not really doing a part; you're not portraying life. There's a famous quote from Michael Chekhov, who said 'There are three kinds of actors. There's the actor who acts for himself, there's the actor who acts for the audience, and the actor who acts for the other actors. The actor who acts for the other actors is the only one who's an actor.' He said 'The one who acts for the audience is at least doing it for someone, and the one who's doing it for himself is not an actor.' Sometimes you just have to stick it out. Sometimes you're dealing with very, very fundamental things in people; it's not a question of giving them notes or asking them if they mind doing it a different way, or rethinking it, it's nothing to do with that. It's so fundamental you can't change it; they're not there to be changed.

Remarkable writers and outrageous characters

When I was first sent *The Caretaker*, my agent didn't want me to do it, and he said 'I can't understand a word of it, and you've been offered something on television'. He said 'The choice is obvious; you can't do a piece of nonsense at the Arts Theatre for six pounds a week.' And I said to him 'I couldn't tell you what this play is about, but I know it's wonderful.' And I found out what it was about – well, what it was 'about'. When Harold (Pinter) says it's about three men, it is about three men in a room. But you don't have to know cause and effect in order for that to be a remarkable piece of writing. You just understand three rather isolated people in life, and understand their need to belong, and to find some kind of purpose. I find them all very moving characters, those three. I understand them, I know who they are.

Mick is a fantasist. He's got a fantasy of the life he wants to lead, and a place in which he wants to do it. His brother is disturbed, he's been given a lobotomy. Mick is instinctively, hugely protective of his lobotomised brother, which means loyalty, in this case. And because he's a protector of his brother, if you like, he's jealous of the Donald Pleasance character; he doesn't like him. I understood all of that instinctively, I didn't need to have anything more specific than that.

You could go to town with *Butley*, he's a complete extrovert, he's wonderfully written. Marvellously witty, wonderfully funny and dreadful at the same time. I mean, it is a gift to be asked to play that character. Again, you have to remain truthful. You can be excessive, you can go too far with anything as long as you're being truthful. But in that, you really can go with it,

Robert Shaw, Alan Bates and Donald Pleasance in *The Caretaker* (1964)

because he was performing within life, and those characters are fun to play.

But then so are people like Guy Burgess (in *A Gentleman Abroad*); he's a real-life character who is also fun to play, because he's larger than life; he's excessive; he's deliberately outrageous. They're not dissimilar at all. Diaghalev is different, but then, it was not, I think, a wonderful film (*Nijinsky*), but it was very interesting and entertaining; I thought it was a very watchable film. I think it should have really been called Diaghalev, and been about Diaghalev, and Nijinksy should have been one of the wonderful moments in his life. Diahghalev's great, you just read about him and you think 'This is one of the great visionaries of the century'.

The value of research

I do research until I feel that there's no room for me; until I feel that I've been almost locked out of it by other people's opinions, say, about Diaghalev. In the end you've got to be him yourself, you've got to find him for you. There's a point at which you really have to know when to cut off, when you know enough to play him truthfully, and bring yourself to it as well. I think I can probably read too much sometimes, because you can pick up opinions, and start playing someone else's idea rather than giving your own interpretation.

I loved playing Marcel Proust (in *102 Boulevard Haussmann*). I knew that I wasn't anything like him, but I felt that I understood that moment in his life, and that particular script. You get the odd critic who starts a review saying 'Now, Alan Bates as Marcel Proust simply will not do', and you think 'Oh, come on'. It's somebody who thinks they know everything, and isn't prepared to just let someone else feel the man out themselves. It's a beautiful piece, isn't it? I think the whole thing was quite gentle and subtle and particular.

Working on stage and in film

I've always said it's the same. I mean, it's a different dimension, different vocal range, different sense of projection, different way of projecting. But you've got to be truthful, you've got to know what you're doing. I think film is wonderful in its ability to pick out slices of life, and when you go between the two – theatre and film – you do have to be very careful that you're not bringing one into the other, that you're not being too subtle for the theatre, or too big for the screen. My views about it are very simplistic, really.

What is great film acting? Well I just know some people who've done it. For example, I've seen ten films of Mastroianni, and I suddenly thought 'I believe this man every time, every single time', and that's true of Mason, and I think Depardieu's terrific. Great film acting is about simplicity, absolute truth, and trusting yourself. Basically, you're asking me what *fine* acting is, and I don't think it matters what medium it's in. In film, it's knowing where that camera is and then forgetting where it is. Monroe is said to have never known where it was; that was probably half her success. You hear stories like that, they're appealing; whether they're true or not.

I used to go to dailies, but then I found I became self-conscious. I started acting for the camera, and I don't like to do that. As I say, I think you have to know exactly where the camera is, and then forget where it is. It's kind of a sixth sense. But if you've seen a bad angle, or something that you thought was too little or too much – I think I've got to a point now where I trust either myself or the director to catch it. And you have to have an idea of how to play a reaction shot. Robert (Markowitz) was wonderful; within three days, he said 'Oh, I love what you did when you rehearsed that. We'll shoot it like that'. So I was rather pleased that he liked what I'd done. Then he said 'Action', and he came up to me, and we both said it together, *at the same moment 'Too much'*. Because he'd liked it, I went slightly too far with it. But that's lovely, when you have that with a director, when you know and he knows.

I think I made a conscious decision not to do some of the things I was asked to in Hollywood. I didn't want to be trapped there. I didn't want to feel that I couldn't get out, or that I wasn't a free agent as an actor. I did work there once, for *The Rose*, and I worked in New York, and all my other American films have been made in Europe. But that was always working on location; I don't care where it is, the great thing is to work on location.

I felt like I did in the very early days when I first left RADA, and Rank was still going. It was in the days when those contracts were just ending, thank god, but I knew that a seven year contract with anyone was a disaster. Because there's no choice, and you have no control, and I never wanted that; I always wanted to be a free agent and to work in every medium, and to be as selective as I knew how. But I did make a conscious decision. I certainly could have stayed in Hollywood after *The Rose*, and earlier, and I didn't.

I think fame – film fame is sort of false fame. What do I mean by false fame? I mean phoney fame, hyped-up fame. I like recognition for what I do. I like to be well-paid when they can afford to pay me well, but I don't really like fame as such. But if people stop you in the street, it means they have seen what you do, and you can't be an actor without wanting an audience. It's quite nice, unless you're in a very bad mood.

Playing with Shakespeare

Just occasionally it really works when you jazz up Shakespeare, occasionally it really comes off. I think you've got to let people do all that; people have to be free. You've got to see new stuff, you've got to see experimental ideas, you've got to. Theatre would die without them. But I'm also very torn, I'm sort of schizophrenic about it. I fall back, and I think 'I really want to see *Richard III*, I want to see it in his century, I want to see it played out then', because I find that's what's exciting about it. I can apply it, you can apply it, it means something to us. I'm very torn about it. I enjoyed Ian McKellen's *Richard III* when I saw it in the theatre, I thought it was pretty exciting.

But I don't think it altogether negates an interpretation, because even if something wasn't intended by a playwright – it may be there. People can get much too clever, and then it becomes just a personal agenda for some directors. You say 'Well, this isn't actually telling me anything, except what he thinks, or she thinks, and I really want to know what the author thinks. I don't want you to interpret the author to a stage where you obliterate or distort that.'

I'm very torn when people do the life of Wordsworth or Tchaikovsky, or whoever it might happen to be, and you think, 'No, tell the truth,' because the truth of these people's lives is what you've set out to do, and it's usually a phenomenal story. Why change it? Why act it, why distort it, why put something in that wasn't there? Let's have that person, otherwise do another story. If you've got a better idea, do another one, do something else.

The current state of British Theatre

It seems to me either the writer's a god or the designer's a god, or the director's a god. The actor often comes fourth in all this. I mean, a design can kill a production. A design that enhances a play, that highlights it, is wonderful, but one that is just there for its own sake, and does not inform you of something . . . what is the point of design for design's sake? I was in a production recently where the designer designed these huge doors. A friend of mine came to it, and he said 'You could hardly open them; they swung you into the room'. He said 'They didn't tell me anything, they didn't inform me of anything; it's a designer's conceit. I don't want that.' I mean, I understand about theatricality. But when you have to time your lines in order to cope with the set, something is wrong. I've been in a production like that, where you had to time your lines to get across the set. You're not doing the play, are you?

I think there is a huge drop in what people want to see. I wish I knew the actual reason. I mean, you can point to a hundred things. Is it education that's dropped? Standards of education, standards of appreciation, or just the hype of the easy and the popular that has taken over. On the other hand, you know, plays are failing, audiences dropping, it's harder and

Alan Bates in *102 Boulevard Haussmann* (1991)

harder to have a play stay on for more than two months or three months. I can have a great night at one of these musicals, but by the time I get out to the street afterwards, I've forgotten what I've seen. It doesn't stay with me at all, it doesn't resonate, it doesn't give you anything. You remember perhaps some pyrotechnical stage management, or perhaps a voice, or a song appeals to you whether it's wonderful music or not; you can enjoy a song that isn't necessarily a great piece of music. But I don't think you can be too elitist about this.

The era of the musical is certainly here, at the moment. I loved *Les Misérables;* I took my two sons to see it when they were about fourteen, and we had a wonderful afternoon. I think there are different contexts in which you can see things, and enjoy them. But you're not seeing anything that really stays with you. What stays with you from that is that it's a great story, great characters and great writing. That's something that pushes through; it has a core. It makes you think. Perhaps people did have higher standards before. There's an awful lot of what's called dumbing down going on today, certainly in the cinema. You look at some of these things and you say 'What is that doing for anybody? What's it giving, really? Okay, this is sort of fun, but it's not taking people on any sort of interesting journey.' You watch it for a rest!

The job of acting

I think there is a whole side of acting . . . I mean, what's so special? I think it's an important job; I hope it is – because I do it – it brings a bit of fun, entertainment, illumination, whatever you happen to be doing, into people's lives. You are there to entertain, and for people to have either a thoughtful or a good night out. It reflects the lives we lead, hopefully it 'holds the mirror up to nature'. So therefore it's got a significant purpose.

But at the same time, people do some incredible things in medicine, they do huge explorative things in space, nurses nursing the sick, teachers teaching the next generation, hopefully! We're not better than that. I think you just have to keep a perspective on it, and not really believe the sort of hype that goes with, I think, the West End or Hollywood. You can't be taken in by it. You just do your job well, you hope. I think everything else that might come with it, like superstardom, if you get it, or being an icon, or a legend . . . you can't go for that. That happens – if it happens, and if it doesn't then you're a working performer, a working actor. It's just trying to keep things in perspective, and the whole thing of not believing your own publicity. I mean, it's the big mistake, isn't it? The Americans do sell their top people, and an awful lot of money goes into selling them in that way. We don't do that, we haven't got a big enough machine to do it. The few English people that's happened to – Sean Connery for example – have done it in America, he hasn't done it here. I think it's how much money is put into it. What do you have to do, what do you have to make? What happens to just spin into orbit? If you're in it, you're in it, and if you're not, you're not.

You may have heard Judi Dench say she's a jobbing actor; you've also heard Marlon Brando say this isn't a job for a grown-up man. Isn't that a different way of saying the same thing? Actually, it is a little different, because I think he's belittling it; here's an extraordinary, unique, great actor saying 'What am I doing?' But I think it's healthy to question what you do, and to say 'Well, it's just a job I do, and I'm lucky to be doing it'. Although I must say, I think English actors are not beyond being knocked out by themselves.

Something in me says it's a little bit more than *just* a job. It's a job, but it's a very visible job, performance. It's a job that needs an audience, which sets it a bit apart. Most jobs don't need an audience. So I think performing is a bit different, and sport is the same. If you're George Best, if you're Vanessa May, or John Curry, or Pavarotti, there's only one of you, you know? And it's public, and for an audience – that sets it apart.

Identifying with a part: emotional effect

I don't know whether the parts I've played have affected who I am or how I live, but I know when I did *The Mayor of Casterbridge*, I had a huge identification with that, identification, sympathy, empathy, whatever is appropriate. Someone who made a hideous mistake in his life, couldn't recover from it, went through parental love, love of wife, rejection of wife, love of someone else, obsession with a protégé, ambition. It's the human condition, it's a fantastic story of how we can't fulfil the ideals we set up, or be this wonderful thing we want to be, or some ideas that youth gives you, and I thought 'This is really wonderful'. How he ends up at the end of his life saying 'I don't want anyone to know I was ever here. Just bury me and don't mark the grave'. I found that whole beginning and coming to that end, so moving. Because we all fail, somewhere, none of us are heroes, really. And I think that really said it.

Simon Callow

'. . . that's what the theatre is about: enabling you to identify the meaning in your life, if not the meaning of life itself.'

Simon Callow was born in London in 1949. Callow made his London debut in a fringe production of *Schippel*. His theatre work includes *The Resistible Rise of Arturo Ui*, the title role in Adrian Noble's production of *Titus Andronicus* at the Bristol Old Vic, *Mary Barnes* at the Royal Court, David Hare's production of *Total Eclipse*, Edward Bond's *Restoration*, *The Relapse*, *Melancholy Jacques*, *Kiss of the Spiderwoman*, *The Importance of Being Oscar* and *Chimes at Midnight*. For the National Theatre, Callow has played the title role in *Amadeus*, Orlando in *As You Like It*, Stafford in Alan Ayckborn's *Sisterly Feeling*, and Face in *The Alchemist*, which originated at the Birmingham Rep. He has also directed a number of productions, amongst them *The Infernal Machine*, *Cosi Fan Tutte*, *Single Spies* (co-directed with Alan Bennett for the National), *Shirley Valentine*, *Die Fledermaus*, *Carmen Jones* (for which he won an Olivier Award for Best Director of a Musical), *The Destiny of Me*, *Les Enfants du Paradis* for the RSC, Snoo Wilson's *HRH* and *The Pajama Game*.

Callow's film career includes four films with Merchant/Ivory: *A Room with a View*, *Maurice*, *Mr and Mrs Bridge* and *Jefferson in Paris*. He has also appeared in *The Good Father*, *Postcards from the Edge*, *Four Weddings and a Funeral*, *Purcell*, *Woman in White*, *Bedrooms and Hallways*, *Shakespeare in Love*, *The Scarlet Tunic* and *Junk*. He has been seen on television as Napolean in *Man of Destiny*, in *La Ronde*, as Molière in *All the World's A Stage*, as Mr Micawber in *David Copperfield*, in *Cariani and The Courtesan*, John Mortimer's *The Trials of Oz* and in *Femme Fatale*. Callow also directed a BBC documentary on the career of Charles Laughton. He is the author of books on the theatre, performance, and biographies of Laughton and Orson Welles, as well as a memoir.

I spoke with Simon Callow on several occasions in November, 1997, in London.

Childhood

My story is a bit complicated. I was born in South London, Streatham, and went to an ordinary sort of primary school, and then my mother became a school secretary, and I spent nearly two years at a very eccentric private school. The school was in the country, near Reading in Berkshire, in a very idyllic country setting, in an old house. An eccentric man called Roland Birch and his mother ran a school for Spanish students, who were about to go to English universities. There was also education provided subsidiarily, but it was very informal, so I got my education mostly from the headmaster's mother. That was a curious interlude in my life, and it was there that I heard my first play, which was on the radio. I heard *Macbeth* on the knees of Mrs Birch, and it evoked something extraordinary for me, that I fell in love with, at about age seven.

My parents separated, and I was then sent to boarding school in Guildford, and spent about a year there, until the alimony ran out. It was a Catholic public school, and I *got God* very deeply, and founded religious societies and things like that, and wanted to be a priest, and had some sort of extraordinary, visionary seizure, where I wanted to grab the host from the tabernacle. Anybody who is brought up as a Catholic will realise quite how blasphemous and wicked that is. I couldn't find the key, annoyingly, so I was prevented from mortal sin. Then, my father most unexpectedly invited my mother and me to go to Africa where he lived. So I went to Africa, and was in a secondary school in Fort Jameson, which is a tiny, tiny place, and then to school in Lusaka. Again, as the alimony lasted, I was sent to public school in Capetown, South Africa, a rather formidable Jesuit college. I lasted for about a year there and then I returned to England, after staying in Africa for three years. I then went to the London Oratory Grammar School, now famous because Tony Blair's son is a student there, and lived again in South London with my mother. Then I went to university.

The impulse to become an actor didn't strike me until very, very late. It didn't really seem at all conceivable until I went to work at the Old Vic, which was after I'd left school. Up until then, I had entertained various ambitions, among them being a lawyer, a diplomat, and a television personality, all of which had an aspect of performing, which I hadn't quite realised at the time. I had a rather unusual school experience in that there was no school drama in the London Oratory School at that time, so apart from the organisation which I founded myself, called the Literary and Debating Society in which we read plays – we did *Pygmalion*, I read Higgins; *Waiting for Godot*, I read Pozzo; *Under Milk Wood*, and I read Captain Cat – that was really the only school drama that we had. There was no sort of 'conduit', as it were, for any thespian talents I might have had.

I remember going to movies in Africa, but we weren't a particularly movie-going family. There was television, which was a novelty when I came back from Africa in 1961; that was the first time I'd seen television. I became besotted with television for a while, then I turned against it. But then BBC2 was invented, and suddenly one started to see the great horror films, I fell in love with those. I had seen and been overwhelmed by Laurence Olivier's film of *Richard III* and Sir Charles Laughton's film of *The Hunchback of Notre Dame*. Those two performances had rather stuck in my mind, and somewhere there must have lurked, in the back of my head, a notion that I could perhaps do something like that. But there was no possible way, within my circles, that you could become an actor. Nobody that I knew had become an actor, nor did I have any sense of the steps you would take. The idea of going to drama school seemed impossible; it seemed beyond one's ken. I had a sort of distaste for the idea of amateur theatricals; I was rather fastidious about that, because I had started to go to the theatre in London a lot on my own.

I went to the Old Vic a lot in the '60s, before Laurence Olivier ran it, and then after. I saw things like Tyrone Guthrie's production of *The Alchemist*, Michael Elliot's production of *The Merchant of Venice*. Everybody knew that the Old Vic was a bit ropy, unfortunately, in those days. It was underfunded and the standards were not very high. Michael Elliot, the man who created the Royal Exchange Theatre, was a director of some genius, and some of his productions were quite impressive. Somehow the energy had rather gone out of the Old Vic by that time, and I started to go to the West End to see rather remarkable actors like Ralph Richardson, and John Gielgud, and so on. But it was Laurence Olivier who was synonymous with acting in my mind. The experience of seeing him on stage was quite overwhelming in a way that's very hard to explain to anybody who hasn't seen him. To see him as *Othello*, Edgar in *The Dance of Death*, actually, later too, as James Tyrone in *Long Day's Journey*, was to experience a blast of sensuous energy, vocal and physical virtuosity, which I think it is perfectly true to say, for better or for worse, has never been seen on the English stage, or any stage, before or since.

I didn't ever get turned off by Sir Laurence, as some did, because I also loved what I thought he stood for. His creation of the National Theatre was an heroic event, which I've written a book about. The idea of him as the *leader* of the company, acting and leading from the stage, was very exciting to me, and I would have loved to have been part of that group of people who worked with him. It was that that finally made me really want to act. I hadn't been able to make the leap of imagination until I got to a theatre and was around actors, and I thought maybe I could be one.

Becoming an actor

I went to Queens University in Belfast, but partly, again, because I just couldn't quite get this idea about drama school. I was only twenty when I went to university, but, funnily enough, I already felt too old. I listened to those ancestral voices which said 'You have to get a degree, otherwise you won't be able to survive in the world', and my mother was terribly, terribly keen on the idea, desperate because she'd had a rather truncated education herself, and she wanted me to succeed. In my heart, I went there just to act in the Drama Society. The great revelation, the blinding Damascene revelation, when I stood on stage, pretty well for the first time, in *The Seagull*, playing Trigorin, was how absolutely god-awful bad I was! I didn't know what the *hell* I was doing.

I just thought 'This is terrible!' I had, by then, a very extensive experience of very good acting. So I knew how bad mine was. So I left university, went back to working in the box office of the Aldwych Theatre, and the Mermaid Theatre, which gave me a considerable background in the realities of theatrical life. At the Mermaid I worked in all sorts of capacities for Sir Bernard Miles. The Mermaid was an extraordinary venture, an unusual kind of rough theatre, exactly the opposite of the Vic, but very interesting.

By the time I arrived at drama school, I knew that I had much to learn, and I was terribly unsure about whether I had the talent or not. I was very blocked in all kinds of ways, personally, but I did know a lot about the theatre. I knew a bit about life, too, it seems to me. I'd been in Belfast when the hostilities broke out again, and all of that. I set myself a tremendously tough sort of programme, which was to say that if the Drama Centre found that I wasn't really an actor, then I would not be an actor, and I had to find some other method of salvation. But I never doubted that acting was going to be, or needed to be, a method of salvation. I never thought of it as just a job.

Drama school, Stanislavsky and Strasberg

I decided upon the Drama Centre because it was the only school that was clear and bold enough to cut through the shit. Because I was full of shit, but I was very plausible. And that was the thing that I wanted to be saved from. I was a brilliant facsimile of a simulacrum of a human being; it was a good performance of being an amusing, witty, sophisticated slightly quirky person. I knew that that way lay madness, because it was a sort of cage of personality that really trapped me. What I sensed from the Drama Centre's prospectus was that they were going to brook no flannel. And I was exactly right. That was one of the two or three very good instincts I've had in my life. One was to leave university because I needed to avoid tricks, or audience-pleasing tactics, and to actually get to the heart of the matter. The second was to go the Drama Centre, because I think that any other drama school would have only buffed up and polished the undeniable gifts that I had. As I say, I was very plausible, both as an actor and as a person, but completely phoney.

One hasn't fully experienced the Drama Centre, unless you've seen Christopher Fettes (the Drama Centre director) or Yat Malmgren at work, because they are very, very unusual people, pedagogically and temperamentally. Within the English theatrical establishment, they are complete outsiders, and completely other. But that's what's so wonderful about them.

Basically the Drama Centre takes on board the familiar divide between Strasberg and Stella Adler – which is much better documented in America than in England – which is an acknowledgement that Strasberg's interpretation of Stanislavsky stopped at the nursery level, and insisted on the primacy, above all, of emotional reality. The Drama Centre taught us all of that, so we started with the ABC of the Stanislavsky system, which was a tremendously good thing for any training actor to go through. But then it took us to the more elaborate and sophisticated variants that Stanislavsky himself never ceased to discover.

I have personal feelings about Stanislavsky, the human being, whom I regard as a somewhat comic figure. A rather charmingly naïve person, which is probably what made him, in some ways, a great explorer, but also a very odd figure. It's very interesting to me that Stanislavsky was regarded by his contemporaries – and particularly by Nemerovich-Danchenko – as a man without instincts, and a man who was possibly over-cerebral, but who paradoxically was also dyslexic, and had a very poor relationship to text. Nemerovich used to go mad with Stanislavsky's paraphrasing. He did not regard the text as the central point. That's very helpful of course, it means that he found his primacy somewhere else, in lived experience, or whatever. But sometimes, it would have nothing at all to do with the text. What we know from the voluminous correspondence of Chekhov, is that Chekhov thought that Stanislavsky had fundamentally misunderstood his plays, totally missed the point. Nemerovich and Stanislavsky didn't talk for the last thirty years of their lives, running that theatre together, because Nemerovich thought Stanislavsky was a barbarian, who had no understanding of the written word. Nemerovich himself was a playwright, and a highly literate man, and a very interesting director as well. I'm not being so simple-minded as to say that Stanislavsky was a bad man, and what he said isn't true. On the contrary, I think he did an invaluable service by thinking longer and harder about acting than anybody had ever done before. The conclusions he came to are, I think, very often not accurate, nor should they be treated as a bible, but as another point of view, an interesting line of thinking that he opened up.

Where I find Stanislavsky off base is that he regards the actor's absolute worst nightmare as self-consciousness. He insists on that. But most actors feel extremely unselfconscious when they stand onstage. Stanislavsky had a personal problem in that regard, so an awful lot of Stanislavsky's work, to do with the closed circle of attention and all that, is devoted obsessively towards the idea of making you forget that you're on a stage in front of an audience. It's not actually very liberating at all, and it results in a kind of inwardness, a sort of narcissism in acting, which doesn't allow you to become very expressive, or release very much. Obviously actors, when they're in that small circle, feel great. But what's coming out is not necessarily coming across to the audience.

Acting is a part of communication. Interestingly, Stanislavsky himself – especially when he started working in opera – became more and more aware of that. He actually distanced himself from some of his early work. But Strasberg was trapped in that early work. It's rather in the same way that some people like Reich, for example, regarded Freud as having *betrayed* his early work, but he was more Freudian than Freud. So Strasberg thought himself more Stanislavskian than Stanislavsky. Strasberg was quite a complex man, too. From a lot of the evidence, he was a very destructive man, very self-motivated, and a personally venomous man. If you read the history of the Group Theater, the great beating, marvellous heart was Clurman, with his wonderful intelligence. I rather unpleasantly compare them to Lenin and Stalin, but I think that's maybe a little unfair, because Lenin was quite a dictator too. Anyway, enough of world history.

The Drama Centre functions in a much more culturally broad context than Strasberg ever did. The Drama Centre is absolutely placed within a context of two thousand years of dramatic history. Because there's such a fascination with the classics, and classical form, there's no sense of the narrowing down of the focus, that you get with Strasberg. Strasberg's work is sublimely suited to soap operas. The best soap opera performances are absolutely, authentically Strasbergian performances, because they're all to do with emotional exposure, and reality and crisis. Unending emotional crisis. They're never to do with ideas; they're never to do with language; they're never to do with form.

I think that one of the most important aspects of an actor's work on him or herself is to develop a relationship to words, and to their implications. And I think I have come increasingly to believe, the older I get, that the most important part of an actor's equipment is his brain, his mind, and that it is the responsiveness of your mind to a text – or indeed, to a situation – your ability to engage it, to see it, that will create the emotion. David Hare tells a good story about Kate Nelligan in *Plenty*, when she goes around the concentration camps, and one of her fellow actors says to her 'What do you evoke to get that wonderful emotion that you get?' and she says 'I just think about the concentration camps'.

The requirement of acting is that you exercise your back muscles, your emotional capacities, your sensuous capacities, your intellectual capacities; you become an extraordinarily apt conduit for whatever you're going to pass through your system. It is the possibility of using yourself, of expanding yourself. And it wasn't a question of the rather mechanical way in which I believe Lee Strasberg uses the concept of substitution, that you just look for something that turns you on emotionally and slap it onto the situation. It's a more general sense of the training of an actor: identify what stirs you, what moves you. When I speak as I am now, about acting, which is a matter that excites me, my voice changes, my body changes,

I become extremely animated. If I talk about money, it is a subject which I cannot understand at all, at any level whatever. But if I were playing a financier, if I were playing Shylock, I would need to understand how that feels, to talk about money like Shylock. But I wouldn't substitute for the words concerning money, words concerning acting, as something that excites me. I care passsionately about food; food means as much to me as money does to old Shylock. But I wouldn't use my feelings about food to get into Shylock's mind. Instead, I need to explore my own feelings about money, and engage with them, amplify them, bring up the temperature on them. There are times when I have loved money, there are things for which I could use money that would make me love it very much. Thus I would hope to enter into Shylock's romance for money. If I mentally substituted my own feelings for food as Shylock every time I thought about money, I wouldn't be engaging in the scene as written, which is the most important thing for me. It would be like a musician saying, the first theme of the first movement of Mozart's Jupiter is not very exciting to me. While I'm playing, I shall think of a tune that I do like; in that way I shall play it with real feeling. This is a kind of mental gymnastics that can only impede the direct communication of the character and the scene. One must always make connections. But not, in a reductionist sense; it's a way of opening up avenues of thinking. One should never be looking at theatre just as a cultural artifact, but as an active thing. One is always pushing further and further into, maybe, the strangeness of it, the complexity of it, but always connecting. Not academic, and not purely theatrical, in other words, not just *theatre truths*.

There is a slightly Teutonic dimension to the Drama Centre. I think their standpoint, basically, is a rather Nietzschean one, 'what doesn't kill you makes you stronger'. Their philosophy is that acting and the theatre are unbelievably tough areas, tough internally and tough externally. It's very hard to make a living when you're in the theatre; there are incredible obstacles and problems on personal, financial and organisational levels. Also, you're dealing with yourself, with your own inner life, appetites, needs, hopes, dreams and memories. You need to be able to have strong and clear access to them, and to be able to repeat them incessantly, and not exhaust the basic store that's there. Therefore, I think that they deliberately create a climate in which people have to toughen up. It's like their idea of a kind of thespian Marines. But if you just look at the list of people who've come from the Drama Centre – Frances de la Tour, Penelope Wilton, Tara Fitzgerald, Helen McCrory, Colin Firth, Pierce Brosnan – we're very different people, very different kinds of actors, not embattled, embittered, paranoid people; we've survived it.

It's also true that in my time at the Drama Centre, people went by the wayside a lot. It is my personal belief, and you may regard it as heartless and brutal of me, that that was a very necessary thing, for them to discover – and for the school – that these students should go. It would be exactly the same if you were a pianist. If your ambition is to be a concert pianist, you need to have not just fingers of steel, but nerves of steel, a brain, an absolutely indestructible mind, and, at the same time, you have to be infinitely sensitive. At the heart of the Drama Centre is an extraordinary idealism towards the idea of the actor and theatre in society, which is that it's an absolutely indispensable part of society's dealings with its own soul, and it's as necessary to life as food or sex. That the theatre is utterly central. It's a religious idea, basically, that if you let theatre go out of your life, you're a diminished person, and that in many ways you'll never be able to come to terms with yourself.

I'm afraid I am completely formed by my Catholic upbringing, though I am, in terms of formal religion, agnostic, I have indeed rebelled strongly against the Roman Catholic church and it's wicked ways. I nonetheless do need to believe in a life with purpose. I've not found that in political terms, because I've found that almost every political movement I've ever been involved with is fundamentally corrupted by its relationship to power. It is a need in me, to believe that I'm doing something important, that needs to be done. To me, nothing could be more important than people's fundamental sense of the meaning of their lives, because a life without meaning is not a human life at all, in my view. Many people manage perfectly well without meaning, it seems. They get their pleasure out of their senses, and that's fine for them. Of all psychoanalysts, psychotherapists, the one that strikes me most of all is the one who just died, Victor Frankl, who created something called logotherapy. He was a survivor of the concentration camps; he was a Freudian originally, but he postulated an entire discipline on the question of meaning; it's also called existential psychotherapy. As long as people find meaning in their lives, their neuroses will either be containable, or perhaps disappear. And that's what the theatre is about: enabling you to identify the meaning in your life, if not the meaning of life itself.

At the Drama Centre, we learned to use objectives and obstacles, activities, and interactions when looking at a text. I think it's something that you always come back to. Always, because there's no question but that drama is action. It's action, that's all it is; it's always things being done in order to get something else. But I hope it's become really grounded in me as second nature, so that when I hit a real problem, and I can't make any sense about why am I saying this, or what the purpose of this is, I can fall back on those concepts. But what you mustn't discount – which I think is perhaps also a Stanislavskian error, or an area of doubt for me – is that sometimes it's an overly teleological conception, so that everything's always goal driven, without allowing for the sheer flourish of personality. In other words, although everything is being done toward an end, it isn't necessarily linear in its achievement; there are all kinds of subsidiary actions and activities. If it's written absolutely true to character, there's always a terrific amount of what you might call the natural *gas* of the character just letting off in an exuberant way. You can't try to channel that and contain that, and put it into a cupboard. It does have a purpose, but the manner of the doing is also important, it's just the natural efflorescence of the personality.

When I'm directing I think the principal obstacle that I've hit as a director – especially with men – is their fear that I'm trying to impose the performance I would have given, on them. I most deeply am not interested in doing that. My whole task as a director, in fact, is to get them to declare who they really are, so it can be theirs. That's all I want. I'm constantly mediating, as a director must, between them and the character and the author. So what we end up with comes from those three people, and not from any one person. There is no such thing as the definitive performance of Hamlet, or Stanley Kowalski, or the leading character in *Hurlyburly*. There's no absolute.

There is no definitive Kowalski, but on the other hand, it's absolutely not the case that Kowalski is you, unless by absolute, extraordinary coincidence, you happen to answer to all the parameters of the character created by Tennessee Williams in 1947. So you have to find a *rapprochement*, and you have to do it in the author's terms. The author is the most crucial presence at all times. That's another thing that Stanislavsky and Strasberg don't pay enough attention to, the fact that someone wrote this. They like to say 'This exists, and Stanley's a real person.' But he wasn't, he was made by Tennessee Williams. He has an organic life because it's wonderfully well-written, but you can't understand it without knowing who Tennesse Williams was, or what he was about.

On British Theatre

There is this whole interesting question of why the English have produced no auteur-directors. They have, but they have been marginalised. For example, Stephen Berkoff is exactly such a person. He's an auteur in every sense; he actually writes his own plays, generally, and he's created a style, an idiom, and imposed things on plays. When he does Wilde's *Salome*, he totally uses the play for his own purposes. It's probably a response to the play in some sense, but it's very far from what Oscar Wilde might have had in mind. It's very much a part of our culture. A lot of British theatre now is in the hands of people who come from a university background; the directors particularly, people like Trevor Nunn, Peter Hall, they're all Oxbridge graduates. A lot of their collaborators, the actors – Ian McKellen, Alan Howard, Derek Jacobi – come from that university background, and that is predominately logocentric; words are the heart of it all. It is a tremendously strong British tradition; our language is outstandingly expressive, and variable, and flexible, and resonant in all kinds of interesting and curious ways. The vocabulary is vast, the grammatical structure is supple and mutable, and all the rest of it. We do use words quite extraordinarily.

But I think there's a very simple question here, of resources, which has inhibited the development of auteur theatre. Because to be an auteur in the manner of Brecht, or Patrice Chereau or Peter Stein, particularly, or even Bergman, who is another such person, you need time and money, and lots of it. Stein rehearses for six months. You can't do what Stein does without rehearsing for six months.

That tradition is an interesting one, because I think that is a tradition of patronage, of court theatre, basically. The court gave you money to enhance its glory. The foundation of all that goes back to the ensemble of the Duke of Saxe-Meiningen, and his famous director, Kronegk who did, indeed, have time to create an ensemble. Tragically, we've never allowed ourselves the time to do that in this country. We've never had those kind of protracted rehearsal periods, and – as a director, I know this perfectly well – when you've got that kind of time, you start to become much more ambitious in terms of the *mise-en-scène*, because you don't have to worry about just getting the show on. So often, my work takes place during a *three week* rehearsal period. Tyrone Guthrie – this brilliant, great, virtuoso English director – once observed that no play in the world ever needed more than two weeks rehearsal, except for *Hamlet*, and that needs two and a half weeks rehearsal. Indeed, when he first directed J.B. Preistley's play, *Dangerous Corner*, in which he had two whole weeks to rehearse, he sent the cast away after three days, and had them come back again after a week, and then did the play in the next three days. And in the British classical music sector, we have English musicians who are unrivalled in the world for sight-reading, because they have no rehearsal time, and still don't. It's shocking.

At places like the RSC, you get eight weeks rehearsal, but it's not a real eight weeks, because it's in repertory. You can only use the actors now and then, a little bit here and there, and you're working around them, and so on. It's really only six weeks, and it's sort of nominal. Unfortunately, under what is known in England as Parkinson's law: 'the work expands to fill the time available'. You do exactly the same amount of work you would have done in four weeks, so there's slightly less pressure. There's nothing that puts a director on the spot more than having a lot of rehearsal time. If you've just got to get the damn thing on, then anybody with a bit of wit and intelligence and drive can do it. Whip up a bit of adrenalin, and bingo, there's a play. But if you're going to take three months, then you really better think of something interesting to say about the play, or have some ideas about how the actors might use their time.

On critics

It's a little hard to speak temperately about criticism, because of the sensation – especially if you do quite a lot of work that involves media, as I do – that you labour and you labour, and you stretch yourself to your uttermost – and for better or for worse, I always do that, then you stand up on the stage, or you submit your book, or show your film to a select group of people, people who write whatever comes into their heads, really, on no known standard, no method of computation. Who just, in other words, air an opinion about your work. And in my case, it's become increasingly *ad hominem*; as the years have gone by, they write more and more about me and less and less about my work, or the roles. They don't review my films, they just review me.

It is, I think, inarguable that criticism has declined rather drastically in the last fifty years, partly because of the requirements of the daily newspapers. You have to earn your place in the sun, in every sense of the word, by making a big splash, so it's always got to be heaven or hell, whatever you see. What most critics reveal is a general ignorance of the processes of the theatre. It's quite astonishing with what regularity things are attributed to the wrong people. When Mr X gives a wonderful performance, the director is praised, but the actor would have given that performance anyway. Mr Y gives a disastrous performance entirely because the director wrecked his work, but it's Mr Y who is attacked, not the director. The qualities of the design are completely ignored, not appreciated, not understood, as are the dynamics of the stage, and the way in which things work.

The great British principle is that the critic is, *in loco*, the man in the street. The critic goes there to report to the man on the street on what's up. So he doesn't need to know anything about it, he just needs to be a good reporter, but they're not good reporters, really. Others seem to think that they're their schoolmasters, and you get this wonderful, richly hilarious situation where the critic of the *Guardian* clearly knows much better than Trevor Nunn how to stage *Macbeth*. If only Trevor Nunn had spoken to the critic of the *Guardian*, because there is a way of staging *Macbeth* and the critic of the *Guardian* knows how it's done, and why didn't they ask him first? Instead of saying 'This is the choice that Trevor Nunn has taken, and these are the implications, this is what wins, and this is what loses'. Then there's a third, even more pernicious kind of critic, who's recently grown up in this country, who is a sort of philosopher/dreamer/theorist, who doesn't mention the set or anything silly

Simon Callow in *As You Like It* (1979)

like that, doesn't mention the actors at all, and treats the play itself as a kind of text of metaphysical speculations, generally revealing how ineffably brilliant he, the critic, is; how widely read, how profound in his cogitations. All of these bear no relation to anything on the stage.

On sex, desire, and self-exposure

I think to show yourself wanting something is a fundamentally and inherently vulnerable thing. It must be, mustn't it? If you say 'I want a glass of water', you're immediately at the mercy of somebody who can give you a glass of water. They may be nice or they may be nasty, but if you want it terribly much, you've revealed it. If by cunning, you never reveal that you've wanted it, but you get your glass, then you haven't risked being humiliated, or hurt or robbed. Culture evolves very quickly. In America, to be in need is now regarded as almost saintly. If you've suffered in some way, if you've been traumatised, if you've been sexually abused, it's a cause for public pronouncement and celebration, and you'll get a round of applause for it. Now that's a big change, and it's certainly becoming common in England, too. But when I was growing up it really wasn't the case; the stiff upper lip was all about *not* saying what you wanted.

And there was the whole sexual and emotional element of being gay, and knowing that I was gay, which was really tough for a child. It was literally dangerous to show that you were in love with another boy in your class; if you said to him 'I love you', or 'I want you', then you'd quite likely get your head smashed against the wall. Part of my strange crab-like journey to the Drama Centre was that I was unable to admit how much I wanted to be an actor. I hedged it around, you know: 'If they say I'm not an actor, then I won't be an actor, and I'll go and join the navy'. Instead of saying, as many people have, 'I'm going to be an actor. Damn anybody'. For better or for worse, for whatever reason, I don't have that attitude. And acting is about wanting. The theatre is a celebration of desire, about wanting things: power, money, fame, family, fortune, sex, whatever. And in our modern world young actors are particularly bad at expressing desire. Because of cool, they mustn't. That's the modern equivalent of my neurosis. It's bad form to show that you'd really quite like to have a game of football. 'Well, maybe, maybe not, who cares . . ..' You protect yourself against the embarrassment of being shown to want something a lot.

On being British and an artist

There's an English tradition, an English embarrassment at the idea of being an artist. There's an American embarrassment concerning it; Robert Mitchum, whom I interviewed – who is a wonderful actor, sensitive and complex – used to just dismiss the whole business. It was like it made him embarrassed even to say 'I'm an actor'. For many English people, if you express yourself and say, 'I'm an artist', immediately, raspberries follow. I made up my mind I would never be a jobbing actor. I wish I'd stuck to that more; I haven't been able to, unfortunately. It's sacerdotal, it's an important job, being an actor, but you're not allowed to say it. In England, above all; only in England could they have invented this word *luvvie*. It absolutely expresses the utter contempt felt by certain of the media, and perhaps by the general public, for any pretensions that an actor might have. When I wrote my book about Charles Laughton, my whole point was that this man did something altogether extraordinary to create images of the human condition which are absolutely on the level with those created by a great painter or great composer. The overture to *Fidelio* is not necessarily a greater creation in its embodiment of that terrible, surging quest for freedom and dignity, than Charles Laughton's performance of Javert in *Les Misérables*. It's as extraordinarily imagined, as rich and complete and as conscious an act of art as the other. Well, I'm king of all luvvies, and I'm scorned in the English press, because I talk like that about acting. They hate it, *hate* it! There's more understanding of the actor who stands up and says – as Dirk Bogarde invariably did whenever he was interviewed – 'Oh, acting is a horse show. It's silly, I've wasted my life doing it. There's nothing to it, just remember your lines when you're standing in front of the camera'.

Callow on his career

I suppose I talk so much about other people's acting, or acting in general, because to talk about my own is quite daunting and slightly embarrassing. I have such ambivalence about my acting, really, I have such a complicated relationship to the idea of myself as an actor, because I expected my life to be so different from the way it's turned out. Once I'd found acting, and then trained in it, and established that there was some kind of talent there, I was lucky to get a job before I even left drama school. Now begins what I conceived of as a fairly steady arc towards the objective of being a great actor – all I ever wanted. I never wanted to be famous, I never wanted to be a Hollywood kind of star, I didn't want to be rich, I didn't want anything at all except to give great performances in what I conceived to be a line, a tradition that stretched back at least as far as Burbage, and well before to Roscius, and even further back. At a certain point I seemed to be well on course for that. I expected to spend a couple of years in repertory, and perhaps go to the National or the RSC, or something like that, and work my way round the repertoire. It all happened very quickly, because I went to rep in England immediately after my first season in the Edinburgh Festival, then I was invited back to Edinburgh to do a season at the Lyceum, then I went to the Traverse. The Traverse was very much a focus of attention at that time, especially at the Edinburgh Festival. We'd had a play which was a huge hit, called *Schippel*, which was picked up and brought to London, to a fringe theatre – Charles Marowitz' Open Space – where it was bought by an English comedian, Harry Secombe, and I found myself in the West End in about two and half to three years, really. So, I'd done rep, I'd done the non-political fringe, and I'd done the West End, and gained a very dominant part that was very well-reviewed. From that I went and did a play at the Bush Theatre, which was in the forefront of new writing, and from there I joined the Joint Stock, which was the political bit. So I'd done all of that, but very little classical work. So, as if my career had been quietly waiting for me to think 'Where are the classics?', I was asked to do *Titus Andronicus*, which Adrian Noble directed. At 27 I played this impossible role. Then better and better: I did a play by David Edgar about a schizophrenic woman called *Mary Barnes*, which is a terrible role to sustain night after night. Then I went to the Half-Moon Theatre and played Arturo Ui, for which I got fantastically good notices, and I started tentatively to do a little bit of television.

Although I had hiatuses here and there, they were all very brief ones. I then met John Dexter, who said that he wanted me to play the leading part in *Amadeus*. That didn't happen immediately; instead, he asked me to go the National Theatre. By the time I was 30, I arrived at the National Theatre, playing Orlando, because of a terrifically good track record only seven years after I'd left drama school. No less a person than Patrick White said, 'I've just seen a young man who is going to play all the great parts, one after another.' After that I met Peter Shaffer, and we got on terribly well, while rehearsing *Amadeus*. I had a little problem with my accommodation, and he said 'Well, we must find you somewhere to stay, an apartment, because you're one of the inheritors, you must be looked after'. So, everything was going astonishingly, and then I did all of Shakespeare's sonnets in front of twelve hundred people at the National Theatre, with an audience that included John Gielgud, and Peter Hall, and all the rest of it.

I was fearless. Fear is something I have only subsequently got to know. I just thought 'Get on with it. This is it, this is life', this seemed to be the way of things. I was in *Galileo*. I personally didn't much care for the production, to be frank, but it was hugely admired, and Michael Gambon was hugely admired, quite rightly. I found it so regimented in the way that John Dexter's work was increasingly becoming. I loved the play deeply; Galileo is a part that I would have longed to play, though, obviously, there was no question of my playing it then. Oh, God, I had such strange feelings about Brecht as a dramatist generally. I had done *Arturo Ui*, which of course is a fantastic showpiece, and a dazzling exercise in style, and you don't look for anything more in it than that. My career at the National began to peter out a little bit; the play that Peter Hall had promised me didn't materialise, and they weren't offering me very interesting parts, so eventually I left.

When I left the National Theatre, it was to do *Total Eclipse*, a play I've always loved and always wanted to do, in a very fine production by David Hare. It won a lot of critical success. I played Verlaine, and a young man called Hilton Macrae played Rimbaud, a very beautiful, rather Mick Jagger-like young Scot. But it didn't entirely work, and in some ways the play itself doesn't entirely work, much as I love it. That was succeeded by Edward Bond's play, *Restoration*, which was, I have to say, his last masterpiece. That was a very fraught and difficult time, but again, a fantastic part. Finally, this wonderful part of Beefy in J. P. Donleavy's *The Beastly Beatitudes of Balthazaar B*. A glorious role of life-enhancing generosity and eloquence, and outrageousness and tenderness and melancholy, and eventually, death. You couldn't ask for a better part. Sadly, not a good play, not a good production. And not a success; bad reviews, and a producer who really was determined to hang on to it, and not let it go, whatever happened. That's when something began to break inside me. I'd had this amazing succession of parts, absolutely unceasing. Acting in things I haven't mentioned: television parts, one-man shows here, two-handers there, all kinds of extraordinary things.

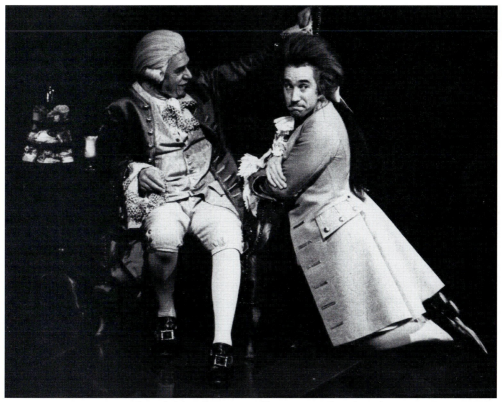

Paul Scofield and Simon Callow in *Amadeus* (1979)

Uncertainty, change and fulfilment

But there was a sort of awful feeling I had that somehow I was getting something wrong, and I couldn't figure out quite what it was. Something happened. I think it was the first time I had the feeling that I was a taste that you either had or hadn't got. Up until then I'd thought 'Well look, I'm just acting wonderfully, so you can't argue with that', but now I began to realise that people might think 'Simon Callow: no thank you'. I'm sure some people felt I was getting my comeuppance. I don't think I felt that in a paranoid way, because my light had not been hidden under heavy bushels. It was then, really, that I began to think, for the first time, the unthinkable – which was if acting isn't making me happy, even though I was, in other respects quite happy in my life, I began to feel, 'Maybe I need to think about something else'. I also had an odd feeling somehow my upward flight had faltered, although in reality, I was doing awfully well. I was playing the main part in a West End play. Not many people realised how badly it was doing, except me, and all the people who were on stage with me. And indeed the producer, he certainly knew how badly it was doing. But I just thought 'It's not working out. I've got to think of what else I can do.' It was around then that I was asked to give a talk at Goldsmith's College about acting. A lecturer said 'The English Society would like you to come and talk to them.' I knew what they wanted, which was for me to sit down and tell anecdotes about what it was like working with Paul Scofield, and how do I remember the lines. I decided instead to make a magisterial statement about the art of acting. I'd started writing, even in my last days at the National.

I got this dream of writing a book about acting. I had no idea what kind of book it was going to be. I went away, bought my first electric typewriter, and went and sat in a Swiss valley, then Cannes, wrote for another week, then went to Spain and wrote some more. So, really, I wrote the book, *Being an Actor*, in those three exotic weeks.

Writing the book had a very strange effect on me, because I thought it summed up my whole life to that point; it summed up everything I knew about acting; and I'd made a statement about something that was happening to British theatre, mainly of the supremacy of directors at every possible level. I really was baffled, not quite sure what to do with my life. It seemed not possible just to go on acting. I'd been to the National Theatre, they weren't asking me back. Of course, there was the possibility of commercial theatre, and I did a couple of fringe plays here and there. Oddly, of all the dreams engendered in me by the Drama Centre, the most eagerly embraced by me, was the concept of ensemble. A tangled structure in which I grow, learn, and continue my project of becoming a great actor, and giving great performances, in whatever role. I passionately loved the company ideal of acting, playing small parts and large parts, mixing it all up. The great strength throughout a company, and the development of people as artists and as human beings within this framework, never has existed, and never will. No English company has ever been formally based on the idea, for example, that it might be associated with a drama school, which would develop a method, an approach, to putting on plays, with a shared language, with tools of analysis, and a series of exercises, systems of rehearsal. So I looked in vain for that, and what happened, really, was that my career has been a series of one-off engagements as an actor, increasingly punctuated by work as a writer or as a director. It had no continuity, no development, no growth whatever.

The self in acting

Some of the best things I've done have nonetheless come out of that pattern, for example, *Kiss of the Spider Woman*, which I did with Mark Rylance, and which was a uniquely gratifying experience. It was actually the dream of an actor, that audiences were completely engaged by the storytelling, and by the emotional journey. I discovered, when I was doing that play, that I found something else in myself when I've been acting as a gay person, or been acting a gay part. I've been able to go deeper and wider. It's a great sense of coming home, playing a part like that. The gay man that I played was very effeminate and had very little to do with me personally, very little to do with the kind of gay man that I am. But nonetheless, I think it's something to do with this sense one has of the audience for whom it's intended, and what effect it might have on them. And it's still the case that it's always an event for a gay person to see a gay person represented, although it's increasingly common, almost systematic you might say, that every play has to have a gay person.

I have done more overtly political work when it was really necessary. But it's not my form of expression, I'm not a person for marches. I would do it if it became absolutely a matter of life and death, but I'm not someone who marches just for solidarity. It doesn't give me pleasure, and, anyway, these marches have become completely hedonistic exercises: 'Let's all get together and remind each of other of how simply wonderful it is to be gay'. Well, I don't think it is particularly wonderful to be gay, and I don't think it's terrible either, it's just a condition of life.

All that's bound up with my changing sense of what it was to be an actor; what I wanted out of acting. It's absolutely the case that when I started acting, I wanted to be as many different people as I possibly could. I wanted to escape as far from myself as I could. If I could have literally got taller, I would have done; if I could have become German I would have done. I just wanted to be possessed, taken over completely, by characters. Character remains central to what I wanted to do as an actor, but my conception of character has changed, in the sense that I most genuinely believed that I could become someone different to me. I now think that's neither possible nor desirable for me. I make no prescriptions for anybody else, because acting is an infinitely varied and variable art. They must follow their compulsions, they must follow their inheritance. That makes exciting acting. Having lived for twenty-five more years since I started acting, a fairly turbulent and intense period in many ways, you could say that Simon Callow has become a character himself. The person who was so unformed when I started acting, has now slowly edged into being the person he merely appeared to be. And I now very much see my work as an actor as finding a meeting point between me and the person envisaged by the audience, or, indeed, the real-life person, because I'm to a degree, unusual among my contemporaries: I've played a lot of people who really existed.

I think it's part of my understanding more what the art of acting, the art of the theatre might be about. I do believe that there's a shamanistic aspect to acting, which you really mustn't ignore. I profoundly disagree with Fiona Shaw, who says that for her, acting should only ever be a reflection of life, a kind of mirror. I don't agree with that; I think that the acting performance is life itself, it's a manifestation of life, it's an organic thing. It's a living, hugely complicated thing with its own ecology, its own biology. It's the baby you give birth to, it's the loaf you take out of the oven. If it's working – as I have once said in an excessively aphoristic mood – it's a point of success when you cease to play the character and the character starts to play you. Then, something's really happening; within the framework that the author has created, the character must have its dangerous life, it must strain to break the integument of the piece itself.

Another actor who's been called dangerous is Tony Sher, and I think Tony and I probably have completely different views of acting. I don't sense in Tony, the autobiographical values. I heard him give an interview in which he said that he'd started to do this with *Cyrano*. But I only ever see Tony's performances as a triumph of the will. For some reason he's decided, exactly as Laurence Olivier did, to turn his body into something else. He's built himself up, he's frightfully muscled and powerful. And I genuinely admire that effort, because it's enabled him to have the stamina he portrayed when he played Tamburlaine, which was extraordinary.

But, in terms of actors' bodies it's quite an interesting thing – so many of our young actors increasingly look more and more gorgeous, and are less and less able to express anything, because everything is pulled up tight, and spread out, and blocked up here (points to chest and shoulders). They churn them out like bionic people; they're on spaceship theatre, and they move around with very curious, and largely martian kind of movements, because that gymnasium culture is absolutely about dragging everything up, pulling it all in. You simply can't do that as an actor. Any more than you could do that as a singer. It starts to make you vibrate with a different kind of wave. The reason why gymnastic movement is not good exercise for an actor at all – dancing is great exercise for an actor, sport of any kind where the pulling up comes naturally – is because to concentrate on the physical culture in that way, is fundamentally threatening to expression. That's the word, that I embrace as a central objective of the performer's art – *expression*. You must be able to express, and to express more and more and more, not less and less.

With actors now, it's heretical to talk about rhythm, shape, phrasing. Phrasing is the most important of all performance skills of an actor. Nobody can teach you that, it's got to be instinctive. The way, not only that sentences or a paragraph are shaped, but a whole performance is shaped, the ebb and flow, the sort of angling metaphors of letting it run out and then bringing it back in and all of that – nobody thinks about things like that at all. Nowadays I'm much denounced, and no doubt I'm held to be an hilariously mannered actor. Someone recently reviewed a reading I did of something on tape cassette, describing Simon Callow as a 'coloratura baritone'. I took it as a compliment, though it was meant as the worst insult she could offer. A true and credible representation of a human being on stage is created not by submission to *the truth*, but by using every skill at your disposal: vocal, physical, tricks of timing and focus. It's no less real than the fascinating and peculiar techniques that Rembrandt – the most directly moving and human of all painters – used to paint a portrait. It's the representation of a human being, a very recognisable representation of a human being, but done by a series of brilliant and devastating tricks, deeply felt, and that's acting too. For some reason, the *art* of acting has always been a sort of dirty word. The 'truth' in acting – which everybody constantly harps on, without seeming to comprehend that art is truth and truth is art – is that neither is much use without the other, they're absolutely indivisible. A truthful performance that lacks art is pointless, and an artful performance that lacks truth is even worse.

My work on Charles Laughton clarified things in my own life, my own work. He tried to dig deeper and deeper, to touch more, to release more in himself, more to the audience. I'm no longer so interested in making the shape of the character. I'm more interested in sounding out all the notes that are in there, and if that means that the line around the character is slightly blurred, that's not important. The important thing is that I always think of the audience. The audience is taken into the heart of the experience, in such a way as they can comprehend what's happening to them while they're having the experience. In other words, I don't want to obliterate with sheer emotion, sheer brilliance, sheer laughter, whatever. I want the audience to feel, 'God, yes. Now I understand better'.

Judi Dench

'I've never realised I had talent. I just feel that I'm a jobbing actor.'

Judi Dench was born in York, England in 1934. She made her London stage debut as Ophelia in *Hamlet* at the Old Vic Theatre, and first appeared on Broadway as Katherine in *Henry V* with the Old Vic Company. Amongst Dame Judi's many roles are: Anya in *The Cherry Orchard*, Isabella in *Measure for Measure*, Titania in *A Midsummer Night's Dream*, Hermione and Perdita in *The Winter's Tale*, Viola in *Twelfth Night*, Portia in *The Merchant of Venice*, Beatrice in *Much Ado About Nothing*, Lady Macbeth in *Macbeth*, Regan in *King Lear*, Imogen in *Cymbeline* and the title role in *The Duchess of Malfi*, all at Stratford-Upon-Avon. At the Aldwych in London, she has played leading roles in *London Assurance*, *Major Barbara*, *Too True to Be Good*, *The Way of the World*, *The Comedy of Errors* and *Pillars of the Community*. At the Oxford Playhouse, Dame Judi performed in *The Twelfth Hour*, *The Three Sisters*, *The Alchemist*, *Macbeth* and *The Rules of the Game*. She played the title role in *St. Joan* and Amanda in *Private Lives* at the Nottingham Playhouse. For the National Theatre, Dame Judi has starred in *The Importance of Being Earnest*, *Antony and Cleopatra*, *Hamlet*, *The Sea*, *The Seagull*, *Absolute Hell*, *A Little Night Music*, and *Amy's View* (which transferred to Broadway, and for which she won the Tony Award for Best Actress). Other performances include her portrayal of Sally Bowles in *Cabaret*, Barbara Jackson in *Pack of Lies*, leading roles in *Waste*, *The Cherry Orchard*, *The Plough and the Stars*, *The Gifts of the Gorgon* and the title role in *Filumena* for the Peter Hall Company. Dame Judi was given the SWET Best Actress Award for *Macbeth*, *Juno and the Paycock* and *Pack of Lies*. She received the Evening Standard Award for Best Actress for *Juno and the Paycock* (for which she also won the Plays and Players and Variety Club Best Actress Awards), *A Kind of Alaska*, *The Importance of Being Earnest*, and *Antony and Cleopatra*. The Olivier Best Actress Award was bestowed for her work in *Antony and Cleopatra* (for which she also won the Drama Magazine Best Actress Award), *Absolute Hell* and *A Little Night Music*. Dame Judi was given the Patricia Rothermere Award for Distinguished Service to the Theatre by the *Evening Standard*.

For BBC television, her work includes *On Giant's Shoulders*, *The Cherry Orchard*, *Going Gently* (for which she was the recipient of a BAFTA Best Television Actress Award), *Playhouse*, *Smiley's People*, *The Browning Version*, *Mr and Mrs Edgehill*, *Ghosts*, *Can You Hear Me Thinking?* and *Absolute Hell*. She has also appeared in *Saigon: Year of the Cat* for Thames and *Behaving Badly* for Channel 4. Dame Judi also starred in the series *A Fine Romance* – for which she won several BAFTA Awards for Best Actress in a Comedy Series – and the long-running *As Time Goes By*. On film, Dame Judi has performed in *A Study in Terror*, *Four in the Morning* (winning the BAFTA Best Newcomer Award), *A Midsummer Night's Dream*, *Wetherby*, *A Room With a View*, *A Handful of Dust* (for the latter two films she was awarded a BAFTA for Best Supporting Actress), *Henry V*, *Jack and Sarah*, *GoldenEye*, *Hamlet*, *Shakespeare in Love* (for which she won both an Academy Award and a BAFTA for Best Supporting Actress), *Tea with Mussolini* and *The World is Not Enough*. For her performance as Queen Victoria in *Mrs Brown*, Dame Judi won the BAFTA Award for Best Actress. She was named Dame Commander of the British Empire.

I spoke with Dame Judi in June, 1996 in her dressing room at the National where she was appearing in *A Little Night Music*.

The right place at the right time

I wanted only to be a theatre designer, that's what I trained to be. And then I went to Stratford and saw *King Lear*. The set was a revelation – simple and spare and everything important for the play. But then my brother Jeffery only ever wanted to be an actor, and I suppose it fired me with enthusiasm about acting. So I thought 'I think I will maybe not pursue the designing line, and I'll try and see if I can get into Central School', which is what I did, and I got in. I went there in a very half-hearted way, I'm afraid.

At the end of the first year at Central when we were meant to prepare the mime, and we got to the class that morning, and I sat down with all the others, and said 'I wonder what we're going to do today?', and Walter Hudd said 'We're going to see all the mimes you've prepared'. I'd completely forgotten. And so I did something, and got the most incredible kind of praise for it. But it was luck. I've never realised I had talent. I just feel that I'm a jobbing actor.

What did I learn at Central? My technique. I expect, a lot of other things too. But entirely my technique. I knew nothing about breathing properly. I knew nothing about relaxation. There's a difference between an amateur and a professional, because an amateur might be able to do a part absolutely wonderfully for a short time, but their voices will pack up even-tually, or their energy will give in, and that's what being a professional is about.

I think that I was very, very lucky in being in the right place at the right time, When I was coming out of drama school, which was three years later, they were looking for some-body to play Ophelia to John Neville's *Hamlet* at the Vic. So I was seen at that time, and I got the part. But I think it's such a dodgy business; I just don't know. I think sometimes you have the trick of it, and sometimes you don't. It's got to be a challenge, because I love the challenge of something very difficult.

The qualities of the actor

I'm sure it takes a certain kind of personality to want to act. I think probably most actors are quite shy people. I know I am. So I put my energies into being another kind of person, entirely different, and trying to understand another person's life. I'm happier doing that. It's no good being an actor if you're unobservant, you can forget it. Forget it even if you consider wanting to be something else, and if you haven't got a huge amount of energy. I do think that actors have to have incredible energy. I do have those things.

Observation to me is like breathing. I think observance is something I do like I wash my hands or brush my teeth. I believe we have a kind of camera lens inside our heads, and when something is required in a character that I haven't personally experienced, I find that at some time I have observed a similar characteristic in another person which remains in my subconscious – in other words, the camera lens. But everybody has this facility, whether or not you want to use it. I think some people don't want it, you see. I'm saying that everybody's got it; I think it's in all of us to be sensitive. Some people absolutely don't require it of themselves. You also have to be curious about everything. We're all rather childlike, I think, actors. We're like children. And I like that about what I do.

If you don't explore absolutely everything you've got, and more, I can't see the point of being an actress, I think you've got to go to the basics with some characters, and then be asked, gradually, to strip away, absolutely. You know how you say one thing – we do it all the time in life, don't we? You say one thing, but in actual fact the meaning is twenty-seven layers down. Or you say one thing, and what you're actually saying is something else entirely. You know that cake, mille-feuilles – well, I always think that that's exactly what acting's like, exactly. It's layers and layers and layers of that minute pastry, which are emotions. I think that's what makes people interesting, and what makes characters interesting. But I never choose parts; I can't choose. So I have to wait until it comes. But very often, there is a kind of extraordinary correlation to your own life. I sense that. Very often, I think, that's the case.

The Method: don't call it theatre

I've seen a lot at the Actors Studio, and I think that is too introverted for me, much too introverted. I mean, I think that's fine if you haven't got an audience, and you're doing it in a way for yourself. I remember going to the Studio and seeing something, and I couldn't hear it. I just couldn't hear it. I thought 'Well, it's fine for them. That's a really private class, it's got nothing to do with me, or anybody else sitting here.' None of us could hear. So I don't know what that's got to do with acting. That's got to do, maybe, with self-examination, but it's not to do with telling the story of a great dramatist. Or maybe not such a great dramatist – and trying to be the sieve for that writer – in order to tell an audience that story. If it's for yourself, then it's fine, but that's not what I think the business is about. I don't think it is for ourselves, I think it's very much to do with our commitment and our communication with other people, that's what I understand it to be. British actors act from the guts, but they go about it in a different way.

I once did a film, *Saigon – Year of the Cat*, with a very famous American actor in it, Frederic Forrest, and he wouldn't say any of the lines that were written. And they were written by a very considerable dramatist, David Hare. He was an absolute sweet man to work with, but he would not say David Hare's lines. And it was very difficult. I was fine, because it didn't effect me so much, because I can adapt very quickly to something. It effected a lot of other people, not least of all David Hare and Stephen Frears, the director. And we can all do that; I've improvised an entire film, called *Four in the Morning*, which won the Critics Award at Cannes, a very long time ago now, and that was fine. But if you're actually going to do a film that is written by somebody, if you're going to do Shakespeare, you must do Shakespeare, or you must do David Hare, or you must do Chekhov, or you must do Strindberg, or Miller, or whatever, unless you want to do your own thing, which is fine, but then don't call it theatre.

A company woman

I think that acting is also not to do with one person. That's why I've always turned down a one-woman show. I turned down *Shirley Valentine*. I've turned down so many one-woman shows, because I don't know who to get ready for! When we get ready here – at the National Theatre – we get ready together for all those people who are coming to the theatre. And I think, that from the very first day, you can give a company an entirely extra dimension by the way you all work together, which the audience picks up completely. If you don't have that feeling in the company you cannot manufacture it. But you can create it by reacting to each other, and listening to people, and finding out why they tick, or why they do things, or why they want to. Have you seen *A Little Night Music?* Well, there is that in the company, I think. A lot of people have said it. Whatever you think of the production, there is a wonderful feeling in the company, and I believe in it absolutely.

That's why I don't like film, because I don't like the process. I really need to rehearse in order to know what I'm doing. I don't like coming to something and meeting somebody for the first time, so that I can't actually create a character or an understanding of that person. And doing a scene several times, the best of which will be chosen, not because it's best, but because the light's right, the focus is right, or something else has happened, or whatever. I admire really great film actors. I think that Spencer Tracy was a great film actor, because he was so human and so utterly believable. Someone like Cary Grant, playing that very light, sophisticated comedy, that's wonderful. And other actors too numerous to mention. Laurence Olivier . . . I admired him. And Sir Ralph Richardson had a kind of carelessness about him, I admired tremendously. And Ian Holm.

Developing a character

I just start to work on it. I have no idea the first day, none at all, absolutely none. Before I start, I don't do anything at all, I just like to be told the story. And then gradually it builds up. I let the subconscious take over. For instance, I do a crossword every day, like my father. I never used to do it, then he died, and the very next day I started to do it. Last night, I finished about eight clues, and I got into my car on the way home – I was being driven home last night – now I hadn't been thinking about the clues at all, I'd been thinking about the show all evening, and then, quite suddenly, that person, the crossword person, who had been thinking about it, finished it off. That's the person that sorts out a lot of problems during rehearsals. Sometimes I think that something only has to be suggested to you by a director, and you don't actually do anything about it. You go home, have a whole night's sleep, and the next day, you'll probably find it's in place. I never underestimate that extraordinary side of ourselves.

I think about how that person would react in that circumstance. You try and think what *that* person might do. I did *The Cherry Orchard* on stage, for Sam Mendes, and when I entered, he had Miranda Foster jumping up and down on the sofa. One rehearsal I came in and instinctively jumped up and down on the sofa with her, and he said 'You must do that'. Simply because that's what I would have done with my daughter. Would she have done it, do you think? Maybe not. Maybe something else entirely. You do it by trying to think of yourself as that person, and then just reacting to the dramatist's story.

I've done a lot of research and reading, but not *before* doing the play. To me, it's about the people who are around me, and the director. It's like picking up a bit of a jigsaw, and not knowing what the picture is. You look at the bit of the picture, and then you see all the rest of the jigsaw all together, all jumbled up. So you recognise colours, in everybody. And quite suddenly, you start putting tiny little bits of it together. I never thought of that analogy, actually, and it is a good one. So very, very gradually . . . sometimes things can go very wrong, but that's thrilling,

Judi Dench and Ian McKellan in *Macbeth* (1976)

that's very exciting. I don't want to know what I'm going to do. Trevor Nunn says I'm always in floods of tears on the first night, saying I'm never going to be employed again. It's good to use real fear. I don't know why I should have that in me. I don't know the process that I go through; but I'm always fearful that it's going to be the last job I do.

Macbeth

I don't really understand about dangerous acting, which I admire a great deal, until somebody suddenly wrote something – Peter Hall, or somebody – said of a performance of mine, 'It's a very dangerous performance', and I was absolutely thrilled. Really delighted.

It was in *Macbeth*. I'd played that before, I'd played it with John Neville, all over West Africa, for the Nottingham Playhouse. We'd say half a line. They howled with laughter. It was their set book. There were no drama groups when I first went to West Africa, and when I went back, years later, there were masses of drama groups, in all the schools, and they were all doing that play, all of them. It was terribly exciting.

When we came to do it the second time, Trevor Nunn nearly didn't direct it. He said 'I've done it three times . . .', Ian McKellen said, 'I'm not going to do it if you're not directing it,' and I said 'I'm not going to do it if you're not going to do it.' And Ian said 'Well, I'm not going to do it if you're not going to do it'. So Trevor had to do it, we forced his hand.

I remember very clearly, walking back from The Other Place at Stratford one evening after the rehearsal. I'm famous for falling down, and I said to Trevor 'We can't crack this, can we?' and at that minute I fell off the pavement. We laughed, and he said 'What were you saying?' and I said 'We can't crack this', and I did it again, fell again. Anyway, we had quite a serious talk then. The next day, he called just Ian and me, and he had the whole place blacked out completely, with this corrugated iron roof, so everything was very dark and very hot, and then he got Ian to go up a flight of stairs, and he said 'Now, just try and start the scene'.

It's in a room, virtually. It was in a room, without an interval, and the intensity of it was paramount. It was very intense, indeed. There was no interval, just the story told, just like that, and, we locked the doors, so the audience couldn't leave.

The British tradition

I left the Vic and went to Stratford, to play Anya in *The Cherry Orchard*, and Peggy Ashcroft was playing Ranevskaya, and Michel St. Denis was absolutely frightful to me. I was kind of a whipping boy. Peggy said to me, about the second day, 'I recognise you've become the whipping boy. Never let him see you cry'. And from that day, she and I became friends, and I just knew her very, very well. I loved the British tradition in her.

Sometimes I see a performance I think is wonderful, and believable, and sometimes I see a performance that I just think is showing off, not acting. But I see that's a kind of universal thing, in any language. I don't know what the difference is between wonderful American acting and wonderful British acting. It all has to come down to the same thing: does it make you believe in that person; do you believe in that person?

Playing the same role twice: *Absolute Hell*

I did it for the BBC and for the stage, and it was much better on the stage. But I had done the groundwork. It was the same with Lady Macbeth. When I played it originally I had done the groundwork of her. I understood what she was about, but not so well as I understood later. So a huge amount of work was done originally on Christine in *Absolute Hell*, but later, on the stage, she was much more louche than on television.

She was more extreme, because I found out more about her, about the real person. I found out also she used to go on the wagon all the time, and go on a diet, and not drink, and she used to sit in the bar with a cigarette, and then she'd go to sleep, and she'd set her hair alight, and they'd always be putting the fire out with a soda siphon.

Cleopatra and Lady Bracknell

I loved it because everyone said I was so unsuitable for it. I said 'Oh, no'. My size, my build, my looks – no one thought were right for Cleopatra. But that's part of the tremendous challenge in the theatre. And that's why I played Lady Bracknell. I was much too young, when Peter Hall directed it at the National Theatre. I was promised a couple of weeks holiday. So he suggested we block Act I and Act III which Lady Bracknell is in – and while he worked on Act II, I could go off to Scotland. It was while I was

Judi Dench in *Absolute Hell* (1991)

in Inverarry that I suddenly thought of Margaret, Duchess of Argyll – that gave me the clue to Lady Bracknell. I used to get very worried, because I needed to know what the person *looked* like before I did a part. But then I heard that Sir Laurence did that, so I didn't mind any more. But I think that's got to do with being a designer too, I like to design exactly in my head what I think that person should look like. Once that's completely out of the way, then I have to start to *be* the person. The appearance of a person is like a dust cover, it's not where I start from, it's what I have to get over with straight away, and chuck it out. I can start from the outside in, get that finished with, and then start at the very, very inside.

Brenda Fricker

'I do think there's three main ingredients you need in this business: talent, toughness and stamina. I'd like more talent, please.'

Brenda Fricker was born in Dublin in 1945. Her theatre work includes roles in *Macbeth*, *TV Times*, *The Accrington Pals* and *The Irish Play* at the RSC, *The Plough and the Stars*, *Lavender Blue* and *Lost Worlds* at the National Theatre, *Up the Sun and Down to the Centre* at the Royal Court, and *The Saxon Shore* at the Almeida. She performed the title roles in *Typhoid Mary* at the Bristol Old Vic, and in *Big Maggie* at the Abbey Theatre in Dublin. For the Gate Theatre in Dublin, Fricker played a leading role in Joseph O'Connor's *The Weeping of Angels*.

Amongst the actresses' films are *My Left Foot* for which she won an Academy Award for Best Supporting Actress, *The Field*, *Utz*, *Home Alone II*, *So I Married an Axe Murderer*, *A Man of No Importance*, *Moll Flanders*, *A Time to Kill*, *Painted Angels*, *Resurrection Man*, *Pete's Meteor*, *The American*, and *Durango*. Her work for television has included a long running role on the series *Casualty*, and leading roles in the specials *The Ballroom of Romance*, *The House of Bernarda Alba* and *Licking Hitler*, several mini-series: *The Brides of Christ*, *The Sound and the Silence*, and *A Woman of Independent Means*. Fricker has also appeared in the television film of Lynda LaPlante's *Seekers*, in Hallmark Hall of Fame's *The Journey*, and the ABC movie of the week, *Resurrection*.

I spoke with Brenda Fricker while she was filming *Pete's Meteor* in the Wicklow Mountains outside of Dublin in November, 1997.

Dublin in the '50s: illness and imagination

What was it like? I don't even remember, I spent most of my young life in hospital; I wouldn't be the person to ask at all. I spent five years in hospital as a child, so I was isolated. My education was scattered. Culturally, the '50s would have been very restrained, I think. My sister, for example, who's very bright, was expelled from five different schools for things that nowadays would be regarded as a sign of intelligence and leadership. But I didn't go through any of that, I went a different route. It was just hospitals with me.

I think that helped form my imagination; it had to be. My illness introduced me to books, most definitely. I got TB, and in those days, you had to lie absolutely still, because they thought that if you moved the bug would move faster through you. So, at sixteen, you're in this place for a year, and for the first six months you're not allowed to move, and you have to go into your head, you have to go into yourself and find something. For the first three months you couldn't even turn a page on a book, you had a little bell in your hand, and had to ring it, and some-body would come and turn the page, so it took me a month to read a book. It made me very self-sufficient, but I don't think it had anything to do with me becoming an actor.

My father was a journalist and my mother was a teacher, so music and books were around. I suppose there were middle-class pseudo-intellectuals hanging around all the time. Influence . . . well, academically, oddly enough, it was my mother – she and I got on very well. There were two of us, and my sister is five years older than me; that's a big gap. She was able to communicate with my father much better than I could, obviously, because she was five when I was a day old. I always had the feeling that he preferred her to me, so my mother, to compensate for that, paid a lot of attention to me.

She did send us all to this woman called Ena Bourke, who is legendary in Dublin. They weren't like acting classes, they were called elocution classes at the time. I went every Saturday morning from ten to twelve, while my mother went off and did the shopping. She taught acting, but she didn't teach you to act, she taught you to go into your imagination, what now would be called improvisation, I suppose. We didn't have a big word for it then, it was just playing games. She had a huge influence on me, again, because by the age of eight, nine, ten, eleven, twelve, we were learning Shakespeare, understanding it, liking it, just as we were liking *Winnie the Pooh*. She never made any difference between them, so that was a great thing. It's amazing how many people in the business here in Ireland went to those classes, like Joe Dowling, who directs in Canada now, Milo O'Shea used to go there, a lot of the actors in Dublin of my generation went. It wasn't an acting school, it was just this woman who was wonderful, and taught us to love language and play. So that would be the main influence in terms of acting.

When we were kids, they sent scouts around the schools, looking for kids for radio plays on Irish radio, and they picked my sister, and she went off, and was doing it. Then she got expelled from the school, and she was sent off to a terrific boarding school in Mayo, quite far away from Dublin. So when the scouts phoned up for her again, my mother said 'Well, she's not here, but there's another one here, if you're stuck, I'll send her, and she might be able to . . . .' Then I did quite a lot of radio plays at that age, from nine on, it was quite early to be doing that. It was great fun, you got paid a pound, a 'guinea', as it was then called. Then I got a job in the *Irish Times* when I was eighteen or nineteen, and got out of all this. I never wanted to be an actress. It didn't interest me when I was a journalist. It didn't appeal to me at *all*. Then one of the men who had been a producer on one of the radio plays, was starting a television series on Television Éireann, and he phoned up out of the blue, I mean *completely* out of the blue, and said 'Would you like to be in this?' I said 'No, I'm perfectly contented where I am,' and then my boss in the *Irish Times*, Ken Grey, said 'Go on, have a go at it. You only live once, and if you don't like it you can come back,' and here I am.

The London years

I fell in love with an Englishman and married him. I left home with my little bag packed. Romance, true love. He was a director, Barry Davis, he died a couple of years ago. That was the reason I left. I don't think I would have bothered going . . . who knows? That was my kind of long stint in theatre, ten years. I mean you learn in public when you don't go to a drama school. I remember standing on a stage at the National, and the director said 'Could you move stage left a little bit?', and I hadn't a clue what he meant! I thought 'Oh, God, I have to stand here, and if I move a little bit . . .' He said 'That's wrong, that's stage right'. So you pick it up; you don't make mistakes twice, because you're doing it in public. I was very in awe of people who'd been to drama school, because they had all the technical language, and I didn't know *what* they were talking about. But you picked it up fast, because you had to. I mean, it was great, I was in love, I was young, I was in London, it was the '60s, '70s, you know, it was terrific, I had a great time. I loved the Royal Court.

I was always playing older than I am, which is funny, how this is balancing out now. At 30, I was playing mothers of boys who were 32, because I was never pretty or glamorous, or whatever. I wasn't an ingénue, I was always a character actor. In that way, I was lucky, because I was never out of work; I got much more work because of it. But the Royal Court was interesting in the early '70s, after the Troubles in Northern Ireland in 1969, they were doing a lot of political plays by new writers which were lovely to be in. I loved being in new plays, because you're part of it. That was very exciting.

Getting into character

When I look at a script, I have a kind of a thing that my late husband told me to do. And that is I read a script the first time, and if it interests me, I will then read it as if I were the director, and then read it as if I'm each character. If there are ten characters, I read it as if I've been offered that part and that part and that part. And then I read it as if I was the costume designer, then read it as if I'm doing make-up, then I read it as if I'm doing the lighting. So by the time you've got to the point of saying 'yes' or 'no' to doing it, you really have an awful lot of information in your head, and it's a terrific tip to give to people, because you need never read it again once you've done that. Once you start working on it, you've got the whole thing in your head. That's the only formal thing that I do.

If somebody asks me to do a part, there must be some quality I have that they like, that nobody else has. You can't 'turn into' somebody else, you know? You can only move differently, or look or sound different, but it's still you, the essence of you. You are the animal you are, and if that appeals to some producer or director or writer, they pick you, and you try and reshape yourself as much as you can. But you can't change! I used to have conversations about why this person did that, or what they're like, their past, what their interests might be, or whatever, but at the end of the day, again, if a script is well-written, you don't need to do miles and miles of research and personalisation and any of that. I mean, if she has to have an accent or something, then you learn things like that, but you just get the meaning and feeling of the words, and put them through your system and out again.

Why do I take a role? It's quite honestly for money at some points. I mean, I'm very lazy, I don't like working, I try not to do it. I do as little as I can. Mainly, I'm very lucky with the two agents I have, both of whom are extremely literate and read a lot of scripts. So by the time something gets to me, I've got the cream of the bunch. It's a bit of a luxury, really. I'm sure people are bored hearing this, but it's the truth, you have to do the script for the writer. Even if it's not a terrific part, if it's a really good piece of writing, you want to be involved, and that's where it all starts. All I can do, or all I think I can do, is do it as sincerely as the writer has written it. That's my job, to travel his words out to the world. That's what I feel my job is.

If the writing is good, it's like poetry. Poetry is like really economical writing, really cut, and cut, and cut again, down into the little poem that's damn good. It should tell you what it means, it should be internationally understood, and if it isn't, it isn't good, or it's too private, or whatever. Same thing with acting. If I read a play, and I think 'Yeah, I think I could be responsible for the thoughts and words of the person who has written this; I would feel brave enough to take them out of the page, as a gift.' But you can go mad with the analysing, and I think you can distort, smash a whole creation apart by over-analysing it. Just do it, fresh. Something'll happen; open your mouth and something comes out, you know what I mean?

My Left Foot

Daniel (Day-Lewis) did a huge amount of research, he was the one who had to be sick, be crippled. We talked to the Browns, yeah. I talked to a couple of mothers who had children with multiple sclerosis and diseases like that. Sometimes I do research just for myself, to help myself get into a thing, but I don't underestimate audiences. I mean, it is fun to really watch the movie, let the people fill in the background, give them that freedom to think 'Oh, that reminds me of me Auntie Mary or somebody', and maybe give less information, just stick to the script. People get very carried away with all this research. I would never deign to understand what makes another person think. I haven't a clue what goes on in my own head, never mind trying to find out what goes on in somebody else's head. Or what influence reading a magazine would have on someone. How would I know that? I can't know that, because we all lie; it's all a game.

My Left Foot was just so well-written. All you had to do was love the boy, really, believe in him. Jim (Sheridan) never gave us any notes, he'd just say 'You love him'. They gave me one note I love. I was carrying Christy up the stairs on my shoulders, and I'm about to give birth, and we get up the top of the stairs, and the line is 'Not long now, Christy'. And I was shagged, because little Hugh O'Connor wasn't as little as he looked, he was quite heavy, and I got to the top of the stairs and I said the line the way I was, heavy and tired, and Jim said, 'Say that in a really light voice, because you love him so much, you wouldn't want to hurt him, to make him think that he's made you tired'. And I thought 'Oh, God, that's a wonderful note, wonderful'. To get a man who knows about that kind of love; I don't think I do know about that kind of love, because I haven't brought up children. I was really moved by that. I mean, the number of people who spotted it, all mothers, said to me 'It was lovely the way you didn't let him know you were tired during that', so that's Jim. That's one piece of direction that sticks out, but there aren't many.

The biggest challenge was not to sentimentalise the role. That's always my one rule, not to sentimentalise things. That was the main one, and it was a razor-edged. I said to Jim at the beginning 'I must never touch him, ever, unless I'm helping him because he is disabled. There can't be any kind of physical touching, no hugging', and he said 'Terrific, I agree with you, good idea'. So even when he was giving me the money, and the little presents, we never touched, until I needed to help him. Daniel and myself said that we have this line of love, it's a string between us, we don't need to do anything, and I said 'Absolutely'. That was good, I think. It was love, it was all about loving.

Any journey an actor has to take to get the day done, and get their work done is fine by me, so long as it doesn't cut across mine, or distract me, or upset or frighten me, and lets me do my day's work as well. They can take their clothes off and dance naked in the street if they have to, to get up. I don't mind anybody's method. I think Method has almost become a dirty word in some way. Everybody has a method. I have a method of doing my work, but I'm not conscious of it. I can't speak for someone like Daniel, who might be considered a Method actor. Obviously, I don't know what goes on in Daniel's head, what he's prepared in his head. I like what happens at the end of it, because it's very good. I don't have strong feelings about it; I wouldn't judge anybody like that unless it seriously interfered with me.

I never talk about acting, you know. Daniel and I got asked to do a lot of talks to students about acting, and we never went, because I can't define acting, I don't know what it is. If I could help them in any way, if I knew *anything* about it, I would go out and help them. I can't. But I think it's such a concentrated form of art that some people have to go deeper in than others and really can't think of anything else. I do think there's three main ingredients you need in this business: talent, toughness and stamina. I'd like more talent, please. A lovely story of Ralph Richardson, who went around the National Theatre one day, looking on the floor. They said 'What are you looking for?' and he said 'Well, I'm looking for a very small thing that's got my initials on it, R.R.' and they said 'What is it?' and he said 'My talent'. As if he hadn't got any, you know.

When I go on a set, I'm giggling and laughing to keep my energy up. Then you turn around and do something really serious, and people are kind of astonished. They don't realise that three quarters of my head is waiting for the call, and the other quarter is playing around. It's my way of keeping myself tense, keeping my energy and adrenalin up, because, as you can see, you hang around a lot. But if you have a director who doesn't have a sense of humour, ooohhhh, you're in real trouble, because they think you're just messing around. So you have to call them aside and do a little barking.

Oscar time

I had a great time, I went for the beer, because I knew I wasn't going to win, and that was fine. I was given free aeroplane tickets, and nice dresses to wear, and I thought, 'This is terrific'. I went to the party, nobody was shocked in the whole wide world but me, when I won. Maybe that's the way to do it. It's kind of innocent in a way, not to realise that you have a five-to-one chance, and Jim Sheridan was phoning, he kept saying 'You might have a chance', and I was saying 'Don't be so stupid'. There was one moment I was walking the dog before I left for L.A., I was walking in Phoenix Park, and I thought 'What if I did win?' and then it was completely gone, because I knew that it was impossible. It was just like saying 'There's a sputnik, go to the moon'. I didn't feel uncomfortable at all, I was delighted with it.

The Field

The interesting thing is, when I heard they were doing *The Field* – Jim Sheridan and Noël Pearson – we all got on so well together, and I arrogantly expected to be offered the part, and no phone call came. So I phoned Jim up, and I said 'What's happening?' I look back at it and I blush, really. There was a long pause, and Jim said 'Brenda, Noël doesn't want you to do the part', and I said '*What??* Why?' He said 'He thinks you're physically wrong for it'. I said 'Oh. Fine', and put down the phone and called Noël, and said 'What's all this about me not being physically . . .' and he said 'You're too fat' – Noël's very direct – and I said 'Well, this is only July, you're not filming till October, I could lose weight', and he said 'Oh, all right then, do it'. So it was a very strange way of

Brenda Fricker in *My Left Foot* (1989)

getting a job that one, because there was no wife in the original stage play, and he had written the part in. All I wanted to do was work with Jim again, because he was just amazing. I did learn from him. 'Less, Brenda, less. You're doing a 100% too much. Less.' That was about the only note you'd get from him.

Again, it's love; she just left her husband alone. It must be worse for him, to live with somebody who won't speak to you because of the death of their son. To carry that guilt must be awful. And when he needed her, she spoke; when push came to shove, she spoke. Oddly enough, I went to a friend of mine who's a psychiatrist, and I asked him, 'Was it extremely unusual that people lived together and didn't speak for twenty years or thirty years?', and he said 'No, an awful lot more of that goes on than you think'.

In that time in Ireland, too, when you were wife and husband, you just stayed together, you didn't pack a bag and walk out in those days. I personally didn't find not speaking difficult. And I made quite sure that Richard Harris didn't annoy me, because he can be extremely distracting sometimes! He's hyperactive. And it was fine, it didn't bother me, it didn't matter; in a way, it was quite nice to shut up for a while.

But I got stuck into the Irish mother syndrome there, I had to say 'No more mothers for a very long time'. I was amazed, it worked! I thought I'd never work again. Fascinating stuff came in over the last two years since I said that. Can't figure out how my agency, Mayer and Eden, find the stuff that they found. Now I'm playing a grandmother! Which is good.

Can a director help?

Ah, well now, that depends who the director is, you know. They can do as much damage as they can do good. Sometimes I send out a signal to directors to leave me alone, to just get on with it, that I know what I'm doing. And if they don't trust you, then it's their problem. There are very few good directors around. It's interesting in America, I always hear these young girls talking about every director they work with: 'He's wonderful, he's wonderful, he's wonderful', and you think 'Hmmm . . .' There's about three that I know who are really good.

It's supposed to be the most democratic job, but it isn't, it's extremely dictatorial – the director's the boss. And some of them are frightened, and through fear they start shouting and screaming. I was married to one for seventeen years, I know *all* their tricks, my love, so I don't have any problems with directors any more. If I see a problem I just step back and leave them alone, and they get the message, which is terrific.

Conflict on the set: a nightmare

Luckily, touch wood, I've only had problems once with an actor, in a television series. I won't name the person, because it would be unfair, but it was a woman, there were two of us playing sort of equal leads, and it was dreadful. Two people left the show. I went through my conscience and thought, was it me? And then I ended up being servile, trying to be peaceful and approaching this person, and then I'm thinking 'Fuck it', you know, this is taking energy away from my work, so I just stepped away, but it still affected me. On the day we finished, I went out at lunchtime, and I turned my car around, I was living in Bristol, and faced the car to the gate, and got all my stuff into it, and when we finished the last shot, I literally ran out of the studio, into the car, drove down, and I got as far as Kew Bridge. I got out of the car, and vomited all over the street. This stranger came along, and the whole story of the shoot came out to him. It's like Blanche DuBois depending on the kindness of strangers. This poor man coming home from his evening's work, and I blubbered about this whole situation, because I'd been keeping it all in. But that was the only one, and I didn't walk out. I was crying in the trailer every day, it was a *nightmare*. And there's one director that I did a film with in America who I couldn't communicate with, but it was fine, that didn't bother me, because the producer was very good and was on the set every day, and I said 'He'll tell you what he wants and I'll tell you what I want', and it'll be very peaceful and quiet that way. But that's all, so I'm very lucky.

In the beginning I got more emotionally affected when I was performing, but now I can find an outlet for my energy. You do dip into yourself, and sometimes it can be dangerous. Like the other night, we were filming a scene where the character I was playing goes out with the knife, and she's drunk, and she's swinging the knife at these junkies and screaming her head off, because her brain has just cracked under the pressure. I was shaking at the end; I got into my car to drive home, and I went to put the clutch in, and my knees were going. I got home, and I was really quite shaken by it, and I was thinking 'God, you know, to be driven to that, it's just awful'. But then you kind of shake it off. It's like the emergency room: a cup of tea and television, distraction, and then it's gone.

But it can work in reverse; sometimes you get up in the morning and you're in a really bad mood. You don't feel in a bad mood, but you are, and then you realise you're doing a scene that day that's a big row, and it's somewhere in the back of your head, unconsciously. It's just there; your life is taken over. But it doesn't take over completely. I mean, I have a life when I go home.

Stage and film acting

I've just finished a play in the theatre, at the Gate, called *The Weeping of Angels*, by Joe O'Connor. It's been seven years since I've been on the stage, so I was a nervous wreck the

Brenda Fricker and Joan O'Hara in
The Weeping of Angels (1997)

first night. I was playing this 80 year old nun. It's set in the future; it's about the last three nuns in Ireland, after all the convents are gone. It's happening as we speak, people aren't joining up, or getting vocations or whatever you call it. I found that very hard, that one. We did an awful lot of rewriting on it. It's hard to put your head into that kind of water, and particularly in theatre, where you really can't stop, you have to keep going. But again, if you have a good writer, there shouldn't be any difficulty, it should be written clearly enough to see.

The only difference, really, between stage and film, is the immediacy of it. Technically, the audience is a member of the cast, which you don't have in filming. The connection there is lovely, and the buzz you get from a good night; the buzz you get from working with good actors, and the flow of just starting and finishing is wonderful. And it is different; I'd forgotten things like about how you can manipulate audiences. I got a really rowdy crowd in one night, and I had this eight-minute speech coming up, which is a beautiful love speech, and I thought, how am I going to control them? They're going to laugh at all the bits; when I say 'his tongue was in my mouth', they're going to go 'ewwww', and I got them, I got them! I don't know what I did, I don't know how I did it, but I got them to shut up. That was a great feeling. I went down to the bar and had three pints of Guinness to celebrate, immediately. It was really great. It's instinctual, I don't know what you do, I don't know how you make them listen. Maybe it's the writing, maybe those words are good enough to get them into it.

I like film because it's a different discipline; it's a different controlling of disciplines, and containing energies in a different way. You're always asked about the hanging around on a movie shoot, how you do that. That's why they spend money on decent trailers, and have people looking after us, so you can be comfortable, and conserve your energy when you're in front of the camera. I mean, the people behind the camera work a lot harder, and they don't have nice trailers to sit in, which sometimes gets my conscience moving. But it is only different forms of discipline, I think: movies, television, the stage. Just using your head in a different way, that's all.

But I hate the camera. I'm constantly getting directors saying 'Lift your head up, Brenda, we can't see your face'. The first time I saw myself on screen I felt like everybody else. I wouldn't look. But again, Barry, when he was working, got a lot of stuff that I had done, and made me sit down and go through it technically, and I used to watch him editing, I used to see rushes of his stuff, so he taught me a hell of a lot, technically. Rushes don't worry me now. In fact, I usually find that I'm not looking at myself at all, I'm looking at something else in the rushes. Because you can't do anything about it then anyways, it's too late. I think vanity has something to do with it, and I'm not particularly vain. If you are somebody who wants to look pretty all the time, then it might disturb you. If I don't like something I will ask for another take. If I think I won't get it, I'll say 'fuck' in the middle of a line, so they'll have to go again, they'll have to cut.

I'm always saying to directors when they want to do close-ups, 'Why? Why do you have to do close-ups, it's a form of terrorism'. Because sometimes you have some of those wonderful directors, with big, wide shots, and you can relax, and you can choose to look where *you* want, and not where *they* want you to look, you know. But you get these in-house styles and, I get very dissatisfied with the way people shoot things, just far too much of the camera trying to do it.

As Glenda Jackson says, if a film is two hours long, and you get five minutes right, you're winning, because it's just so hard. But sometimes you think 'That wasn't too bad, that was lovely, yeah'. You do get it right sometimes, that's kind of an accident, and it's quite nice.

Ireland, England and America: attitudes toward acting

I wouldn't really know about England, because I'm Irish and they're the enemy, so that's a political question (laughs). But I don't think we have a celebrity mentality about acting. For example, I just bought a house in Wexford, which is two counties down from Dublin, and in between is County Wicklow. And County Wicklow is now like Hollywood, all the American movie stars have bought houses there. The reason they've done it, I think, is because it's very difficult to impress the Irish, they're not going to go '(Gasp) There's Brad Pitt walking down the street'. It's different, Brad Pitt can happily go out and have a quiet drink, which is what we all want to do, or have a nice meal, or go out and walk without being attacked. Maybe our dreams are different, or our sense of achievement is different, or our need for recognition and privacy is different. It's just a culture gap, isn't it, a cultural difference? I mean, America's gone mad about celebrities, those talk shows where people go up and become celebrities because they committed incest, I don't know. It's maybe not as bad as that, but it's frightening.

There is a difference between Irish acting and British acting, and there is a difference about French acting, and American acting as well. But I think because of the *stiff upper lip* of the English – which is, I think, loosening a little, but certainly, the British movies of the '30s and '40s, you couldn't do them now. I mean, you try and do it as a joke, to imitate them, but I don't know how they did it. Maybe, the clothes they wore, the rules they obeyed in their head; they had no freedom. It was all very starched and extremely repressed, which I think the English still are, in many ways. It's all just people being different in different places, isn't it?

I thought Colin Blakely, who's dead now, was a quintessentially Irish actor. Any actors who are terrifically instinctual, that's what Irish actors have, because they don't take it all that seriously. I don't mean that in any insulting way at all, but it is a job. There's a freshness about Irish actors. I've been watching some of the young ones that have come up when I've been away living in England for a long time, and there's some wonderful talent around, I mean, they just bounce off the screen at you. And they're not big-headed, and they're not ambitious in the sense that they only want to be stars. They're going to work, and they love their jobs, and maybe that's what it is, loving it is part of the energy.

I don't think there's any difference when you get through all the flak that's around films, and get down to the moment when the director says 'action', and I do what I'm paid to do. I think that's the same everywhere, it's just what's around you is different, the attitude of all the people is different. It's beginning to get good here. Actors have a little more input in things than they have in England. It depends on the group. If you have a director who listens to you, then that's great. But I kind of live in a bubble; I just go in and act and go home, it doesn't make any difference where you are, really.

Nigel Hawthorne

'Most directors will want to work towards an opening night, and that's the thing I want to work away from. I don't want an occasion, I want more of a happening.'

Nigel Hawthorne was born in Coventry in 1929 and raised in South Africa. He played the title role in *Macbeth* and Falstaff at Sheffield. At the Hampstead Theatre, Hawthorne played leading characters in Peter Handke's *The Ride Across Lake Constance* (which transferred to the West End), Michael Frayn's *Clouds* and the title role in *Uncle Vanya*. At the Royal Court, he performed in John Osborne's *West of Suez* and *A Sense of Detachment*, as well as in *The Double Dealer* and *Bird Child*. For the Young Vic, the actor played in *The Alchemist* and *Julius Caesar*. Hawthorne's performance in *Privates on Parade* at the Aldwych won the Clarence Derwent Award and the Society of West End Theatres Award for Best Supporting Actor. He played in Tom Stoppard's *Hapgood* at the Aldwych as well. For the National Theatre, Hawthorne played leading roles in *The Magistrate* and *Jacobowsky and The Colonel*. At the RSC, Hawthorne performed in *Peer Gynt* and Tartuffe. He played C.S. Lewis in the West End production of *Shadowlands,* and won both the Tony Award and Outer Circle Critics' Award for Best Actor when the play transferred to Broadway. For his leading role in *The Madness of George III* at the National, Hawthorne won the Olivier, Evening Standard, Timeout Readers' Award, and Plays and Players Magazine Award for Best Actor. The play later toured the U.S. Other theatre work includes *As You Like It* for the National, *The Doctor's Dilemma, Otherwise Engaged, The Heiress, The Millionairess,* and *Oh What a Lovely War* (for Joan Littlewood). He also appeared in Edward Bond's *Early Morning*, the last play to be banned by the Lord Chamberlain.

The actor repeated his role in *The Madness of George III* (renamed *The Madness of King George*) for film, winning an Academy Award Nomination for Best Actor, BAFTA Best Actor Award, Empire Best Actor Award and the London Critics Circle Best Actor Award. His other film work includes *Demolition Man, Richard III, Inside, Twelfth Night, Murder in Mind, Amistad, The Winslow Boy, The Object of My Affection, Madeline* and *The Clandestine Marriage*. Television work has included *Yes Minister* and *Yes Prime Minister* for which he has won the BAFTA Best Actor Light Entertainment Award on four occasions, the Broadcasting Press Guild Television Award for Best Actor (the latter for his performances in *Yes Minister, Jesse* and *Rod of Iron.*) Hawthorne has also appeared in *The House, Madame Curie, The Knowledge, Mapp and Lucia, The Barchester Chronicles, Relatively Speaking, Tartuffe, The Miser, The Shawl, The Fragile Heart* (for which he won the BAFTA Best Actor Drama Series Award) and *Out of Darkness*. Nigel Hawthorne was knighted in 1998.

I spoke with Sir Nigel in October, 1997, in London.

A dreamer in South Africa

We moved from Coventry to South Africa in 1932, when I was about three and a half. I was brought up there, educated there. My father was a doctor, and we lived by the seaside. Cultural milieu? There was none. I had no contact with anybody from any of the arts until I went to university, really. My father had been at Cambridge, Clare College. He'd also been a member of the Footlights Club, which is the Cambridge dramatic society, and had written an operetta, which was the nearest, in fact, he got to understanding what my ambitions were pointing towards. After going to school, I didn't know what I wanted to do with my life. He said 'You know, you need a good solid background in something', so I went into motor insurance, which was probably the least appropriate direction for me to take, particularly as I didn't learn to drive a car until I was nearly fifty! I had no interest in cars at all. I did that for a year, and I decided that it might be a good thing to take a degree at university, and then I realised that I wasn't particularly academically-minded.

My trouble all my life has been that my concentration on anything which is mundane or technical is diverted by my imagination, and I used to take off and dream. I'm a dreamer, I suppose. So in this academic world at the University of Capetown, I slid into an English course, and as part of the English course, there was the occasional English Department production, the first of these being *She Stoops to Conquer*. I played an incredibly old man, I remember. Sir Somebody-Somebody, the first in a long line of Sir Somebody-Somebodies. From there, I did *Twelfth Night*, and I played the smallest part – Curio – who has, I think, two lines: 'Will you go hunt, my lord?' 'What, Curio?' 'The hart'. That's all I had to say. But it did start me off on an adventure, and a love of my work which has never left me. I'm very lucky in that; I do enjoy my work enormously. I'm not saying the people who watch it enjoy it, but I'm saying I do. I think that the relish of one's craft is good, and that's remained with me.

I decided then to leave university before I got my degree, incurring the wrath of my father, to join a professional company, because by that time I'd been bitten very, very badly by the bug. So I went in for three pounds a week, and did everything, which is the best way to learn. But I didn't have training as an actor, in so many words, although I did go to some voice and movement classes that my friends attended; I snuck into things. That was really my background as an actor, and finding a way of expressing myself. As a child I'd been rather plain and shy, very self-conscious, as I say, coming from no artistic beginnings, really, being a beach boy – and then suddenly found that I could hide behind a lot of strange characters. I remember, I was about seventeen, playing a sophisticate, you know, lying back on a settee, dangling a cigarette and drinking a martini. My mother came to the production, and said 'It isn't neces- sary to drink the martini in one go; you sip at it'. It was only by immersing myself in these strange characters that I found some sort of personality.

Nobody really encouraged me. I sort of knew I had talent; I don't know how you know these things. I worked with a group of students; we were very much of the same way of thinking, and in fact, they were wanting to do a production of *The Glass Menagerie*. This was in 1948 or '49, and a director who'd been in America was coming over; there was a big fanfare about this. So a group of us said 'Well, we'd like to be considered for this', and we put on our own show. We phoned up a charity, and we got them to give us some money to present the show; we took a hall with a stage, and invited the director along, and he agreed to audition us for *The Glass Menagerie*. I didn't get any of the parts – much to my huge disappointment – I became the stage manager. But that started to be the pattern of things, that I was always going to be, not the ugly duckling, exactly, but someone who was going to find it harder to establish myself than some of the others who were better-looking, or prettier, or had more character. Those sort of people went ahead, and I was rather scrawny and a bit spotty, and found it not as easy. But then, in the professional company, someone was fired about two days before the opening night of the very first production, and they asked me to take over, and I did all right. Not wonderfully, but all right. That encouraged them to give me more roles. I think had I been considered a genius or a prospectively great actor, someone would have probably said 'You should go to England'.

It was really the only route one could take. The opportunities in South Africa in those days were very, very small. They'd just formed a national theatre company, and they were touring a verse play called *Hassan*, by James Elroy Flecker. That took almost everybody that was interested in the theatre in the whole country. And then, there was the repertory company in Capetown, which I joined – that was the three pounds a week thing. It gave me a training in popular theatre. They were farces, and boulevard comedies, and the occasional drama, but mostly very lightweight West End stuff.

Moving on to England: an unpredictable career

We were all going to England together, about six of us, and there was a big article in the paper, 'Is this country such a terrible place? Why are these interesting young people leaving?' – I decided to go and see the senior critic, who was an alcoholic, and say goodbye to him. It was a couple of days before the boat sailed, and I eventually found him at the bar at the Café Royal, and I said 'I've come to say goodbye'. He said 'Where are you going?' I said 'I'm going to England to continue my career', and he said 'See you back in six months'. That sort of spurred in me a need to succeed.

I then came to England in 1951 to pursue a theatrical career – or hoping to pursue it. I worked quite a lot of the time in repertory, but it was not necessarily the sort of work I wanted to do. Sometimes we did a play in a week, and sometimes we did it twice a night for a week. That meant a very truncated version of the play, because you had to fit in two performances a night, and rehearse in the daytime for the next one. I didn't do that very long. It's very good for your memory, but the quality of the work is not necessarily of the highest standard.

Just over six years later – not months, you notice – I came back to South Africa, because things weren't going well, and somebody offered me a job there, and I thought 'Oh, yes, go back . . .'. So I put my tail between my legs and went back and my family said 'It's all right, don't worry, you're back home'. And then I knew that I had taken the coward's way out, and I had to go back yet again. So I saved some money, and four years later went back to England, where I've been ever since. It was a need in me – if I was going to be considered anybody of any talent – that I had to pit my talent against what I thought was the best in the world, and go back.

Nigel Hawthorne, Paul Eddington and Derek Fowlds in *Yes Minister*

I don't consider myself ambitious. I play tennis, but not to win, I play because I enjoy getting better, improving. I don't play any competitive games. The only thing that's in me is a pride, I suppose, to do as well as I possibly can, and to be accepted by my peers. That's really all I need. I don't need audience approval, praise from an audience. And it's odd, because with most actors, if you say 'Why do you do it?', they say 'You know, when you hear the audience laughing, and the applause at the end, the curtain calls'. To me that's the least interesting, most embarrassing part of the business.

When I returned to England, I did a lot of understudying, and playing small parts, some West End. The Royal Shakespeare Company wouldn't have me. And, in fact, there's a story that is perfectly true. They had these mass auditions, and when I first came to England in the '50s, I used to go, because everybody used to go. Every year they'd give their auditions, and you'd have your two pieces of Shakespeare, and a piece of modern, or whatever – I can't remember now quite what you had to present. I was never very good at taking things in isolation; I was always much better if I could share with somebody, and so to just get up and do a speech seemed to me to be a totally false way of behaving. I never got a job, I didn't even get a recall. Years later, in the late '70s, I did a play; it was the first time I'd ever worked for the RSC, and it was a modern play called *Privates on Parade*. And Trevor Nunn, who at that time was running the RSC, came into the dressing room one night, threw his arms around me, and said 'Please, please, please, promise me that you'll join the company and come to Stratford'. I should've said – and I didn't – 'I've been trying to get to fucking Stratford since I was 21!' I didn't ever go. In hindsight, I think that I'm not an actor in the grand manner, and the way things have happened – the way I've moved more and more towards doing films – is the way it should be, and should have been. I don't have a huge voice, and I don't have a huge personality; I work better on a small scale. I don't think Shakespeare, therefore, would necessarily have suited me – not at the huge theatre in Stratford; perhaps in the smaller houses where I could be more intimate.

I haven't followed the route that most actors follow. Most actors have gone to RADA, or one of the big drama schools, and then they've joined the RSC, and then their careers have gone up like a stepladder. My career has never done that. It started from almost nothing, and then did a sort of little squirt, and then went *bleah*, and then another little squirt, and then *bleah*, and then did a little hop and a skip, and then sat down for a while. But that's how it's been. It's not been predictable. I love that, I love it. The unknown is always much more interesting to me.

It's strange, in the old days, I didn't choose the roles, they were chosen for me, and I was asked if I'd like to do them. Nowadays, I can actually choose; I can say I would like to do something, and it's conceivable that somebody might say 'Oh, all right then, you can'. But it's very hard; they've been trying to persuade me to do *King Lear*, and I don't want to do it. Not necessarily because of the things I was saying earlier about the need to be smaller – because I wouldn't choose to go into a big house, I'd go to an intimate theatre if I did it – but because I would then follow somebody else's path. I'm thinking, of course, of Ian Holm. Ian's a very good friend, he's a wonderful actor, and I admire him hugely, and I love him as a man, you know. He's made his mark in that. I need to make my mark in my own way. And when I did *King George*, that was a sort of *King Lear*, although it wasn't *King Lear*. And perhaps, without being conceited about it, that's really the way things should be. I should do things that are unexpected, rather than follow a familiar path.

The Madness of George III

I suppose I'm a bit unconventional. When the script first came to me, it was very, very long, about four and a half hours. And Alan Bennett, who'd written it, had used about eight different typewriters, all of the most ancient variety – an old Royal, and an old Olivetti, and the o's were up there, and the a's were down there, and the t's were everywhere, and then when he got a little bit that he thought he liked, he would snip it out of the page, and stick it on there, and build up a sort of collage, and that's what we got. And then they were put into the photocopier, and we got these pages of strange happenings. Nick (Nicholas) Hytner was the director, and decided that he would give a reading of the play at the National Theatre Studio, and invited a lot of people, not who were going to be in it, but whom he knew, or worked with, or liked, or admired, or whatever. So all these people came along; it was very nerve-wracking, and I was the only one who was cast.

I didn't know what to do. They all sat around, and Alan Bennett was there, and Nick, and all these actors sat around in a circle. And I knew, just as it came my turn to speak, that I had to go for it. I just put all my energy into it. I didn't know what I was doing. I was working off the top of my head, and I'd turn the page and go, 'Pop!'; whatever came to me, I did. It was very unsculptured, but it's the way I like to work, and it infuriates most people who have to work with it, including directors. But I think Nick understood what I was doing. What was incredible, what actually happened that first day, was that Alan Bennett, who thought he'd written a play – almost a satire – about the medical and the political factions in the eighteenth century, set against this mad king, suddenly realised he'd written a human document about the King. These issues were peripheral, and the King was central. And that was just from the reading. So he then started to structure the play, so that the King had a throughline. We had a bare stage; I asked Nick if I could have some clothes – just a dressing-gown, and a pair of slippers, a hat or a cloak – and right from the very first rehearsal, I started to put on these clothes, and it was this that started to shape what we were doing, and also to catalogue the illness that the King had. You understood the degrees of the severity of the illness. So it was really done off the top of the head, and I think probably that's the way I work best. I know that if I take a script home and go over it and over it – and I do learn my scripts before I rehearse, and I know them quite well – but if I work on them too much, I can spoil it and lose the spontaneity. I work a lot on them and I keep them in my head, because the words go over and over in my mind. I'm finding out ways of doing things, finding an approach to something that isn't necessarily the conventional way, but something dangerous. I like to try things that are dangerous.

On research

Of course, I read a lot about the actual King; there were lots of books around. Alan wrote about porphyria, which I think has since been disproved as the cause of the King's malady. But there were books written about the Royal malady, about the course of the King's illness. Incredibly detailed medical reports of the time, in which every breath that the King took, day and night, was recorded. But you know, there's only a certain amount that you can put in.

I once did a production of *The Heiress*; I was cast as Doctor Sloper. It was written by Ruth and Augustus Goetz, adapted from the Henry James. When I read it, I thought 'Oh, this is a wonderful piece'. And then I went back and of course I read the Henry James, and I realised that they were poles apart – I mean *poles* apart. And I thought that the Henry James was more interesting to do, and that *The Heiress* was actually 1940s melodrama. So I then started to go back to the novel, and say 'Well, you know, instead of doing what the Goetz family have suggested, this is what Dr Sloper really felt, this is how he behaved, we should do it like that.' And I screwed the whole thing up, because what we were doing was the play, which had its own arc. And you had to play those climaxes which were artificial in the '70s, but were expected in the '40s. It was a very good lesson to learn. I got to a stage where I knew that there's only a certain amount of research that you can do, and then you put it aside, and you never look at it again, because you've learnt enough. You can't play the research. When I've played real life people like Pierre Curie or C.S. Lewis in *Shadowlands*, I do a lot of research about the period and the people, and then discard it, and play the play. Play the script. It's a very good tip and one I learned the hard way, and one which I now do.

Rehearsal: 'I've got an idea!'

We rehearsed for *George* quite a lot. I think Nick knew at a very early stage, that the best thing with me was to just let me go, and the more he let me go, the more I would come to terms with the role. In fact, I was told much later that the members of the company had decided that they might organise a t-shirt, and on it was written 'Nick, I've got an idea!', because apparently I used to say that every day. I was totally unaware of it; it was my enthusiasm for finding different things to do, and new ways. And then, also, the disease didn't progress from A to B to C to D, but from A to B to D to C, to A. You kept the audience not knowing whether he was improving, and so there was a sort of jagged inconsistency about it, which meant it was rough around the edges.

You didn't know what the throughline was for the character, because he was going through this turmoil. But he did know that he wasn't mad. 'I'm not mad,' he said; 'I'm ill. Nobody believes I'm ill.' You see, I think you can work best if you have a solid framework. It's like a film script: if you get the film script right, you can make a good movie. If you don't get your film script right, you'll have a terrible movie, you'll never get it right. It's always got to be structured, and when you get the structure right, you can go anywhere within that area. You can just take off, because the structure will make you secure.

Switching gears: acting for the film version of *King George*

It's always very difficult, the most difficult thing, to translate from one medium to another. So I think all you can do is really wash your brain. Uppermost in my mind – and I rang Nick, the director of the film, and said 'I've got to totally rethink the part'. It is the most difficult thing. You have the huge advantage of knowing the lines – most of the lines, anyway – and then you just have to give yourself into the hands of the people who are making the film.

The parts had been recast, as well, and I'd never met Helen Mirren before. I loved working with her, and she was wonderfully helpful to me, because it was my first leading role in the movies. She said to me one day – because I was worrying about a scene, I wasn't doing as well as I wanted to – 'You've got to let go. Do something, then let go, get on to the next, because the next is more important'. And she also said another thing, which contradicts the first, but which is also somehow true, to make sure I was happy with every single shot, and never to let the director say 'Okay, that's all right for me'. If you're not satisfied, go back and ask for another take, because what you do will be seen for the rest of your life, and probably everybody else's who's around. She was so helpful to me, and great fun, and naughty, all those things. She's good news.

Charting a role

You start off with the King perfectly all right. But then, somebody who knew him would think there's something odd about him, he does something unusual, (makes stammering and harrumphing sounds), or some trick of the voice, and then doesn't even react to it. And you start introducing these inconsistencies, and gradually build to a state where he gets up at four in the morning and wakes up all the pages, and then starts to talk filth and rubbish. Alan Bennett said to me once 'Oh, just say whatever you want to say,' and I said 'Alan, I can't, you've got to give me lines.'

And so he then went to an expert on madness and got the idea – I was going to say the logical way a mad person would speak, but, the illogical way a mad person would speak – and found how they harped on certain words, and kept returning to them, almost like a Lewis Carroll fantasy world. So I learned all these lines, but said them so that nobody could really hear; they were just around, but it was all part of the texture. And then the King went into the really tragic part of the illness, and was wrenched away from his wife and family. I've always been a great believer that no matter how harrowing something is, you have to moderate it with humour, and *Shadowlands* was a case in point. I tried to make *Shadowlands* as funny as I could, so that when Joy Davidman dies, and his explosion of grief happens, it comes out of a real person,

Nigel Hawthorne in *The Madness of King George* (1994)

that you've got to know and laugh with – and that he's immodest, absurd sometimes, quirky, boring . . . all those things, you just have a big melting pot, and you throw everything in, and out of that comes somebody that's got legs and feet.

The most touching moment for me is when Helen is running across the grass at Windsor Castle, and it's snowed, and the King has been put in a strait-jacket, and thrown into the Royal coach, and as the coach goes past, he looks back at her, she looks at him, and this man is wrenched away from his home and his family, and you don't know where he's being taken. There are very often things that just came out when you walk on to the set. Nick (Hytner) is wonderful at that; he is so open, he'll take suggestions. That's what every good director should do, and every good actor should do: be able to take what the situation gives, and just go. We did quite a few of those. I remember one instance in the film of *King George*, when Ian Holm opens the door, and the restraining chair is in front of the King. For some reason, it really upset me to see that chair, and my eyes filled with tears just at the rehearsal, and every take we did, I cried. I just knew how the King must have felt, being confronted by that, with those goons around that appalling instrument of abuse. It used to upset me, and I can't watch the film – I haven't seen it for a long time now, but I couldn't watch the film without being moved by that moment, because I knew that I was moved when I made it, and it's still there.

There was a bit, right at the end, where the King comes out of the coach, and he goes to the Houses of Parliament. He's helped out, he's frail, and I look at myself – and I know it's only two days since I did one of the other scenes in which I was running around earlier on in the picture – and I can see I have physically changed, and become more frail and thinner. I don't know how I did it, except I thought it, and I was it, and I suppose that's what it's about. That's what Alec Guinness was so brilliant at.

I've always admired Alec Guinness, but I could never equate myself with him, because he's much more technical than I am. He contrives his performances, as does Scofield. Scofield knows he looks good, and he's got this fabulous voice, so he doesn't really need to do much more, so he just sort of . . . talks, and that's it. But Ralph Richardson was always the person that I was most likened to. And I'm flattered that they say that. I worked with him in a play called *West of Suez* in 1970. But I never wanted to be like him, because he was just too dotty, you know. It was wonderful to watch, but I didn't want to be his sort of actor. Olivier was the person that I'd most admired as a young actor. Then, I started to see the wheels going around, and it shattered; it was like my hero had feet of clay. It was a terrible shock, seeing that, and I never recovered from it.

Academy Award nomination: Best Actor

Obviously it was very exciting, and the news that I'd been nominated was totally unexpected. I was at a memorial service at the National Theatre for an electrician, and someone came up to me and said 'Hey! You've been nominated for an Oscar!', 'What??!!' And then suddenly, press appeared from nowhere, and there was a great hoo-ha about that.

When we went to Los Angeles, I suddenly realised that it was an American celebration, and I felt a real foreigner. It was most odd; it was almost as though I'd come to the wrong party. It was not my scene at all. It's not that people weren't very nice – they were absolutely fabulous to me – but I got the feeling that I didn't belong. In fact, when Tom Hanks won, a friend leant across to me and said 'What a relief'. I laughed, you know, I didn't smash his face in or anything, but we were in the wrong sort of atmosphere, it wasn't right.

It was wonderful being there; I'm a huge star spotter, you know, and I was talking to people like John Travolta, and Jodie Foster. I just didn't believe I was actually there and speaking to these people. That was the most exciting part, seeing all these people really close up, and peeing next to them in the lavatory. Steve Martin was in the next cubicle to me.

Asking the director for help

There are very many cases – in fact, most cases – where I'm on the wrong track, and I have to be put right. The sort of directors that I work best with are those who don't try and pin me down, who don't say 'Yesterday you did it like that, and I like that way', because that hems me in. Most directors will want to work towards an opening night, and that's the thing I want to work away from. I don't want an occasion, I want more of a happening. I think directors either steer clear of me, or they go along with it. I'm making myself out to be some sort of strange being; I don't think I am. But I don't think that I do my work conventionally.

I was doing a Chekhov play once, and the director rang me up and said 'I'm calling you to tell you to stop interfering!' And I said 'I have no idea what you're talking about', and she said 'Well, you keep telling the actors to do things I don't want them to know for another three weeks', and I said 'Why? Why don't you want them to know?' She said 'That's my business; I'm the director.' We've come from a school of autocratic directors, where I began, who said 'You move there, you sit there, you do that, you say it like this, and these are the notes', to directors who are democratic, where everybody joins in, and they say 'Hey, let's try this'. And then you get the directors who suddenly say 'Hey, just a minute, who's in charge here, you or me?' Then I can't work, because I have to have that freedom to participate, to make suggestions, to join in, if I want to. If I know that there's something bugging me, I'll just say, 'Why are we doing that?' Mercifully, very few people say 'Mind your own business'.

To go down the same journey, night after night, for a year or eighteen months, I find increasingly difficult to do. It's such an unnatural way of behaving, to go in every night, and to say exactly the same words, maybe in slightly different order, or with different emotions attached to them. And also, the people you work with, must necessarily, because they're different to you, work in different ways. Sooner or later, you're going to come into conflict with somebody who works in a different way from you, and what you're doing is upsetting them.

I'm not really that technically adept, you know. I just go for it, and I know exactly what I'm going for. I have a very good instinct, and I'm very lucky about that. It sometimes lets me down, like everybody's does. But generally speaking, I know what's right, and I have a certain amount of taste: 'No, that feels wrong, I don't think I'll do that', and then I'll start to change things. In the course of a play I'll totally change my performance, every night, totally. Moves, everything, which always angers a number of my colleagues. I had a terrible row with this English actress. She said 'I think you change things just for the sake of changing them', and I said 'Yes, of course I do'. She said the art of acting is to be able to come into the theatre every night and give exactly the same performance that you gave the previous night, and I said 'I don't agree with that, it's boring. Surely the important thing is to keep it fresh, I would have thought'. Once you've left the rehearsal, it's out of the director's hands, it's in your hands as a group, to maintain the thrill, the danger, the spontaneity of it. You make it a happening every night, and you get people who don't agree with the way you're doing it.

The Hollywood megafilm experience: *Demolition Man*

I did *Demolition Man* because I wanted to do the screen version of *King George* and I had no credibility. I always thought Tony Hopkins would get the part, because he got the role I originated on stage in *Shadowlands*. Joel Silver, who was the producer, came over and saw *The Madness of George III*, the play, and called up my agent, and said 'I WANT HIM! GET HIM!' So I then thought, well, maybe if I did this movie, there would be a chance of playing the King, because they were talking about the film at the time. So I went over, and I think I got a bad deal in all sorts of areas.

I shared my caravan with a gigantic 358-pound man. He was on one side, I was on the other. He's a good friend of mine, Glenn Shadix, a most lovely man, but when he breathed, the whole thing moved quite a lot. Also they used to take me onto location in a mini-van, and I just didn't think it was right. Then I was paying my own accommodation, and so I knew I had a really bad deal. I got to know, during the film, that if they know that you've agreed to a deal which is bad, they'll walk all over you, the big boys, and they did. And (Sylvester) Stallone used to keep me waiting on set for forty minutes, never say good morning, just sort of stroll on. And he was always arm in arm with the producer, with a bimbo on the other arm, strolling in with a cigar. And it's got nothing to do with anything, anything, anything. I watched with a certain amount of amazement that it existed. It was quite an ordeal by fire, if you like. Particularly so, as I was burnt to death at the end of the film. I played an old man called Cocteau, and he was the bad guy that ran the strange world that they were all in, and I was dressed like a sort of Mandarin Chinese. It was quite cynically done, to get myself some credibility. And it didn't. Zilch. Served me right. It was totally foreign to me, a foreign experience.

You never know what the outcome is going to be when you're making a film. I suppose if we did, we'd all be millionaires. You read a script and you say 'Yes, that looks interesting, and that part suits me, and there's a good scene there . . .', and then you get onto the set, and they say 'Okay, here's some new lines, and some new pages . . .'. And you suddenly find your part being totally altered, and the scene which really convinced you that you were going to do the film, that's gone long ago, and there's a whole new end, and this and that. And there's nothing you can do about it, you just have to go along with it. I suppose you could sue them. I get impotent with the frustration of not being able to change it. And you can say to yourself 'All right, I'll be an executive producer', and I've been that for *Murder in Mind* (1997), it doesn't do you any good at all, nobody asks your advice. I didn't do anything, and I had, again, absolutely no control over that picture at all. When I read the script, I thought 'Oh, that looks interesting', and then the directors dropped out like that, nine or ten directors, and I thought 'Okay, that's not going to happen', and then suddenly a new director comes along, and you're in a totally different ball game, and you either pull out, or you say 'Well, let's try it'. But I've never seen it. I've got it at home, and it's still in the cellophane, as is *Demolition Man*. I've never looked at it. I don't like seeing myself on film. In fact, I have to be dragged forcibly, screaming, just to do looping, which I hate. Looping is horrendous to me, because you see yourself there, and sometimes they stop the frame, and there's this awful person, frozen in time. Actually going to the film itself is a nightmare.

A Method man?

I'd worked with an actor called Arthur Storch some years ago, and we did some William Saroyan plays in London, in 1962, and he was a Method man, and I liked the way he worked very much. I hadn't really done Method acting before, although I knew exactly what it was, and what one was aiming for. But it seemed to suit me very well, and still does. I can work as a Method actor.

I suppose the essential thing about the Method is that you know everything about the person that you're playing. You know what they have for breakfast, how they think, why they think. I don't necessarily go along with all that, because I think that makes you too insular. But similarly, I think to work in a more traditional way, where an actor says 'Okay, this is my part and this is what I do, and I sit over here and I do that', to me, is rubbish, because acting seems to me much more of a communal experience, and that we work best when we take ideas from one another, and spark off from one another. Now, Mike Leigh works very much, I think, in the Method way. I'm not quite sure that I'd have the patience any longer to work for such huge stretches as he wants. He demands your undivided attention for long periods. I worked with Joan Littlewood, whom I regard as my mentor, and she was the person who said 'We all have it in us, and all you've got to do is to be brave. There's the high diving board, just jump. Jump. The world is your oyster'. And exploration of character is fascinating, of course it is. It's wonderful to find out every aspect, every breath. But then it's quite good to throw all that aside, and start working with your fellow actors, and evolve something. That can be a million times more exciting than anything else. I find sometimes that Method acting means that you become too self-aware, and I don't think it's about that, to say 'Look at me, look at me, look at me!' all the time. It's never appealed to me, that. Obviously, if you're playing a leading role, the audience *will* look at you, because you happen to be on the stage for rather longer periods than anybody else. But it shouldn't just be about how best you can display your talents. It should be about telling the story, and I think sometimes that's forgotten.

Acting in Shakespeare: to cut or not to cut?

I think now, it's become almost obligatory to re-think any Shakespeare play. You couldn't do a Shakespeare play in its natural setting in its period. The critics wouldn't stand for it. The critics get so jaded – because they have to watch a play every night, most nights of the week – that they want to see a new angle. But, it's not necessarily the right angle. Like *Othello* – Othello is an acting part. There's no reason on God's earth why it should always be played by a black man. It's an acting part. There's no reason why Shylock shouldn't be played by an Aryan, you know. Why not?

I'm not bothered by cutting Shakespeare, as we did for *Richard III*, not at all. It was cut, but it was reasonably sacrosanct. But Clarence's big dream speech is quite famous, and so perhaps it was left alone for that reason. I don't feel that any text is sacrosanct, and I know that Harold Pinter would probably reach out and strangle me if he was near enough, and so would Edward Bond, and say that I was wrong. But I think that when a writer writes something, it's really only the beginning, and then people take it over, and start forming the characters, and you gradually find, very, very often that some lines are unnecessary. And John Osborne, I can remember him walking out of the theatre when somebody suggested cutting a line. He said 'Fucking charming!' and the whole theatre reverberated with the sound of the door slamming, and he didn't come back for three weeks. I suppose I've been, if you like, contaminated by what I learnt with Joan Littlewood, because she had really no respect for the text. She saw that as a starting point and then her imagination would take off. And sometimes, it was awful, it was embarrassingly bad, but sometimes, it was absolutely extraordinary, and you saw people coming out with their faces shining, because they'd been through an experience with her. That's why she's my mentor, my guru.

The British: success and vulgarity

We have, of late, developed – and perhaps it's been going on for a long time – a distrust of fame, of success. We really don't like it. You'll notice that when anybody – and it's happened to me, it's happened to everybody that I can think of – becomes famous, for whatever reason, they will slap them on the back of the legs and say 'This is who you really are, and don't you forget it'. They won't let you become successful, because they think that there's something vulgar about it. And perhaps that is what we really believe, that there is something slightly vulgar about it. Perhaps one of the reasons we distrust success is that our background is very often theatrical, from traditional theatre, where you were taught to conform, certainly in my day. There were a few starry people, of course, who threw their weight around, but you always looked at them rather askance, and with slightly disapproving eyes. It's hard to say what it is. It's something in the national reserve. We admire success very much in other people, and we have our heroes, you know. Our heroes are not English actors, they're American film stars. And it seems crazy that our industry isn't, if not as big as the American industry, at least as important, because we speak the same language. We have wonderful actors. I know we have problems with distribution, which is the great spanner in the works, but we should be making films of a huge international appeal, as we used to, and as we are capable of doing. So it's quite sad, really, that we can't stand up and be proud.

Taking stock

I don't see my work changing at all, although I'm pretty sure that I was dreadful when I began, and a lot of people think I still am. The arc is really my age, my experience. The arc has been fractured here and there, and is supported by staves and things like that where it's starting to get a bit weak, but it hangs in there. You asked me at the beginning was I an ambitious person, and I think I'm not. I don't think 'Oh, I want to play this, and I want to play that, and I'll take the world by storm.' I don't have that; if the right thing came along, then I'd look at it and think 'Yeah, maybe I'll do that', but I don't really have that personal drive, I suppose it is, to achieve fame, notoriety. I just want to be good in whatever I do, as best I can.

I see myself physically changing; my appearance is something I've never been at ease with, and so that's I suppose why I don't watch myself. I'm not saying I want to be handsome, but I'm always slightly appalled when I see myself, I think 'Oh, Christ, is that it?'

But ultimately I think all the quirky things that I have in me, all my oddnesses and my mannerisms and my absurdities and my shortcomings and my faults and my weaknesses, are all useful. They're the things that I tap into when I'm working on a role, trying to find ways of putting them all in, sprinkling them around a bit. They're what make up what I am, and I know them very well, and I can infiltrate them into my work.

Jane Lapotaire

'I think more female actors than men draw on the personal-emotional memory bank, and use their own pain and experience as a filter for the role ... Women don't have a history of mimicry or imitation like men do ... [They] have to struggle to find their own voice ....'

Jane Lapotaire was born in Suffolk in 1944. After two years with the Bristol Company, she became a member of Laurence Olivier's National Theatre Company at the Old Vic in London. She performed leading roles in productions of *The Dance of Death*, *The White Devil*, *The Way of the World*, and *The Captain of Copernick*. She also played Jessica opposite Olivier's Shylock in Jonathan Miller's production of *The Merchant of Venice*. Lapotaire was a founder member of the Young Vic Theatre where she played Jocasta in *Oedipus*, Kate in *The Taming of the Shrew* and Isabella in *Measure for Measure*.

The actress joined the RSC and played Viola in *Twelfth Night*, Lady Macduff, Sonya in *Uncle Vanya*, Rosaline in *Love's Labour's Lost* and the title role in *Piaf*. She subsequently performed the latter role in London and New York, winning the Society of West End Theatre Award, the Plays and Players Award and the Variety Club of Great Britain Award as Best Actress of the Year, as well as the Tony Award in New York for Best Actress. Rejoining the National Theatre, Lapotaire played lead roles in *Kick for Touch*, *Venice Preserved* and *Antigone*. Other theatre credits include the lead in *St Joan* for Compass Company, *Misalliance*, and *Greenland* at the Royal Court. She won the Variety Club Award for Best Actress for her portrayal of Joy Davidman in *Shadowlands* in the West End. At the RSC, Lapotaire played Gertrude opposite Kenneth Branagh in Adrian Noble's production of *Hamlet*, Mrs Alving in Katie Mitchell's production of *Ghosts*, and Katharine of Aragon in *Henry VIII*. She performs a one woman show entitled *Shakespeare As I Knew Her*.

Lapotaire has appeared in many television series and plays, including, *The Barretts of Wimpole Street*, *Macbeth*, *Antony and Cleopatra*, *Marie Curie*, *Blind Justice* (Broadcasting Press Guild Award, Best Actress), and *The Dark Angel* (with Peter O'Toole). She has appeared in two series of *Love Hurts* and the six-part series *Big Battalions*. Her films include *Lady Jane*, *Eureka*, *Antony and Cleopatra*, *Napolean and Josephine*, *Surviving Picasso* and *Shooting Fish*. Her autobiography, *Grace and Favour*, was published in 1990. Lapotaire has a visiting fellowship at Sussex University, and was awarded an Honorary Doctorate of Letters from Bristol University.

I spoke with Jane Lapotaire at her London home in November, 1997.

Childhood: dramatic contrasts

Cultural milieu, hah! There was absolutely none at all. I was a foster child brought up by an old-age pensioner who'd been a foster mother to my mother, a French orphan, who had been shipped over to England. We had no money, there were no books in the house. We never had a television, ever, or a telephone, or hot running water. There was an outside toilet, and the bath hung on a hook on the wall by the coal-shed. I was one of seven foster children that this old lady brought up. If I read a book, it was a sign that I was sickening for something. Like a lot of working-class children, my passing into grammar school was the key to a completely new life where I was introduced to music, literature, art. They were state-run schools, for children who presumably had an above-average intelligence, and they were the only way that working-class children could get a public school education.

My childhood was balanced against this perhaps stereotyped picture of poverty by the fact that my mother made a bid to get me back when I was about 12. I chose to stay with my foster mother, but the child welfare department of the Suffolk County Council – the area of England in which I grew up – decided that my mother did have some claim on me, although my foster mother had brought me up from the age of two months. So I went to see my mother three times a year. My mother was then married to Lapotaire, whose name I have, and he worked for various French oil companies in North Africa. So against this rather austere, very poverty-stricken background, I had a complete contrast in North Africa where my family spoke French, there were houseboys, they had cars, they went to the French Embassy for drinks, and like all colonials, their lives revolved around the embassy. So I had these two extremes.

I can't say that my mother and stepfather's life was cultural either. I hadn't realised this before, but there were two strands in both of those existences, which were similar. I would steal money from my foster mother's purse to go to the cinema, and lie about having gone to visit a friend or to the youth club at the Methodist church. My only social outlets were church on Sunday morning and evenings, Sunday school in the afternoon, and as I got older, the youth club on Saturday nights. For me the cinema was a total wonderworld, a total escape – three, four hours of complete escapism – it was longer then, of course, because there were big A features and B features. My mother, stepfather and stepsister were also film crazy.

I wanted to be Audrey Hepburn more than anything else in the world. When I was younger, before my hair went grey, I was very, very dark-haired, and I always had a fringe, so I thought there were lots of similarities. She was a particularly popular icon for most young girls my age. I was born in 1944, so by the time I was 12, in '56, she was in her heyday in films. I also liked Danny Kaye. I was very taken with his incredible – I wouldn't have put it this way then – versatility. I don't think I laughed much as a child, there wasn't a lot to laugh about in my life with my foster mother. Although I loved her deeply, life was a struggle, and it was hard for her with no money, and my mother never sent her any. I probably laughed more in the cinema than anywhere else.

Theatre takes hold

When I was 16, I was dared by some friends at grammar school, to go along and muck up the school auditions for a production of *Toad of Toad Hall*. My group and I were rather third-class rebels, but the joke backfired, and the teacher taking the audition got me to read for Toad, and then gave me the part. I got German measles, so I didn't end up playing it, in spite of my pleas to assure my foster mother that the red spots wouldn't show under the green Toad make-up, but by then the die was cast. The next year there was a production of *Romeo and Juliet* at the boys' school, and I got the role of Juliet. So by the time I was 17, all my ideas of being a writer, and going to university to read English and becoming a journalist, had gone through the floor. I lived, dreamed, breathed, walked, and talked theatre.

I auditioned for RADA, but failed to get in, and cried all weekend. By then I was ironing costumes and running errands at the local repertory theatre in my spare time, much to my headmistress' disgust, and somebody at the theatre recommended that I audition for the Old Vic school in Bristol, as it was away from the pressures of London. I was very aware then – I'm not sure it's the case for drama students now – that RADA was very much beyond my social background. At the time, most county councils would give children a grant to go to drama school. Now, of course, most students have to work to finance themselves, or sadly – because I teach in many drama schools – there is an influx of only middle-class children whose parents can afford the fees. But at that time, if I did well in my A-levels, as I did, I would have had the right to a full grant for drama school. It's interesting in this country that you still can't do a degree in the performing arts, even in 1997. A drama degree was only instigated in the early '60s in Manchester and Bristol Universities. That's really an indication of this country's attitude toward theatre and cinema.

Having had the disappointment of RADA, I thought 'Well, I'll give it one more go, and if Bristol doesn't accept me, I'll give it up and go to university and read English, and write'. But at Bristol, the Old Vic school and the university drama department worked very closely together, even then, which was 1961–63. The programme I entered was a two-year course at the time, now it's three years.

The Bristol Old Vic: the golden years

Any question about drama schools being good is very dangerous, because I think drama school is largely about what you put into it. One can look back and say 'I was lucky, I was there in the golden years'. I do think, like the director of a production, or the leading actors in a production, it all comes down from the top, and I was very lucky to be there in Nat Brenner's years, who was an exceptional man. A visionary, a great working-class conscience, a man who saw theatre as a huge weapon for social good and social improvement, and also someone whose working-class roots allowed him the joy and the pure entertainment value of say, music hall or pantomime. It wasn't all hard, intellectual 'Let's use theatre as a means of changing people's perceptions'. So, I can be very brief and say I really do think drama school is about what the individual student wants out of it, and what they put into it.

You cannot teach acting, you *cannot*. People either have it or they don't, it's as simple as that, and as hard as that. You can teach them how to speak better, to breathe properly, to move properly, to analyse a text, but the actual spark that transmutes words on a page into a living, believable human being, as a functioning organism, in its own right, is a process of mystery and myth, that no one can analyse. That's what makes it so magical.

I wasn't a particularly good student. It was my first time away from my foster mother and my mother and stepfather. I partied most of the time, I spent my money immediately I got it. I had two of the happiest years of my life! (laughter) I don't think I learned much at all! But, I was one of the lucky two that were taken from the school into the Old Vic Company, and then I realised, of course, I had to start learning. Drama school doesn't get rid of short-comings, it just presents your problems to you, deconstructs you, if you like, and the rest of your life is spent trying to hide the faults and reconstruct. And those are only technical short-comings. People who go to drama school think that they're going to leave being this kind of spanking new person, who speaks beautifully, and moves beautifully, and hasn't got any flaws at all. The truth is you leave drama school knowing where those flaws are.

The business is a hungry machine for new faces. It's after the first two or three years that those new faces are not so new any more, and are replaced with those who have been regur-gitated from drama school. And they're coming into a business where there's something like 85% unemployment. I've just directed one of my son's plays, in a staged reading at the Globe Education Centre, and one of the young men that I got to play the lead is someone I helped sponsor through drama school at the Bristol Old Vic. Since he left, he's only done two jobs in three years.

What's interesting in the Royal Shakespeare Company is to notice the deterioration in the way that the language is spoken; most drama schools now train youngsters for television, so they don't know how to project or handle blank verse. Most of them, when they come to the RSC, have never been in a Shakespeare play. Our system of provincial repertory theatre where Shakespeare's plays were also done, has largely broken down. When I was at the Bristol Old Vic in 1965 we were doing a different play every three weeks, in two theatres, for fifty weeks of the year; that's about thirty plays a year. Now they're lucky if they do six. And of course Shakespeare was always part of that. So we're getting young British actors who can't speak, who don't know how to handle classical text, so all our cultural inheritance is being undermined.

Foreign queens and great women

On film and in television, because I have a foreign name, I have tended to get the Spanish queens, or the Italian this or the French the other, because I did look, when I was younger with dark hair, very un-English, and no one in their right mind would have cast me as an English rose. In the theatre it's different, because one can be much more of a chameleon. But most film directors want the character to walk in through the door, no acting required. I often used to long to say when I was younger 'Look, I'm an actor. You're talking to Jane now. Give me the script, and I'll turn into who this person is, or I'll use the characteristics that are in my personality that are relevant to the part.'

I tend to have played a lot of 'great women', a lot of indomitable women: Piaf, Eleanor

Paul Jesson and Jane Lapotaire in *Henry VIII* (1996)

of Aquitaine, Elizabeth Barrett Browning, Marie Curie, Katharine of Aragon, a lot of queens. It must be something in my aura, in spite of my working class background, something of the French style must have rubbed off. I tend to play tragic roles. I actually think I'm quite funny, and my family think I'm quite funny too, but there's a danger in this business that you get hung on a hook, and that label stays.

I remember journalists in the States being fascinated by my childhood, and hanging me on the same hook as Piaf. Now, hang on, I wasn't born on the sidewalk, I didn't grow up in a brothel. I actually went to grammar school and had a very loving foster mother. It's a journalistic tendency to want to align you with the part you're playing.

Playing a part: instinct and integrity

What I do when I first get a script is I read it to see how big the part is! I read it completely instinctively. If something in me goes 'Yes, I know this woman', then I want to do it, it's as simple as that. I turned down an Edward Bond play years ago, not out of any arrogance – in fact the director hauled me in and said 'You're turning down a new Edward Bond?' I said 'I don't know who this woman is. I don't know where she comes from, I wouldn't know where to begin.' So my instincts have to respond to what's on the page; I have to have an empathy with the character. I could play a fascist if ultimately the film or the play was anti-fascist, but on the whole I wouldn't want, and I don't think I would empathise, with a part that perpetrated principles that I didn't believe in. That sounds very sort of hifalutin', but I do think you have a responsibility to more than just your career. I think, rightly or wrongly, actors who do have a public profile, can be in the vanguard of other people's changes of opinion, and effect people's attitudes, and one has to be really careful about what you're perpetrating, particularly on television.

There was a series (*Love Hurts*) where I played a rabbi, and I refused to have an affair, and it cost me the third series; they wrote me out. I'm not Jewish, but a lot of my friends are, and I went to synagogue for three months to learn some Hebrew, and to understand the services on the Friday night and Saturday morning. I said 'No, I won't do that, this woman is a spiritual leader. Her husband has just left her for another woman, and you're going to have her jumping into bed with this Russian concert pianist? I'll fall in love with him, but I will not have an affair with him. I will not perpetrate adultery when we've got an audience viewing figure of twelve million.' It cost me my job. However they dressed it up, they wrote me out. That makes me, again, sound extremely serious. But I do believe that an actor has a responsibility to more than just his or her own track record. Single-handedly, that series did more about removing anti-Semitism, hopefully, from a lot of people's minds, when they saw that she was just an ordinary working mum with the usual sort of harassments, stresses and strains any other mother had, and that she was also a social worker, as well as a spiritual leader, and a teacher and a guide. Lots of people might have said, 'I didn't know that's what rabbis did'. The Reform Synagogue has had women rabbis for twenty-five years, which is more years than the bloody Church of England has had women in a similar position.

Of course, I do take parts that are fun; it's good to have a laugh. In fact, even on the serious stuff, you laugh. In fact, you laugh more at the serious stuff, because there's a natural balance that comes into play. The more serious a script, the more appallingly you behave off the set! Or the more jokey you become in order to find an equilibrium.

Non-fiction characters: the covert student

If I'm playing a character who actually existed, I'm a great one for research, I do everything I possibly can. I read every book written about the person, I look at all the photographs. If it's something medieval, I'll listen to the music of the period. I think you have a double obligation when you're playing someone who actually existed, and that's not to make false value judgements. You've got to open up every possible area of understanding about that person's life, and then by a process of osmosis, all that information kind of stews inside you, it seeps through the pores and informs every aspect of the character. I love non-fictitious characters. I love the idea of putting my head into a book or books, and listening to music, or looking at paintings of the person. I did six months of research for *Piaf*; my son had just been born when I did *Marie Curie*, so it was probably a little bit less. I even learned the theory of relativity when I played Marie Curie. I couldn't tell you what it is now, because you have to wipe the slate clean in order to make space to go on. But I needed to know how bunsen burners and pipettes worked, I wanted to do it myself, and in fact, I did indeed wear newspaper inside my shoes, as she did, because of damp laboratory conditions. This is, of course, not surprising for American actors brought up on the Method. For me, that is the privilege and the gift of playing someone who actually existed, getting to learn, to know all the stuff, and being paid to learn it.

It's the covert student in me that loves it. There are people like dear Tony Hopkins with whom I did *Surviving Picasso*. He virtually read nothing, he said 'I just do the script', but you see, Tony also is a great mimic, a great impersonator. I love him dearly, but his way of working's very different from mine. I see this as a sort of privilege, as a bonus when you get to find out all this information. For Katharine of Aragon, for example, there's a scene in Act Four where the Cardinals come in for the next round of the divorce proceedings, and before they arrive, she says to her ladies 'Sing me a song, I'm feeling low'. The words of the song are 'Orpheus with his lute made trees/ And mountaintops that freeze/ Bow themselves when he did sing.' And they played me this madrigal tune, and I said 'Hang on a minute. This is a Spanish princess who was married to Henry VIII's brother, who then died. She was marginalised into dreadful castles on the borders with Wales. Henry VII, who was still alive, said "You haven't got enough money? Sod it. Eat the money from the dowry that your family never completely paid." She was then married to Henry VIII and ousted in favour of Anne Boleyn. She's alone, isolated, her daughter has been removed from her, she's been downgraded from castle to castle – and she says "Sing me a song", and you sing her an English madrigal? Why can't we have a Spanish song?' Gregory Doran, the director, said 'What a great idea'. I said 'Why don't I learn to sing two of the lines of the song in Spanish?'

That's the way that research can inform. A lot of people who've seen it say that it's the most wonderful moment. It sounds like I'm kind of patting myself on the back, but this only illustrates how, when you really get into the skin of this other person, that you can come up with things like that. And it is a privilege to walk in the same footsteps of some of these great women; I've learnt an enormous amount from them.

'Where's your charm Marie?': playing *Marie Curie* for the BBC

I was trying to play the passion of the pursuit of pure science. Even towards the end of her life, she simply wouldn't have it that women were dying of cancer of the jaw in watch factories where they were licking brushes with radium paint on the end. She just said 'Oh, well if they got out at lunch-time and had plenty of exercise and fresh air, they'd be perfectly all right.' At both her and Pierre's grave, the Geiger counters went bananas, because of the radioactivity that their bodies contained. But I would never make a value judgement about her, because I was still travelling the journey. Marie was so intelligent, I think she's the only woman that ever won two Nobel prizes. When you have that kind of single-minded pursuit, because you believe passionately in the purity of science, and pushing back the horizons of discovery and invention and experimentation, then the audience can draw whatever conclusions they like about her personality.

That is the hardest kind of acting of all, keeping things inside, as indeed, she did, because she was a very internal person. She was also not emotionally expressive, because she didn't function in that area of her psyche at all. There's a scene where Marie has to do her

Jane Lapotaire and Nigel Hawthorne in *Marie Curie* (1977)

presentation to the Academie Française, and as I came off at the end of the shot, Nigel Hawthorne (Pierre Curie) said to me 'Oh, where's your charm, Marie?' As an actor, you still have to provoke the emotions, but you have to put the lid on them all the time, and that's the most wearing of all, because it has no outlet. During the filming of *Marie Curie*, I heard that a girl that I'd worked with had committed suicide. And after one scene, a few days later, I couldn't stop myself crying; her death had triggered the release of this incredible multi-layered emotional repression that was Marie Curie, and I, Jane, just simply couldn't contain it any more. I'm not like Marie at all. I'm very much a heart on the sleeve person. So I find those kind of contained characters very wearing. She didn't have a lot of small talk, Marie Curie.

Nicolas Roeg's *Eureka*

I spent most of the film completely flipping out of character, because I was so amazed at what an astonishing, brilliant actor Gene Hackman is! He is just one of the nicest men; he asked me to play his wife in another movie immediately afterwards, and the company wouldn't have it, because they felt it was too cliché, having done it once. He spent most of his time talking about his chances of playing Lear at the Royal Shakespeare Company! I so admire him, I think he's one of the best actors in America. I went back to being 16 years old and wet behind the ears, I was so in awe of this great god of American cinema. I don't often watch my work on video or film, but I did go to see *Eureka* several times.

It was Nic's (Roeg) masterpiece, really. But we were the unfortunate prey of United Artists and MGM over that merger. MGM would come down and cut things and change things and then UA would come down and put them back, or cut different things, so there was nobody, really, to baby it when it was in post-production. So it really got marginalised, as a sort of arty movie.

I loved working with Nic. He's completely barking mad. I remember one morning, Gene got the Gettysburg address, and I got a poem by Matthew Arnold called *The Sea*, and those bits were to help us play the scene! I don't have very constructive thoughts when I look at my performance in that. I had come straight from Broadway doing *Piaf*. I was very tired. It's very hard to play drunk on film, and I hadn't done much film, five or six, before that, and as I said, I was very much in awe of this great icon of screen acting. And he would be so real, and so truthful, that I was simply drawn into his vortex. I had to play the scene where they tell me that he's dead on my first day of shooting, and I hadn't even met Gene! I was very in awe of Nic, too. I didn't feel comfortable, I couldn't believe I'd got the part, and I wasn't really prepared for it. I was very flattered that they wanted me, but it wasn't a comfortable experience. There were frictions between Gene and Nic, which it's not my place to discuss, but I picked up some of that, because most of my stuff was with Gene. I spent most of the film being terrified about the nude scenes, and when it actually came to it, Gene wouldn't do them, and I just wished he'd told me earlier! I could have spent six weeks in Jamaica and had a better time than going 'Oh my God, I've got to take my clothes off!' I'm very pleased and proud to have been in the film, but I wish I could do it all over again and do it better.

Art mirroring life

Whether or not roles mirror the state of your own life, or the state of your own perception, is inevitable. Take a really trite example: if you're old enough to play Gertrude, chances are you're at the stage in your life where your own son is at university, as Gertrude's son is. There is a kind of factual inevitability about that. At a deeper level, I think one draws towards oneself parts that echo the level of awareness that you have, because your life experience has opened those avenues up to you. For example, I got divorced when I was doing *Piaf*, and I remember thinking 'Why am I worried about whether there's any washing-up liquid, or loo paper in the bathroom, when I'm playing this extraordinary, gigantic, voracious little woman who ate men, and drugs, and alcohol, and every experience she could get her hands on!' It seemed to be such a paradox to be worried about the banalities of running my home when I was playing this – as Charles Aznavour called her – *monstre sacrée*, which she was.

Of course a part influences you. You don't drop it at the front door when you come home, it lives in your psyche, mostly in your subconscious when you're performing, but when you're rehearsing, it is much more in your conscious mind. I think it's a question of chicken and egg: is it because of those perceptions that one attracts similar parts, or does one attract those parts because there are things that one has to confront? I mean, acting is playing with fire, psychologically. You are sticking fingers in scars that otherwise would have healed, if you're playing tragic roles. I once did a course of transactional analysis, many years ago, and we got to a point where the analyst said to me 'Do you want to go on?' and I said 'Well, I don't think we should, because you're going to start to heal the equipment with which I work, and I can't afford to have you do that'. I think part of my being unsettled at the moment about 'Do I want to go on doing this, or shall I write full-time?' – is to do with 'Do I want to put myself through the emotional shredder?' I like peace, I like quiet, I like harmony, and I'm not sure I want to be food, sacrificial food for the audience any more.

Female actors: the struggle to find an authentic voice

I think more female actors than men draw on the personal-emotional memory bank, and use their own pain and experience as a filter for the role, or at least the role is filtered through that. Women don't have a history of mimicry or imitation like men do. To use a very banal example, if you asked a lot of leading female actors in this country to imitate Glenda Jackson or Peggy Ashcroft or Janet Suzman, we couldn't. But if you asked male actors if they could impersonate Laurence Olivier or Ralph Richardson or John Gielgud or Richard Burton, they could do it. That's often intrigued me.

In the classical theatre, the female roles are outnumbered by the male eight to one, and often, as the leading lady in the play, you'll be surrounded entirely by men. The director will be male, the lighting designer, the costume designer, and all your colleagues in the cast will be male. Even in *Henry VIII*, there are only two other women in it: Anne Boleyn, who only has one scene, and a character that the director has compiled out of three other characters, called 'the old lady'. So you're very much alone, as a strong female lead. Because you're so alone, and because you are in such isolation, the 'voice' that you have to find is a struggle, and, consequently, has to be unique. I think women have to struggle to find their own voice, because there isn't a tradition of mimicry or imitation.

Une Certaine Age

I hate being marginalised simply because of my age, and I'm at that very difficult stage between 45 and 60. When I'm 60, I'll be able to play the grandmothers. At the moment, on the whole, I am too young to be the leading lady's mother, and too old to be the leading lady. I was quite shocked, after about 45, how suddenly my leading roles diminished. As an actor, what would I like? Like most middle-aged women, I'd like to see more leading roles for middle-aged women.

Sometimes it is hard to believe the last 30 years of feminism have happened, when I still see the money men in Hollywood perpetrating the baby-doll myth; the pretty, pouty-lipped blonde. I remember with great warmth and admiration, people like Meryl Streep, and Sissy Spacek, and Glenda Jackson doing a lot to break that chocolate-box image, and now here we are right back in it again, with the Julia Roberts and Melanie Griffith. Madonna as a feminist icon? Don't give me that shit. This is a woman who simply used titillation; she's actually perpetrating negative stereotypes of women. Camille Paglia, go stuff yourself, Madonna's no feminist icon. She's just simply marketed and packaged what she knows will sell: the titillation, and pandering to the sexuality of the heterosexual male. So I'd like to see more women writing, more women directing, and more roles for middle-aged women *as the protagonist*, not as somebody's mother, or somebody's wife, or somebody's sister, but as the woman around whom the story revolves.

And what's interesting is how different it is in France and Italy and Spain – not so much Germany, because of course they suffer from the old Anglo-Saxon puritanical streak too, Lutheranism. When I go home to France, I'm always shocked, without fail. The other week I sat in an airport lounge and this guy was looking at me, and I thought 'Oh my God, I've probably smudged my make-up'. So I slapped my compact out, and I looked fine. Then I realised he was giving me the eye! He was a man of about 60. And that's because I had just crossed twenty-two miles from the UK into France. Women of a certain age, have value in Latin countries. We're mature, we're independent, we know what we like, we like ourselves, we've gone through bringing up children. In England, and in America to a certain extent, mature women frighten men, because they want this little androgynous 'Yes dear, no dear', girl-child of a partner. Whereas in Latin countries, middle-aged women are respected and revered, and their opinions are sought. So it's got a lot to do with the sexuality and sexual leanings of the men who hold the purse strings. I'm coming off like a militant feminist, and I am a feminist, because I would find it hard for any intelligent woman not to be, any person who's aware or concerned about the world. I have to try hard not to be very depressed by what I see.

I teach and I write, so I've got other strings to my bow. Acting is an interpretive job, it's not *essentially* creative – the seeds of germination come from the writer. I think the actor's job is a great privilege, to be able to touch the lives of other people. The actor is a vessel through whom the playwright's words travel. But I think something happens to people who are reasonably intelligent and aware, in their forties and fifties, and that is the desire to hold the reins a bit more, because it is such a passive job. I really am now balking at the fact that my future depends on some guy saying 'Yeah, we'll have her', or 'No, we won't'. Especially when the American film people come over to this country. You have to interview on video! I've been in this business for thirty years, what an insult! There's a wonderful story of one of our greatest actresses, Athene Seyler being asked by a casting director, 'What have you done?' and there was this long pause, and she said 'This morning?' Often, I think women with intelligence and integrity frighten the money men, because we won't take the bullshit.

Many, many more English female actors are having little nips and tucks and face jobs. A wonderful Anna Magnani story, who I adore, when she was first flown out to Hollywood for a screen test, they wanted to make her into an international star. This make-up artist started work on her face and she said 'What you do?' and she said 'Well, Miss Magnani, I'm just lightening the little crows feet here, and lifting the down lines here on your mouth', and Anna Magnani grabbed her hand and said 'You no touch-a my face. My face-a my life, you no touch-a my life'. And that's the truth of it. Thank God for people like Jessica Tandy, and a few others.

On class and power in acting

In this country, we tend to underplay the importance of our job. In America, as you know, the actor's power is equated with how much money he or she earns, and consequently how much they can throw their weight around. We don't have that in this country. In fact, whenever I've done a multi-national production – i.e. Spanish, German, Italian, French, American money in it – nine times out of ten, the make-up people – which of course is the area of the film where the small talk and gossip gets aired – have always said 'We much prefer working with English actors'. I've had a French production manager say to me exactly that, when the French actors arrive on the set, they want to know how long they're going to be, when their first day off is, when they can go home. I did a co-production in France not long ago, and all the English women were dressed and made up true to the period: terrible, Empire, hard, red mouths, very, very formal curls on the forehead, not the most attractive look. The American women in the cast went back to their caravans, on with the lip gloss, out with the combs, soften up the hairline, and you would look round at the cast and know exactly who the English actors were, because they were the ones who looked like they actually were from Napoleon's time, and the others just looked like they could have come out of an American soap opera. They just happened to be wearing Empire-line dresses!

A lot of this has to do with our class structure, you see. I hate this whole thing about the British class system. There is as much of a class system in the States. I lived in the States: what labels you've got on your clothes, what part of New York you live in, what kind of car you drive, what restaurants you eat in, that all says what level of income you're at. Money is the class divider in the States, and here, it's where you were born, and where you went to school, and what your accent's like. But that's all now being deconstructed, because a lot of people who go to public school, (with lower-class accent) all 'talk like that now', because they don't want people to think that they're upper class, that they've had a privileged background. It's now a complete reversal of what it used to be when I was a child, which was anybody from the working class strove to get rid of their accent, and strove to emulate well-spoken English.

Can Americans do Shakespeare?

I've taught Shakespeare in the States now for about four years, and it's a complete fallacy that the Americans aren't capable of performing Shakespeare. It's the same thing when young English actors start to do Shakespeare, there's no depth of experience behind the handling of the language, and it's the same in the States. If you want to do Shakespeare, then keep doing it. You start off with your Laertes and you progress to your Hamlet. You can't expect, as Daniel Day-Lewis found out, just to go wallop into the role of Hamlet. However good Mel Gibson was, it was a one-dimensional performance, because he simply hadn't got the history of speaking that language over years and years. Of knowing that you run that line through, and this is where you take the break. That all sounds very complex. But you wouldn't expect to say to a graphics artist who's been trained in acrylics, 'Okay, here is a palette of oils. I want you to paint me this van Gogh'. There simply isn't the multi-layered gone-before experience that informs the act of painting. Of course you can say 'You do a dash of yellow here, and a dash of brown there', but there is a history behind the yellow and the brown. There's a history behind the way you say the lines because you've done twenty years of speaking Shakespeare.

The whole thing about the American accent is neither here nor there, because you speak English nearer to the way Shakespeare's audience would have heard it spoken than I do. As you know, the Plymouth Brethren came from a part of England where (with middle class English accent) they speak like that and you can hear all the burring and the rolling of the r's, and that's where the gentleness of the accent comes from. So if you want to do it, do it and do it, because it's only by practising it and hearing it, that your ear begins to acclimate itself.

It's like when you hear a piece of music, you can go 'Oh, that's Mozart', or 'Oh, I think that's a bit of Beethoven', and it's only because your ear has been attuned over the years to recognise Mozartian phrases or Beethoven-type phrases. And it's the same with Shakespeare, you can hear when somebody's not *on* the line, or when they're playing the wrong words, or they're not allowing the energy to flow through to the end of the line. So no, do it, and do it a lot, if you want to do it. I'm always very moved by American students who discover the joy in that language, and who then want to continue working on it. I love teaching in the States, I find the energy in America very seductive, as well the spontaneity of the students. The trouble in America is the opposite to England; you have to go 'Hang on, could I just have five minutes?' I put my nose out of my study door in great trepidation on campus in America because I know I'm going to be jumped on by thirty students who want advice or to share ideas, whereas in England, you have 'Okay, come on now, who's going to go first?' No one. You have to put a stick of dynamite up their arses in order to get them to go first.

The Method: behaviourism vs. classical style

There's so much bullshit talked about the Method. Good acting is about being truthful, whether you're truthful to a camera that's three feet away from you, or whether you're truthful to an auditorium that holds two thousand people, and you've got to let that truth reach the back row which is eighty feet away from you. A lot of American students can't cope with the little truth that they find between themselves, and having to share it with two thousand people. I feel very passionately about this. Good acting is about truth. All good classical acting is based on the Method, whether one chooses to use that word or not. You need to know what state Juliet is in, what her relationship to her mother is, what her superobjective is over the entire play and what her objective is in each scene, if that's the way you choose to analyse it. But there is a difference between the demands that the syntax of a classical text, that is up until 1911 – Chekhov, Shaw, Strindberg, Ibsen, Shakespeare, a consciously structured line of writing – will make on you as an actor, when you have to project it and share it with two thousand people, and what I would call *behaviourism*, which is what happens in front of the film camera. You don't have the demands of that kind of syntax in a modern film script. You can go 'Um, I . . . uh . . . well . . . um'. You can't do that with Shakespeare, because you think as you speak Shakespeare. If you do *behaviourism* with Shakespeare, you'd be in the theatre for four months.

You have to marry the demands of the language with where the public ear is; where classical theatre is at *now*, i.e. Ken Branagh's *Hamlet* was very different to Laurence Olivier's *Hamlet*. Classical theatre isn't a dead object; it moves and grows and changes with each generation's input, and with the way each generation handles the language. Now, of course there is a difference between the demands of that, and what I'm calling *behaviourism*; you just behave in front of the camera.

I mean – to say the bleeding bloody obvious, to quote John Cleese in *Fawlty Towers* – Shakespeare wrote with such perception about the truth of human interaction, that what would hold in 1616, holds in 1997. The closet scene between Gertrude and Hamlet is rife with potential Freudian interpretations, and that's why Shakespeare is a wonderful writer. The way that a young man who's angry about his mother having found a new lease of life, and a new sexual partner, who happens to be the brother of his dead father, muddles up his own personal grief with his own sexual expression, and his, either lust for his mother, or his *denial* of his lust for his mother, all those kind of Oedipal complex things are true. You can psychologise a text out of existence, if it is a classical text, but ultimately, you've got to do it as you speak. You don't do the acting and then speak.

Text, image and physicality

Let's face it, we in the UK are a word-based culture; we always have been. America is a visual image-based culture; the home of the visual image. It's not for nothing that Hollywood is the birthplace of the movie. We're very text-based here, especially in companies like the National and the Royal Shakespeare Company. If you go to Poland or Czechoslovakia they say 'We have a Hamlet who can juggle and stand on his head'; the physical side of our theatre is sadly way down on the priority list. I'm ashamed when I direct English actors. Their sense of spatial relationships, their sense of the picture they create on stage is zero! Have you seen Theatre de Complicité? Because they've done more single-handedly to break through that physicality barrier, but again, they've had an enormous amount of French and Italian influence.

I don't think one must be *precious* in the real sense of the word. Many things have a part in the spectrum which is called theatre, as does standup comedy. Theatre isn't just a text-based classical thing. But I think there is a great rift in this country between word-based theatre and physical theatre, we have very little of it, and I think that's a lot to do with English repression. Often, when I teach, especially Shakespeare – which has to be text-based in order to code-break it, so they can understand and get into it – I'll do very physical exercises with my students in order to open it up. Because it isn't just the words. Often, I'll say, 'Okay, everyone freeze in this class. Just move your eyes and take in the position of everyone in this group.' They all get a bit terrified about that. And I say 'Now, look. Every single physical posture that everyone is in, says something about their mental attitude, doesn't it? It's just to remind you that what you do physically on stage says as much about your character as what you're doing with the words, and with your voice.' But it is a huge lack in this country, and something I feel passionately about. A movement teacher is only brought in if there's a special dance to be done, or a special type of movement. We are very inhibited physically in this country.

In the world of French theatre, you see, they have the whole commedia dell'arte history and inheritance, where for a large part of the 17th century, theatre was purely physical expression. You donned this costume and you moved in the way that Harlequin moved. We don't have that in this country. Because of our history of the written word, and because English was an extremely seminal language – apart from the millions of Chinese – English was, and is the most spoken language in the world. I agree, that language is used sometimes to the detriment of physical expression.

And also so much of young writing that you have now, you think 'Well, this could be done on television'. What is it that makes a piece of writing intrinsically of the theatre? It can only be when it is not able to be expressed in any other medium. You know, you throw a bale of silk over upturned chairs, and call it *Snow Covered Forest of Arden*, and then you're talking theatre, even though that owes a lot to Japanese Noh Theatre. But the minute that the theatre starts to compete with Spielberg, we're doomed, because theatre is, in essence, very simple magic, and very bold magic.

Janet McTeer

*'I couldn't give a performance that was less than 125%
... My creative self just wouldn't let me, and I live my
life like that. I cannot do it. I cannot live half a life.'*

Janet McTeer was born in Newcastle in 1961. She made her
London debut at the Royal Court Theatre as Mary in *The
Grace of Mary Traverse*. Other stage roles have included
Elizabeth I in *Vivat! Vivat! Regina* at the Mermaid, Cecilia in *Simpatico* at the Royal Court,
Beatrice in *Much Ado About Nothing* at the Queen's Theatre, Yelena in *Uncle Vanya* at the
National Theatre, Rosalind in *As You Like It*, Imogen in *Cymbeline*, and Masha in *The Three
Sisters* at the Manchester Royal Exchange. For her London performance as Nora in *A Doll's
House*, McTeer won the Olivier and Evening Standard Award for Best Actress, as well as the
Tony Award for Best Actress when the play moved to New York.

The actress' film and television career includes *Precious Bane* (for which she won the
Royal Television Society Best Performance Award), *Miss Julie*, *Portrait of a Marriage*,
102 Boulevard Haussmann, *Dead Romantic*, *A Masculine Ending*, *The Governor*, *Saint-Ex*, *Waking
the Dead* and *Tumbleweeds*.

I spoke with Janet McTeer in Montreal in March, 1998, where she was filming *Waking
The Dead*.

The odd one out: growing up

I grew up in Newcastle until I was 6, then we moved to York, where we lived until I was 17.
Then I went to London. My young schooling was ordinary, a bit like everybody else's, a little
village school. My grown-up school, my grammar school, from 11 to 17, was an all-girls
school. Looking back, it was a very good school, in a beautiful old Victorian building. Lots
of amenities, and all that sort of stuff. I got very good grades, but I don't seem to remember
enjoying it very much. I made some very good friends, all of whom I've kept, which is pretty
cool.

I had two English teachers that were spectacular, both of whom I'm very fond of; I am
still in touch with them, because they helped me enormously when I decided I was going to
be an actress. They gave me the audition speeches, and without them, I would never have
gone to drama school. The rest of the school didn't really encourage me.

My family occasionally went to the theatre, but that was a rare event, rather than something that was part and parcel of everyday life, the way it is in my life. I'm the odd one out.
Theatre wasn't really part of my childhood, although we all had music lessons. Because my

parents were war children, they very much wanted us to have the opportunities they hadn't had. They're great people, my parents. But they'd never had that sort of cultural upbringing; it was slightly alien to them. They didn't have an academic background, and I was very much an academic kind of girl.

I only did one play when I was about 12. We didn't have theatre or an amateur dramatic society. So, I sold coffees in the York Theatre and met all these people and thought, 'These are my people. These people make me feel comfortable'. I'd always felt like a fish out water. So, I decided to be an actress, having never been on stage. I decided to audition, and my parents said, 'All right, then'.

I have a few of what I call my *revelations*. Where I have known something, and I've known it absolutely, and I look back and I have no idea where I got the courage to follow it through. One of them was when I thought I wanted to be in stage management, and we had the Mystery Plays at York every few years, and I painted scenery and other things, along with six million other school girls. I just had a blast; I loved the whole thing. Of course, when I look back, these were little pointers. Also, I read a story once in assembly, which became famous in my school, because it was funny and all that. So, I can say, 'Yes, the pointers were there'. But the biggest thing was I felt the odd one out everywhere, in my family, in my home, in my school. And to an extent, I think that's the same as absolutely every young person. I think everyone feels like an odd one out, because they don't really know who they are. Then I started working at the York, and decided, somehow, I would work in the theatre.

The emphasis was very much on security when I was growing up, that sense of safety and security was totally ingrained in me as a necessity for life. It was a quite fearful kind of place to come from, as opposed to the sense of feeling, 'Oh, fuck it! What can go wrong? What's the worst thing that can happen? I'll have to phone home and say, "Will you send me some money to get me home, please?"' But the idea of taking life by the balls and having a go at it was not something that was bred into me. That was very much *me*. The idea of going to college, getting a degree and a secure job was very important. And that's what I intended to do, because I'd obviously inherited that fear. When I was 16 or 17, I started going to see everything I could at the theatre. This would be the late '70s. I remember one night, watching *She Stoops to Conquer*, and the lights went down. There's that buzz you get just before the lights come up on stage, and it's a real palpable sensation – and I remember thinking, 'If I don't have a go at this, I will regret it for the rest of my life.' That night, I decided to become an actor. And the rest is history. Here I am.

London and RADA

This particular night, after the play, I asked the actors the best places to go to drama school. And like all actors, they gave me the list they would have given to every young sixteen year old who wanted to be an actress, the best schools of England, about eight of them. And I wrote away, got their addresses and prospectuses, and applied. I remember calling one of these actors, about six months later, at the Scarborough Theatre, and saying, 'You know those schools?' He said, 'Yes . . .' I said, 'I've got into five, and I don't know which one to go to. What do you think?' And there was this stunned silence, which

I can now understand, because so many 16 year olds want to be actors. I decided to go to RADA because it was the one that he'd been to, and it was the only one I'd ever heard of, simple as that.

I think I did my entire growing up in that one moment. It was very frightening. Luckily, one of the actors I'd met in York found me a bed-sit in the building he was in, for eighteen pounds a week, which was quite disgusting. I was very nervous and very shy, I felt too tall, and all of those kind of things.

York is such a little town. It's such a small, white, middle-class environment. And to be honest, not a lot goes on there. For years I said that I could never live in a small town again. And I never have. I like being in the mish-mash of life, and you don't really get that in those kind of places. So, the whole social and cultural part was huge to me. I'd virtually never known anybody who was not white. I'd never known anybody who wasn't heterosexual; all of these things were completely new to me. Plus the fact that you're an 18 year old who's run by your hormones, and you're surrounded by boys, and you've got no parents at home. Of course this was pre-AIDS, the worst you could catch was herpes. Everybody slept with each other, and it was fantastic! You learned about yourself in a wonderful way. It's only by making those kind of mistakes that you learn anything.

I went to London wearing straight-legged jeans and mid-length brown hair, and about a term later, I had white dreads and the Camden Town version of Vivienne Westwood. So I went kind of 'Whoo! This is freedom, and I like it!' Every now and then I'd be absolutely in terror and stay in bed all day, and think, 'What am I doing? I'd quite like to go home to my mummy'. But I think that's the same as everyone else, really. Because my family's very, very different from me, as much as I love them. We're like chalk and cheese. We all laugh about it. We're quite comfortable with it, but it was pretty hard then. I found it hard to find out, for myself, what my rules and regulations and boundaries were. Because so much of what my family believed, I didn't.

One of the things I really liked about my training was that you didn't go in front of people for quite a long time, which I think is very good, because it's so terrifying when you do. If you leap to the presentation point too early, you miss out the process. It's like you're racing a racing car when you haven't properly learned how to control it. That was very good about RADA, for a start. And there was a lot of body work, and different ways of using the Laban Technique, which I found incredibly useful. I've never forgotten all of the stuff I learned there. That is the groundwork for the way I look at characters. Every character I play is six foot tall, but every character I play has a different way of moving, because she has a different way of thinking about her body. Your body is your vehicle of communication in many ways, or part of it, so you have to be able to use it. 'Being centred' I remember was a concept that used to drive me nuts! Literally, I remember screaming once, 'I don't understand what you mean!!' And of course, the answer is that you just keep practising, and you'll know it when you feel it, like anything else. I eventually got it, and the difference was huge.

There was a lot of improvisation, which I thought was brilliant, putting yourself in situations in various ways. Voice work, of course. In America, I found they don't have as much voice work as we have over here. It is absolutely shocking! Along with your body, it's the second vehicle of expression. And how you cannot make your voice a finely-tuned instrument is extraordinary to me. So, you get people going on stage, and they're in trouble, because they don't know how to project, or they don't know how to do it without hurting themselves. I suffered from bronchitis a couple of times, and it's amazing how it throws me off when I feel I can't project to the maximum. Or it's a struggle, and you lose that sense of control. So, we did a lot of voice and body work, a lot of work on pieces, and work on speeches with various voice coaches. I remember it being very diverse. There were lots of different sorts of teachers, and I had a couple of people who were my gurus, who I thought were spectacular.

There was one guy called Malcolm McKay, who was one of my tutors. He was this fierce, wonderful English maverick. I liked him because he wasn't a grown-up, first of all, and I'd been brought up in a very kind of 'grown-ups are grown-ups, and children are children way', and I kept thinking I was going to turn into a grown-up. Then when I came to London, I met these grown-ups who were just people, and that radically changed my thinking. He was one of those people. He'd come out and drink beer, and smoke fags, and say 'fuck' a lot, and just talk.

I remember all of my teachers there with great affection, but I think what was wonderful about him – and this is me, personally, he might not have worked for other people – was that he was a driven perfectionist, and that appealed to me, because I am also a driven perfectionist. One of the things I think that's a huge lesson for people to learn at drama or art school, or anything that isn't business-orientated, is that you go in as an amateur, and you come out as a professional. And the difference between being an amateur and a professional is enormous. And basically, it's the cognizance of the fact that you are a professional artist. It's as simple as that. I remember people would come to rehearsals a bit hung over, and Malcolm would go fucking berserk! A couple of times he walked out. I felt a huge shift because of that. You'd say, 'Okay. Right. I'm a professional actor. That's what I do.' And that's a big leap, because professionalism is really important.

Having said that, I think that sense of professionalism has fuzzy lines around it. Essentially you are employing somebody for their creativity – and sometimes that means you can't leave yourself at the door the way you can if you have to file cabinets, or you have to do a business deal. If you're very upset about something, and you have to do a very upset scene, the lines can get fudged. Issues have to be dealt with within the creative environment that aren't necessarily professional, because you're dealing with emotions. But you're still a professional, and that means dealing with the other actors and other people in the profession – whatever their job is – with respect, with professionalism. And Malcolm taught me that.

There was a great turning point with him, when we were doing a piece, and I was working my bollocks off. And I was terrible. We were doing a dress rehearsal, and he was known for being really vicious and ruthless. I was sitting looking into my dressing room mirror thinking, 'That fucking bastard's going to come in here and he's going to fucking tell me off. I was terrified.' He came in, and he looked at me, and said, 'You don't know what the fuck you're doing, do you?' And I said, (tearfully) 'No'. He said, 'I'll take you out for a pint later, don't worry about it.' And I burst into tears.

He was very wise at recognising where I was in my process, in my life, at that time. He told me how I was staying out of the frightening centre of the part, and how I was compensating for people who weren't where I was. I remember Malcolm saying to me, 'You must understand that a good actor is like a Rolls-Royce, and you are a Rolls-Royce. You will get better and better, as you get older and older. So, you've got to think long-term.' He was spectacular, one of my biggest gurus.

Preliminary adventures in the theatre

I got my first job in Nottingham, and they were wonderful. Richard E Grant, Hugh Grant and I got our Equity cards, but we had nothing to do. Little parts, that's how you got your Equity card. They were very kind and let me go when I was offered some very nice parts at Sheffield for a few months. Then from there, I went to the Manchester Royal Exchange, and that was where I really took off. They were sensational to me, I played Rosalind in *As You Like It*, Masha in *The Three Sisters*, and a team of things. It was in the days where you had a six-month contract, and we had a fantastic company, and we all had a blast. I've been back there a few times.

I didn't want to work for very long anywhere. It wasn't my kind of thing. I worked at the RSC, where I did Titania and Hippolyta in *Midsummer Night's Dream* on the big stage, and this wonderful play called *Worlds Apart*, in the tiny theatre – before the Pit was remade. And I loved that. I had a whale of a time at Stratford. Then we came to London. I didn't like London; I didn't like the RSC theatre. It's totally actor non-friendly. I didn't want to be there, and I wasn't very well, so I left. But I thought Stratford was a glorious place, the challenge of working in different theatres, being part of a big company, living in a city that's as beautiful as that. I had a 16th Century cottage two minutes from the theatre. I did so many plays. And the directors were totally delightful: Bill Alexander, John Caird, Richard Eyre, Trevor Nunn, everybody. If they're British and they direct, they were there.

I've always wanted to play challenging, interesting roles. I've never really wanted to play the second fiddle to a man. You know, the wife at home, that kind of thing. That doesn't really appeal to me, not unless it's interesting, and about her. I've always considered myself very lucky in a way, because I've never been part of that young-pretty-blonde set. I've always been somebody you can't necessarily categorise. I think that if you have anything that's extreme, you can do a lot with it. Being six foot tall is very extreme. I've been very gawky, I've been ridiculously elegant. I've always toyed around with my looks, because it's very interesting. And I've always looked for roles that are well-written. And like any actor, you want to work with good people. So, projects come along and they're not necessarily the greatest parts in the world, but you're working with great people. Sometimes that's enough.

Developing a character

I think the greatest challenge for a professional actor, as you carry on, is to be consistently at a point where you know nothing. And you have to assume when you begin a part, that you know nothing. It's too easy to fall into being comfortable with certain aspects of yourself as a performer. I've never particularly wanted to do that. I've always wanted to do something dangerous.

I read Uta Hagen's book, *Respect for Acting,* when I was at college. Her book was very important to me. I think there's a great misapprehension, which I find very interesting, about English versus American acting; and I do think there is a great difference. But I also think the truth is exactly the same in either country. If an actor believes themselves to be the character in a very deep way, then, in essence, it's simply a question of how it comes out that is different. As I said, I'm shocked that American actors seem to have so little technical training compared to us. But having said, that, I believe that an essential truth is an essential truth. It doesn't matter whether it's Japanese, English, or American or Indian. That is what you're looking for when you're trying to play the character. So you have to assume you don't know anything about the character and start from scratch. An absolutely blank page, a whole new picture, and you paint it on yourself, or in yourself. You always work from a position of chaos, and I think that's the best place to be, because if you do that, everything is possible. If you have a very particular way of working, I think it can become constricting. So, I try to always stay as open as possible to wherever it leads me.

Obviously there are certain things I know. I know what the story is. I know what my function in the story is, so that I don't throw off the balance. 'There are no small parts, just small actors', is bullshit. A small part is a small part for a very good reason, because it's not as important as a big part. You need to make it a full person, but I can't stand it when you see someone coming on and saying 'This is my chance to shine!' No, it isn't your chance to shine. It's your chance to come on and fulfil the function of the scene, and it can imbalance things if you don't understand your function. Doing what is needed within the function of the piece is what's important, adding to the flesh of the piece. I'm open to ideas every time. But in Uta Hagen's book, there's one big thing I remember, she says the first reading of the play is very important, and I've never forgotten that. I never read scripts on the run. I read them properly.

I don't work as specifically as Uta Hagen suggests, charting the character's basic wants, desires and obstacles. I probably do all of those things, but I wouldn't be as concrete about it as she is. I always go through a script and read what I say about myself, and what other people say about me, and then I look at certain facts and say, 'Are they true? Do other people think they're true?' For example, when I played Yelena in *Uncle Vanya,* she's this archetypally beautiful person, who everyone thinks is beautiful. That is a huge fact about her, and you have to ask, 'Okay. Do I think I'm beautiful? If I do, do I like it? Am I worried about being beautiful? Does it cause problems for me? Do I use it ever in a manipulative way?' I ask all of those things. You can't fall into the trap of thinking, 'Oh, how lovely, you get to play somebody beautiful and wear beautiful clothes, which automatically means that you want to be beautiful.'

For that particular part, you are dealing with somebody who's always been told that they're beautiful, and the pressure that puts on them. People probably don't listen to them as much, because that's all they are. They can feel lost behind the shell that everyone puts their imaginative projections onto. All of those things are not things I particularly feel in my actual life. So, that was quite interesting. And also, if you're very beautiful – especially if you're a woman – it must be much harder as you grow older, because people always focus on your beauty.

I felt Yelena was thinking, 'Here I am. I'm nearly 30, and it's all going horribly wrong, and I've got this old husband who was fantastic ten years ago, and isn't any more.' The one thing I always do is work out what somebody's belief system is. I think that's very important, and has a huge effect. What do I think about women? What do I think about men? What do I think about husbands? What do I think about furniture? What do I think about curtains? What do I think about pets? What do I think about sex? One thing I do, when I'm rehearsing or thinking about something, wherever I am – this morning I was in a book shop – I suddenly said, 'If my character was here right now, what would I think?' And if I don't know how my character would think and feel, then I note it, and I think about it. And you build the character like that.

A Doll's House

I think there comes a point where something has been completed in your life, when you know it at a very deep level, and you can use it in a part. I've just played *A Doll's House*, which doesn't dovetail with my life now at all, but you could say that it was an encapsulation of the first ten years of my adulthood. I got to the position where Nora is, in a more modern, less obvious way, when I was about 27.

My mother wanted me to have all the opportunities that she never had. She was taken out of school when she was fourteen, because girls didn't get educated, and it was war time. She will now say if she'd been born in a slightly different time, a bit later, there were lots of things that she could have done. She didn't utilise her skills. And I think she very much wanted us children to be able to do that. Having said that, I still think I was brought up to be a wife and mother. I had an inherent sense that you needed a man to complete your life. That was something to be attained, and however wonderful a career might be, without that, you had nothing.

And I always had great charm, as a child. One of my early school reports said, 'Janet must learn to realise that she cannot get by in life on charm alone'. I've always had an ability – which is a great actor's thing – to empathise with people. I can sit and talk to absolutely anybody, and get along in a way that some people find very hard to do. Consequently, I was always a bit of a chameleon, because I didn't know who I was. Essentially, when I was young, I made myself into what I thought people wanted me to be, especially emotionally. And I would put up with all kinds of nonsense from the boys I was going with. Eventually, of course, I tired of it. But it took me a good few knocks to be tired of it, to finally say, 'Hang on a cotton-picking minute, I deserve better than this. Fuck you!' or 'Could you listen to me?' So, basically I used a very early form of myself in the role. I was never as bad as Nora, obviously, but I was able to turn my experience into early Nora.

I related easily to the sense of repressed anger that Nora has. We didn't really get angry in my house. Anger was considered to be a bad, non-Christian emotion. I totally disagree with that now. I'm a highly passionate person, I get very angry sometimes, and I get very happy. Now to me, anger is just another colour.

And the other thing is that as an adult, a real grown-up, you've been through shit, you've seen life in its many colours, much of which is great and joyful and much of which is really hard. And certainly for *A Doll's House*, you get to a point as an adult when you know that there is no split, no divorce that happens without an extraordinary amount of pain. It doesn't matter who's right, or who's wrong. It's extraordinarily painful. And the destruction of confidence that goes along with trying to make something work, trying to convince yourself that it's all right to stay. Trying to convince yourself that all the shenanigans that we go through in an effort to make a marriage work are worth it. Sometimes it works, and it sorts itself out, and sometimes it doesn't. The point where you finally say, 'I'm leaving', is so unbelievably painful. And the point where you walk out the door, the first thought you have is 'Did I really do enough to make that work?', especially when there are children involved. I think it's mixed up and confusing, and only as a real adult, could I have understood that sufficiently to be able to play the last act of *A Doll's House* the way I thought it should be done.

Janet McTeer in *A Doll's House* (1996)

Researching a role

We commissioned an absolute literal translation of *A Doll's House* as well as using Frank McGuinness' new version. Go right back to the source all the time. I read it in Norwegian even though I don't read Norwegian. But I read everything. We wanted the translation to be very modern, without being in the vernacular, and it's all Ibsen. There are no additions. All of it is absolutely Ibsen. People have been taken so far away from what was originally there. All of Ibsen's sentences are short when they're written in Norwegian. The words are short. They're not long, convoluted Victorian sentences. That wasn't what he wrote. He wrote a humanist piece of drama, encapsulating every idea of its time, about men and women, and love. It was extraordinary. I think it could be played in six million different ways, because it's such a beautifully-written piece.

I read a lot about Ibsen, about his life, and the ramifications that the real-life incident of forgery had on his life. Why would he write something like this piece in the first place? Why was it so fucking brilliant, especially for its time? Relating to a forgery is very hard, because it's not something that could make me want to kill myself, or anyone else. In terms of the actual playing of it, sometimes forgery wasn't enough, I would have to give myself something else as an actor. Cherry Jones (the lead actor in a long-running Broadway show) made this wonderful comment, by the time she finished *The Heiress*, she'd imaginatively killed her entire family, and most of her pets, and everyone she ever loved. Because if you're playing something for a long time, sometimes you have to find a new imaginative starting point that will heighten the stakes.

It goes back to the belief system. I would think 'Okay, what was different about being in Norway than being in Victorian England?' And I very much wanted that difference. There was a very different sense of physicality, the style of clothes, everything was very different. There was not that sense of female repression, sexual repression certainly, that there was in England. Then, within that interpretation, I would look at what I thought Ibsen intended, what I thought he was writing about. I think a lot of the received notions about *A Doll's House* in particular, are rubbish, or at least an intellectual opinion taken too far.

For example, the idea that it was the first great feminist play. It wasn't. It was never written with that intention. Ibsen was furious when it was taken as the first great feminist play, because what it does – to take Nora as a feminist character – is to remove her vulnerability. It takes away humanity, because she becomes this kind of strident quitter. For many years, that was how it was played, and I think that was very wrong. Like any great work, you can translate it in many ways because it is so deep, and rich and wonderful. Nora is a much more complex, complicated character. I think it is a humanist play, from which you can draw feminist conclusions, which is a completely different way of looking at it. It gives it back its humanity, and that's what I wanted to do with our production of the play. So, that was the kind of research I would do, because that would lead you back into the imaginative brain of the person who sat there and actually wrote it down, and what he was trying to do. Why would you write about somebody who left her children? Why would the situation get so bad that you would do that? Are you saying she's a bad person? Of course not, otherwise why write three hours of drama about her? So, how can you – as an actor – justify that? How do you leave your children?

I didn't have a problem with the last scene. To me, the scene played itself, and it was the scene I least rehearsed. It made perfect sense. Nora did love her husband, she still loves him when she leaves. But she's saying: 'I don't know who you are. You don't know who I am. How can I possibly say that I love you? Because I'm locked in myself, this little game I've played, and you're locked in – and I don't know who I am.' And the worst lesson you can possibly teach a child is to not know who they are. And how can she ever help her children if she doesn't know who she is? The only way she can ever help her children is to know who she is, because then she can teach them how to be themselves, or rather allow them to be themselves, rather than teach them to be brought up to be these proper little people, and fit into this cardboard cut-out town.

The idea is not to give away the secret to the audience at the beginning. Not letting the audience think that actually you're this really big person who's playing a small person. That's what attracted me to the part, and that's what's dangerous about it. It's frustrating for an audience, but actually much more true-to-life, that Nora is a big person who doesn't even realise that she is a big person. That this secret she'd had, of paying for her husband's medical care through an act of forgery, was something she was secretly proud of, but would never dream of revealing in front of anybody. And she would certainly never dream of tipping the balance in her relationship with her husband. I know tons of people who still do a version of that. I think everybody does. I wanted to make it modern and real enough that it would touch people's lives. So they wouldn't look at it and say, 'Gosh, how awful it must have been to live then. Wasn't she marvellous?' I wanted people to say, 'I do exactly the same thing', about women who earn more than men, for example. They slightly fib about the amount they spend on clothes, or the fact that they pay the bills. That is certainly not equal. The fact that men may do the same amount of housework as a woman, but who makes the roster? Who divides the jobs? Who actually writes the to-do list? Chances are, it's the woman. That kind of thing still goes on in subtle ways.

Rehearsal time

I've never liked blocking; I've never done blocking. I've constantly believed that if a move is right, it will happen. And if it ain't right, then that's what rehearsals are for. So, if it's uncomfortable, it's much more than a problem with the staging. I've very much forged my own personal way of working, which, I think, is absolutely in-between England and America. Having spent quite a lot of time in America, I think I've drawn from the best of both worlds.

For me, blocking is exactly what it says, it blocks. It blocks me! And so, in a scene, with a bunch of actors, you come in and just do it! And you do it without the fourth wall; you do it for real. And if somebody does something, you deal with it. Nine times out of ten, it doesn't work. One time out of ten, something wonderful happens. And then once you've been rehearsing for a while, you pick out every one of those 'one of the ten', and you have something that is rounded and spectacular. Because I believe that, again – this is very English – because of the training that English people have, it becomes about generosity. We can rehearse a scene in a certain way, but I know fine well, because I trust you and you trust me, that when we come to doing it, when it comes to a week before we actually open, and you say 'This isn't going to work', we change it. You work it out totally organically, *then* you do technical things, like leaning forward to listen when it's her line, and leaning back when it's yours. These actions are purely technical, but now they come out of something organic. But for me to *start* doing by doing those things, is to totally block my instincts. But that's purely my way.

Other actors like something to hang onto, they like to be blocked from the word 'go'. There are as many different ways of acting as there are anything else. But I cannot stand it. And I have to say, I swear to God, since I was 20 – when anyone says, 'Okay, Janet you come in from there, he'll come from over there, and we'll all meet here', I will literally, every time – because I can't stand it if somebody tells me where to walk and where to go – do something different until they realise that I'm not going to be pinned down. At the same time, I try to be sensitive to the fact that other actors need that sort of direction. When I was doing *A Doll's House*, I remember John Carlisle who played Dr Rank, at the beginning found it really hard, because he comes very much from a certain kind of training. I think for the first week of rehearsals, he thought I had no idea what I was doing. After a while, as he saw this real performance begin to emerge, and he realised that I did know what I was doing, and then there was a sense of, 'Oh, okay. I'll go along with this'. And he had much more fun. Having said that, I liked the stability he represented as well, because that was really good for me, too. You need a sense of security. But my anchors are inside. If I'm having a bad day, and I think, 'Oh, I'd just rather be watching *Coronation Street*, quite frankly,' or 'I've got period pains, and I *really* don't want to be here, and I most certainly don't want to cry.' On those days, you have this third eye, and it goes, 'Right – I will get from here to there'. If I have to do it technically, if I'm not feeling it deeply that night, the truth is, nobody will notice, because that's my training. But my anchors are deep inside, they're not on the surface.

I'll always ask for help during rehearsals. If I reach a point where I'm stuck, I'll just say, 'I'm stuck! I'm stuck! Anybody with any suggestion, help!' Because sometimes you can't see the wood for the trees. I'll happily listen to anybody who has a suggestion, anybody at all. I'm not very precious about the way I work. Anybody can say anything, as far as I'm concerned. I often get stuck in the process. It's a bit like a computer. You put in so much information into your emotional, psychological, physical banks, that suddenly you just have no idea what the fuck you're doing. No idea at all. I've since learned that this is the wonderful part. This is the part where you go out and watch Bruce Willis or Arnold Schwarzenegger in a movie, you don't think about it. You don't watch anything clever. You never watch anything with great acting in it. You watch complete shite, or you read a really bad novel, and the computer does all its work, and you walk into rehearsals two days later, and suddenly, something's moved. It's gone through that barrier of your skin, and it's on the inside. Then you're in the next phase of rehearsal.

Keeping body and soul together: a long run

That's a hard one. You learn that over the years, and every year it gets better, hopefully. For me, the key is to have a very strong perspective. And my perspective was: at this time in my life, I am doing this wonderful piece of writing, getting these wonderful reviews, having full houses every night. It is a totally gratifying, fulfilling creative experience. And it's happening right now, and it will never be repeated, not this one. If you give yourself to that, you can do it. There's so much gratitude for that. I can't tell you what it's like to give your soul to a performance every night. You come out, and you see these enormously moved people all standing on their feet, crying. And you think, 'Jesus, what a gift. What a precious, precious gift in my life be able to touch a thousand people, every night.'

I didn't do a mid-week, because I couldn't do it. I did them at the beginning, and I collapsed one day, in tears, on a Saturday afternoon, and said, 'I can't. I'm not going to last five minutes. I cannot do this'. And so we cancelled the matineé. And when we came to America, they were adamant that we did the mid-week, and I said, 'I really can't do it. I cannot compromise like that'. But even Saturdays killed me. But if you have that perspective on it, then everything you have to do in order to achieve the performance becomes less of a sacrifice.

I felt that very, very strongly. I was on a very strict diet, I ate protein and a shit-load of vegetables, and I didn't drink apart from Saturday night, when I had some champagne, religiously. I ate incredibly well. And during the days, the phone was off, and I didn't do very much. That's what you have to do. And warm up every night for a good half an hour, so that you don't break anything. It was a seriously full-time job. I've never been so tired as I was by the time I finished *A Doll's House*. There were many times when I'd think, 'I so absolutely don't need to be here'. Because the journey every night was so huge, but every night I was glad I did it. You have to take incredibly good care of yourself, and realise that in order to give that amount, you have to be completely focused on *it*, and it alone. Again, I don't have children, and you say, 'If I do have children, I may never be able to do this kind of job for a very long time, so enjoy it while it's here'. And every night after the show, wonderful people came to see me, whether they were in England or in New York, and that was lovely, and a trip, a real joy.

I've always had this ability to focus on a performance from about five o'clock in the afternoon; your emotions are somehow working and waking up in a sense-memory kind of way, and you do the show. I've always been slightly shocked at myself, really. We did *A Doll's House* which ends with that intense emotion. I'd finish the show, walk off and it would be completely finished for me. Owen (Teale), who was magnificent as Torvald in *A Doll's House* would sometimes come off sobbing, because it would touch him in a way that would make him cry. I've never had that. Leading up to a performance, or in the middle of a performance, it might touch me very deeply, or remind me of certain things, and get me very upset. But as soon as it's finished, it's gone. It lives in its own little magic bubble. I don't know how I do it, but I have always done it.

Playing real-life characters

There's a different kind of research that goes on when you're playing somebody real. I spent an enormous amount of time, I read everything there was to read about Vita Sackville-West (for the BBC production of Nigel Nicholson's *Portrait of a Marriage*). I spent days and days and days at Sissinghurst literally sitting in her room just feeling her presence. The same kind of thing, building up, reading what everybody said about her, because obviously her life is interpreted by different people in different ways. It's like putting a jigsaw together when you have a real person. So, you have little bits here, little bits there, and eventually you try and find a piece in the middle that is you, that you can connect with, that makes all the pieces and lines in the jigsaw puzzle disappear. And suddenly you have this three-dimensional picture. So, you meet somewhere in the middle. Vita had a whole different way of holding herself, of walking, her sexuality was different from mine, all those things were very important.

I remember she has a painting above the arch that goes into the little turret at the back of her writing room. I loved this room, and I could see why everything was there. Then there was this painting, and I just didn't understand it. I think if you don't understand somebody's art, you don't understand their soul. I must have spent *hours* looking at this fucking picture! Until eventually, it clicked, and that was a really important moment for me. In actual fact, we weren't allowed to film in her room, so we built a set and duplicated it in a studio in London. I remember going into the set, saying, 'God! That's extraordinary!' And if you didn't look up and see the bank of lights, you would've thought you were in her room. And there was this painting, and I thought, 'Did they buy it? No, they couldn't have bought it'. Of course, somebody had copied it. They gave it to me as a present, and I still have it at home, and I love it.

But the central piece for me, with Vita, was, again, 'How could she leave her children and go off with her lover'? A lot of that was about the time in which she lived. She herself wrote that she didn't realise that every woman *wasn't* gay. She thought everyone felt like her. There's a wonderful speech she wrote in her diary to her husband trying to explain to him why she did what she did, why she went away. And the speech was 'I fish, and I fish, and I fish, and sometimes I catch a lovely little trout, but never the great salmon that lashes and fights, and convinces me that it's fighting for its life'. And the lady who wrote the script put it in, but she didn't understand it. I was thinking, 'This is really important'. And eventually, of course, what it meant was that she had an uncompromising spirit. She couldn't help herself. She couldn't help but jump off the high beam. She couldn't compromise her soul, because to do that would be to kill it. And there was nothing she could do about that.

And, that for me was the bit where I connected, because I'm like that. I can't help it. The reason I was so unbelievably exhausted by the time we finished *A Doll's House* was because I couldn't give a performance that was less than 125%. Not because I felt any pressure from the people who were coming to see it, not because of anything external, but because I just couldn't. My creative self just wouldn't let me, and I live my life like that. I cannot do it. I cannot live half a life.

On being a woman and an actor

I've constantly been asked 'When are you going to start directing?' And I've constantly said, 'I'll start when the menopause hits'. Because by Christ, this business hates you then. They don't know what to do with you, they don't like you, because it's still mostly run by men. And I'm not going to sit around and get miserable about not working and feeling low on myself. No, thank you very much. While the work's still here, this particular work, I'll do it. You never know, it might not dry up. Chances are, it will. Who knows? And then you come back as an accepted older actress, like Vanessa Redgrave, Judi Dench, those people who are mature, not at the wrong end of 40, which is what most people seem to think women in their 40s are. They're the right side of 50. I think it's a horrible aspect of this business.

I was brought up in a time which allowed me to facilitate my actions and beliefs. My sense of being a strong woman is less rebellious, I think, than women of an older generation. I don't have a sense of 'men this, and men that'. I don't see it. If I see it, I deal with it. I've always had this tremendous debt of gratitude, from the time I was very young, to the women who fought the fight.

I've often thought as well that a lot of what I am, or a lot of the way I am treated, comes from being six foot tall. I can't remember the number of times people have said to me when they've got to know me, 'God, I was really frightened when I met you!' Because I'm this big, striking, strong, noisy, vibrant person. I remember when I was playing Masha in *The Three Sisters*, we were doing a dress rehearsal, and I just couldn't do it. I was 24, and I burst into tears in the dress rehearsal, and I said, (mock-cries) 'I can't do it!' Niamh Cusack, who was playing Irina came up to me and gave me a big hug, and she said, (in an Irish accent) 'I don't believe it! You're a little person, just like me!' I think people just assume because of your physicality, and because you have a deep voice, that you are this huge, towering,

Janet McTeer in *Portrait of a Marriage* (1990)

feminist big person, even if in actual fact you're thinking, 'Oh, Christ, I'm six foot. I wish I was five foot-two, then nobody would be looking at me'. Which I do often when I walk into a party. So, I think a lot of my feelings come from that. I have many gifts that have helped me along that way, that are totally unworked for.

Films vs. theatre

I love absolutely everything about filmmaking, and I love everything about rehearsing and doing a play. I love working with people for six weeks on a rehearsal, privately. Having all that time to really explore a character. You don't get that time in a film, you have to do that on your own. I love that interaction in a play, going to the pub, everything about it. I love the excitement of the technical rehearsal, the terror of dress rehearsals and public previews, and going in front of an audience for the first time, when you'd much rather kill yourself. I love it all.

On films I also absolutely adore being picked up at six in the morning by some tired driver, who's just as exhausted as you. You go to the set and the film unit becomes – because there are such long hours – a real family, and I love all of that as well. I love them both. I do try to go from film to theatre to film.

The difference between film acting and theatre acting is minimal, I think. Some actors work from the outside-in, some work from the inside-out. If you work from the outside-in, you'll find film much harder, if you work from the inside-out, it's easy. You say, 'Here's your kernel of truth', and it's like a lens, you just open it, this far for film, this far for a 500-seat theatre, and this far for a 2000-seat theatre, but the essence of truth is not different, you're just opening the lens bigger. Of course, the first time I ever saw myself on screen I thought I was the ugliest person in the world. Hideous. I cried, I seem to remember, and got terribly drunk.

Classical acting and the Method/British and American acting

I think if you're a good actor, you're a good actor. The way that acting is taught is ultimately, slightly immaterial. If you're really good, you'll get at the truth. Perhaps the way it comes out may be slightly different with a different training, but essentially it's no different. Look at Charles Laughton, one of the best Method actors that has ever been. Spectacular. There is a moment in *The Hunchback of Notre Dame*, where Esmerelda gives him water, and this classically trained actor, tips his head away from her because he thinks she's going to hit him, and then he looks to her in this hugely stylised moment. She gives him the water – he looks at her, and falls madly in love with her in that one second. And he leans forward, and opens his mouth for her to pour the water in. It is one of the most exquisite moments I have ever seen on film. You literally see this simple man falling in love. And that's totally Method. There's nothing un-Method about that. I think, in terms of certain techniques of training I talked about, the voice/body work, a lot of that doesn't seem to be done as much among Method actors.

A lot of American acting that we see in Britain, is obviously on film. And a lot of film scripts that you work on are about stories. The dialogue isn't that well-written; it's not classical text. So, when you come on to the set, you improvise, and that is very American in its way. That desire to be totally, totally real in its essence is something that we don't really do in England, or certainly not to the same extent. I suppose there's a difference between being yourself in a given situation, and being a character in a given situation. A lot of American actors, especially the young ones, play themselves in endless number of given situations. But then, to a certain extent, all stars have done that all the time, because that's what it means to be a star. I consider myself to be somewhere in between. I've always been drawn to the kind of thing that's considered to be very British: the wonderful speaking of text. But for me, if the wonderful speaking of text has no heart, I'd rather read it.

Confidence, final fancies

I think every good quality has its opposite, bad side. You can't enjoy the laid-back quality of somebody without also getting pissed off at the fact that they might not be on time. I think my greatest quality is my courage, and the opposite of that is without my courage, I have nothing. When my confidence goes, which it sometimes does for absolutely no reason at all, I'm desperate, and I have nothing to fall back on. Without that, I feel invisible, I feel totally guilty, and I can't do it. The amount of times I've forced myself to go on stage, the number of times I've had to have the nearest and dearest come to a performance for several nights, usually at the beginning of a run. When I've frightened other actors by crying in the middle of a scene, because I think I shouldn't be on stage. And then it'll go, and that's the opposite side of being as brave as I am. It's because I act without a big safety net. I have millions of nets in many other ways, but if I feel I haven't quite got it, my confidence is low. I do master classes sometimes, and the thing I say to actors is that there are really only two things you need as an actor: one is talent, and the other is confidence, and you cannot have one without the other. I can't say I would change it, but I've learned to accept that when I hit those lows, I say, 'this too, will pass', and just keep going, keep saying the lines, and hope for the best, and know that tomorrow it will be easier. That's just a bit of maturity. But there have been times when I've drunk myself into a stupor, or smoked 75 cigarettes, or contemplated not going in, and withdrawing, and all of those things, and then that feeling just goes away. You walk on and suddenly, you're okay. I suppose, if I could change anything, I would change my ability to deal with that, but I seem to deal with that better and better every time it happens.

Anything else? Oh, I would sometimes like to be man. I would like to be short and blonde. Simply because then you could play everything. You know, there are so many fantastic parts that are written for men that you really can't play. I'd love to play King Lear. When I was younger, the only classical young role I never played was Juliet, because nobody would ever think of me as a 14 year old ingénue. I had no intention of playing it; it's not a part that bears any resemblance to me at all. But still, it would've been nice to have played it. If I could be a hologram and change the way I look totally, I would quite like that, yeah.

Stephen Rea

'... *any artistic process is a difficult undertaking, and painful in many ways, but art is meant to re-define, and to turn the bad into the good.*'

Stephen Rea was born in Belfast in 1947. For the National Theatre, he has appeared in *The Playboy of the Western World*, *The Comedians*, *Tales of the Vienna Woods*, *Strawberry Fields*, *The Shaughraun*, *Making History* and *Piano*. At the Royal Court, Rea's work includes *Freedom of the City*, *Endgame*, Sam Shepard's *Geography of a Horse Dreamer*, and the Royal Court production of Pinter's *Ashes to Ashes* at the Ambassadors. Hampstead Theatre productions include *Killer's Head*, *Kingdom of Earth*, Mike Leigh's *Ecstasy*, Shepard's *Buried Child*, Brian Friel's *Translations* and *Someone to Watch Over Me* by Frank McGuinness, which transferred to New York. Other major theatre work: *High Society*, *Miss Julie*, *The Cherry Orchard*, *The Duchess of Malfi* and *Shadow of a Gunman* in London, and Richard Eyre's production of *The White Devil* in Nottingham. In Derry, Northern Ireland, Rea formed the Field Day Theatre Company with Brian Friel. He has acted in all Field Day productions except *The Three Sisters*, which he directed. Amongst the Field Day productions in which Rea performed are: *Translations*, *Boesman and Lena*, *The Riot Act* (which he also directed), *Double Cross*, *Pentecost*, *Making History*, *Saint Oscar* and *Uncle Vanya*. Rea has appeared at the Abbey Theatre in Dublin in *Aristocrats* and *The Blue Macushla*, and at the Gate Theatre in the 1991 Beckett Festival.

Rea's film work includes eight films with Neil Jordan: *Angel*, *The Company of Wolves*, *The Crying Game*, *Interview with the Vampire*, *Michael Collins*, *The Butcher Boy*, *In Dreams* and *The End of the Affair*. He has also appeared in *Loose Connections* (directed by Richard Eyre), Mike Figgis' *The House*, *The Doctor and the Devils*, Mike Leigh's *Life is Sweet*, Robert Altman's *Prêt-à-Porter*, *Bad Behaviour*, *Citizen X*, *Trojan Eddie*, *The Crime of the Century*, *Still Crazy*, *Guinevere* and *This is My Father*. For television, Rea has done Ken Loach's *Days of Hope*, Stephen Frears' *Early Struggles*, *Professional Foul* and *The Seagull* (both directed by Michael Lindsay-Hogg), *The Plough and The Stars*, *Joyce in June*, Mike Leigh's *Four Days in July*, Danny Boyle's *Scout* and *Hedda Gabler*, directed by Deborah Warner. He has also read the poetry of James Joyce and W.B. Yeats for Channel 4.

I spoke with Stephen Rea in Dublin in May, 1998.

Growing up in Belfast

Belfast was bleak, I'd say, very bleak. I think it's improved now. It was a squalid little sectarian city, and not conducive to an artistic imagination. One lived a very narrow life. I went to a state school; there was the odd reasonable teacher, but nobody very inspired. We can get through this area fast; I don't really like to talk about it. I don't think I was influenced by anyone in particular; I just had this instinct and urge to show off. Becoming an actor is a matter of whether you respond to an instinct, or not. I don't think there's any particular kind of background that would encourage it, necessarily. I was at a show last night and Ameilia Fox was there, and her father is Edward Fox. Inevitably she's going to be an actress, but apart from that kind of obvious influence, it's hard enough to find something that you're good at. I suppose when you do, you go with it. I was always good at reading aloud; the teachers always used to ask me to read more than once in a class. I knew I was good at it because they always got round to me twice. The way some kids read would be unbearable, and I read with some interest in what I was doing. So if you were good at something, you just stuck at it, and that was the only thing I was particularly good at.

I kind of got a degree at Queen's University in English and French. But I wasn't academically inclined, really. My mother would like me to have been a teacher, but that wasn't a very thought-out thing on her part, it was just that if you had an arts degree there wasn't much else you could do. I never intended to teach, that was an idea my mother had. I wouldn't have been very good at it. At that time, teaching was a secure job, but it ceased to be very quickly. I suppose I was nervous about becoming an actor, but that's just because of the apparent insecurity of it. In the end, you realise everything's insecure.

I went to the cinema, but I was never in a theatre, probably, until I acted in one. I had an urge to act, and acting was then channelled into theatre, because theatre was what existed. You couldn't be in the movies because there weren't any movies to be in, in Ireland. So I went into the theatre.

Reflections on acting for film

I've always had a great love of Robert Mitchum. I can't think of it with the vision of a child, because I don't really remember. It's a bit more conscious now. What it is I admire about his acting is that he's one of the great narrative actors. Nowadays everybody wants to 'show emotion'; everyone since the post-Brando Italian actors wants to scream the house down and show their innards, and Mitchum simply *thinks*. He must have been wonderful for a director, because all you do is cut to Mitchum and he thinks something, and then you can take the movie in any direction you want. So, that's the kind of acting that I really admire, Bogart, Tracy, and those kind of guys.

I very much like the acting that Brando used to do, because he had a wonderful imagination and wonderful restraint as well. Look at the inroads that Brando, in his heyday, had into his own feeling, in the most staggering way. But I think that there was a lot of misunderstanding of what he was doing. He was devastatingly sexy as well as being a brilliant actor, so everybody really wanted to *be* him. After Brando, there's a movement away from the kind of actor that Mitchum and Tracy and Bogart were. I prefer what they did to what came after Brando. The Italians . . . I don't want to name them. You know, in *Raging Bull* there are sequences where Scorsese should cut. He doesn't cut, he allows De Niro to go on displaying character, whereas the great screen actors like Mitchum were very economical;

they knew that the movie had to have a movement. They constantly move it on, which is what theatre actors have to do, because you can't hang about. And you can't leave actors alone to do things.

Taxi Driver, I think, is great and perfectly judged. But by the time you get to *Raging Bull*, he's indulging De Niro, and I don't think he should. I don't think any director should indulge any actor, and I don't think actors should indulge themselves, and those guys, like Mitchum and Bogart, in the most seemingly casual way, really knew about the movie, in the way that a musician would know a piece he's playing. It's so boring hearing someone do a virtuoso solo, when really you want the piece of music to move on. But I didn't know all this when I was a kid.

I saw a movie that Rod Steiger did, called *Al Capone*, a black and white thing, and I saw that maybe eleven times. That was before Steiger went crazy. He was hugely inventive back then, and it was a wonderfully structured performance. You saw this guy go from being a little Sicilian greaseball, to being at the top of the tree, and then the collapse. So it was very Shakespearean somehow; it was epic. That had a strong effect on me, because, in those days, Steiger was very intelligent. He charts it very, very well, and I found it interesting, because I was very shy, so I learned to be more extrovert as an actor on the stage, because I would imitate what he was doing. It's a wonderful performance. The treachery that he employs, the way he gradually nudges his way to the top. I liked Steiger very much, but he became indulgent, and it seems to happen that great actors lose control. They stop taking direction because they become so powerful, and the egos become inflated, and they start reading the script for the purposes of their performance and their career. They end up having their own writers, all this stuff. There's a limit to the amount of control an actor should have in a movie.

I can only speak for the people that I know, that I've really loved working with – obviously Neil Jordan, and Robert Altman with whom I've only done one picture – they're always so mindful of the needs of the movie, and the thrust of the script. Neil doesn't direct me as an actor, he doesn't try and orchestrate my performance, he just reminds you of what the story is, and where he wants the story to go. Altman gives you huge freedom, but you know very well that the freedom's within a structure that he has in his head. It's tiresome to be directed by somebody who doesn't know what they're doing. Sometimes not very good acting remains in the movies nowadays, because people are impressed by it.

British beginnings and the formation of Field Day

I went to England, and I worked there for a number of years, playing leading roles at the Royal Court and the National Theatre, all the stuff you should be doing. And I did a play of Brian Friel's at the Royal Court, called *Freedom of the City*, which was a response to the Bloody Sunday killings by the British Army in Derry. We got on well, and I always had a strong feeling about what was going on in Ireland; I was very politically aware. I always knew that I would form some sort of company of my own at some point, so around 1980 I approached Brian. Somebody in the Belfast Arts Council said they had money around and they didn't know what to do with it. Imelda Foley worked there, and I was talking to her; she knew how I felt about the thing, and said 'Why don't you apply for some money?' So I went to Brian and asked him for a play that we would tour together. I'd only met him once since we'd worked together, but there was a kind of unspoken respect between us, and he said 'yeah', and the play happened to be *Translations*, which is a very great play indeed. So it launched Field Day in a big way.

We toured Ireland, North and South, East and West, and we started to have an agenda which was to probe the condition that the country was in, and to ask questions about it. We were sometimes attacked for being narrowly nationalist, but we were far from that. Usually, when we were attacked in that way, it was by people who were narrowly Unionist. And the thing expanded to being more than plays; we were doing publications, because we were involved with Seamus Heaney and Seamus Deane, and Tom Paulin, and for a time, Tom Kilroy. That was how it happened, and we toured for ten years with it.

We did one production annually, and took it to London. Part of the intention was not only to do plays about particular areas of interest to Ireland, but to do them at a level that could survive in a big theatrical metropolis. I'm very proud of that fact. Nowadays, plays transfer very easily from Ireland to England, but they didn't do it then, I can tell you. It's now considered normal, and the traffic of actors between Dublin and London, and Belfast and London is very simple and very easy, but it wasn't then. When I first went to London, it was a very difficult transition to make from being an actor who worked in Dublin, to being an actor who could find his way around London, and be known and respected. It was very, very difficult indeed. Now it's more straightforward, and Field Day had a lot to do with that. It became automatic that our plays transferred, and that wasn't as a provincial company looking towards the metropolis; there was a belief that we should be able to survive in the most theatrically sophisticated circles.

I toured Ireland; one of my areas of pride is that we toured into some parts of Ireland that hadn't seen a professional production for over thirty years, since Anew McMaster, the last great touring actor/manager. We used to joke that I was the new Anew McMaster. We did a couple of productions after Brian left, and three years ago I got Frank McGuinness to do a version of *Uncle Vanya*; it was a very uplifting translation, wonderful for actors. That was an attempt to get back on the road, and confound everyone who said we were dead.

The distinctiveness of Irish speech

Part of that deal was, because I'd worked in England, I had the notion imposed upon me that you had to speak in a particular way if you were working in English theatre. Particularly if you were doing translations of foreign classics. It seemed totally stupid to me that I should pretend to be English in order to pretend to be Russian or German. I resented it very much, and it robbed me of all the colour and emotion in my own accent. Because the standard English accent is part of a culture which is designed to conceal emotion, and the Irish way of speech is more emotional, more poetic, more colourful; they express emotion in their language. Lots of English accents do too, but the standard English accent is part of the Hanoverian influence in England. It's not Shakespearean English, it's Hanoverian. If you listen to the Queen of England, she sounds German; it's a Germanic mode of speech, and it's (in upper crust English) all held back, and absolutely everything's concealed. It's part of the caste that ran England, and actors had to pander to them by imitating their speech. Well, I hate it, so I won't do it. With Field Day we did translations of *Three Sisters*, we did Sophocles translated by Tom Paulin, Molière, translated by Derek Mahon, and Seamus Heaney did a version of *Cure at Troy* by Sophocles, in the language of South Derry. The whole idea was to release Irish actors into these great classic plays, without restraint. We had girls playing in *Three Sisters*; two of them were from Dublin and one of them was from Belfast, but nobody even noticed. They just spoke how they spoke; one spoke with a Belfast accent and two spoke with Dublin accents.

The British actors can do what they like, as far as I'm concerned. They've had it all their own way in terms of world classics. But they do Chekhov very badly, in my view, and the Irish do Chekhov more interestingly. The Field Day versions of Chekhov have been more Russian in the sense that they're more emotional, more volatile, and the English are rather restrained and depressed. That's not the point of Chekhov; the characters are never depressed, they're very alive, they're grappling with their problems. They're going crazy with their problems, but they're not depressed.

When I did *Vanya* I was able to really go at it with my own speech patterns. I've played Chekhov in England – I played Trofimov in *A Cherry Orchard*, and it was difficult. It's a problem role, it's a bit hard to get a handle on anyway, but trying to do it in standard English was doubly difficult – to find a way of speaking that doesn't make everybody think of Belfast rather than Moscow. That's the trick. But Frank McGuinness achieved it, and I think you forget that we were Irish actors.

I love Chekhov, they're great plays. If you understand Russian, the experience of Chekhov in the original must be staggering, because like all great writers, his use of language is the most important part of his work. It must be wonderful to hear Chekhov in Russian, and it's not so wonderful to hear it in a flat southern English. It's very vibrant in Hiberno English, or whatever it is Frank and Brian write in. And Tom Kilroy, who started it all with his magnificent version of *The Seagull*.

I did a production of *Hedda Gabler* for the BBC, with Fiona Shaw. I don't think that was a successful experiment. I didn't like the fact that there were English actors in the play doing Irish accents. That just seemed stupid to me. That's imposing a different standard; saying 'Okay, we don't have standard English any more, but we'll impose another standard: standard Irish'. Well, I'm not in the business of replacing one cultural oppression with another. The idea is to release actors into the text. It's different if you say 'Okay, we're going to set *Hedda Gabler* in Tipperary', then everybody does it in Tipperary accents. Well, they didn't. It was precisely as Ibsen had written it. So I didn't see why they should get an English actor to pretend to be Irish. That was exactly the same as I had to do when I was doing Chekhov, or Von Horvak or Strindberg in England. Why didn't he just do it in his own accent? It's too literal-minded to have everyone speak with the same accent. Or else they should have had an Irish actor playing that role.

At a certain point, I just lost the energy to tour with Field Day, because I have a family, and I decided that if my interest in acting had been originally stirred by going to the movies, it was time I did some more movies. I'd done a couple, but it was almost coincidence that they happened. For instance, my very first movie was *Angel* with Neil Jordan, and that was when I happened to be free of my commitment to Field Day. *Angel* happened when I directed

Three Sisters, which toured with Field Day, and had I acted in it, I wouldn't have been free to do that movie, and maybe I wouldn't have had the kind of relationship with Neil that I do. So in a way, important as it was to me, Field Day had prevented me from pursuing a movie career. I had to call a halt to that at some point, and I said 'Right, I'm not going out of the house until some movies happen', and then *The Crying Game* came along. So I was lucky.

Working with Neil Jordan: *The Crying Game*

Neil and I have an almost unspoken relationship, because we know each other very, very well, and he knows what he can get. He knows I'll do the script; I don't have any other agenda than to do the script as well as possible. I know all actors say that, but not all of them are entirely truthful about it. Anyway, I'll tell you why it's fun, because his sense of narrative is so highly developed that you're very

Stephen Rea in *Hedda Gabler* (1993)

secure as an actor. The story is being told; you don't have any other responsibility than just to be the person that you're supposed to be. Sometimes, when you're doing a script that's less polished, less thought-through, you're having to make it work as you're doing it. You don't with Neil; it works. A crude example is you're walking down the street; you don't have to do anything because everybody knows that someone you thought was a woman, is a man. But his movies are always like that; you only have to walk down the street, everybody knows who you are. Sometimes, in other cases, you feel you have to be offering information, you're helping make the thing work, but you're very released when you're working with Neil. In terms of composing the shots, he really does make it up as he goes along, so every scene is shot the way that scene should be shot. He doesn't predetermine, he doesn't come and do master shot, reverse, reverse, reverse, tighter lens, he doesn't run through the lenses in that way. He maybe does one really interesting developing shot, and does a reverse on it, to match it, and some closer stuff, but you feel very involved in it, because you know you're contributing. The completeness of whatever you have to offer is used. That's why you don't get bored working with Neil.

I always knew *The Crying Game* would be a good film, but it had a huge success, and how could you anticipate that? You couldn't. Miramax marketed it very successfully, and that contributed to the whole thing. It was a good movie, it caught the moment. It caught the whole gender thing, and it caught it in a way that was humorous as well as touching. And it was such an unusual setting, a very unlikely story of a transvestite and an IRA man. Almost anyone else you can think of would have done that very clumsily. If you read a treatment for it, you'd say 'What?', 'A tranny meets an IRA terrorist? Please . . . .' But, as Neil said at the time, the last taboo was gender. All the class divisions had dropped, and racial divisions – although he had an element of race in it as well – but that's gone as a kind of barrier to relationships.

It was very clever of Neil to maintain the ambiguity of the relationship between Fergus and Dil. I mean, Fergus is definitely heterosexual, that's why he had the relationship with Miranda (Richardson). I remember at the time, Neil saying 'I don't know if we need to have this scene outside with Miranda', and I said 'You've got to see him kiss her, because you've got to be sure that he's heterosexual.'

But I think it is an ambiguous relationship between Fergus and Dil, and deliberately so. After he knows that Dil is a man, they never consummate the relationship. They kiss, but it's never actually consummated. That's Neil's way of avoiding the potential prurience and squalor of it. But, when he kisses Miranda, it's definitely in the audience's mind that they're lovers. Part of the deal, why she comes after him, is that she's a spurned lover, as much as Fergus' running away from the movement.

Fergus is completely naïve. There may be gay bars here now, but there weren't any at the time that movie was set. Around the north of Ireland, he wouldn't have seen a gay bar, and it wouldn't have occurred to him. Actually, the first time he goes into the gay bar, it's not as apparent as when he goes in the second time. It's much more ambiguous. The second time he goes in, it's apparent; they've got hairy chests, and all that. That's the film-maker tampering with the material to help the audience, so that the audience feels the way Fergus feels when eventually it's revealed that Dil is a man. And then when he goes into the gay bar the second time, the audience laughs, they say 'Jesus, how did we not notice'? But he didn't notice.

Building a character

I don't have any fixed idea or method, or a fixed approach to acting, because I don't think you can. Each role is a different project. Sometimes you just have an instinct about how it should go, and it works. Other times you have to do a little more probing and a little more work. I respond to scripts. If you read a text like *Translations*, *Dancing at Lughnasa*, *Someone to Watch Over Me*, you know within seconds or minutes that they're great. The tone is so individual, you know it will be sustained right to the end; I have known that about certain pieces of work. You know that unless the writer has had a nervous collapse before he's finished the play, it's bound to work.

I wouldn't create a backstory for a character like Fergus. Some people might, but I think it's too literal. You can make it work just by saying, 'Yeah, I know where he would have come from', but you don't work it out. I wouldn't work out who his cousins were, brothers, his granny; it's not necessary. The text already exists with Neil, and you have an emotional understanding which you bring to the piece. If you were doing Shakespeare, you don't work out Othello's auntie, you know what I mean? I think you do whatever you need to do to make the thing real for you, as the actor. I'm not challenging anyone who wants to work out a backstory. There's a current fetish for research; everybody says 'How did you research that role'? Sometimes you just read the script, and if the scenes are really well written . . . . If I was doing *Streetcar Named Desire*, why would I have to research it? The fucking stuff eats you off the page; the poetic language is so intense, Williams is such a poet, what's there to research?

The emotional journey is that Fergus realises that you can love anyone. He goes from being a man who's got a very rigid code about who you can offer love to, and it doesn't include British soldiers, it doesn't include the British, it doesn't include loving other men, and it probably doesn't include black men, or black people. So by the end of the movie, he knows, and we all know and all feel it, you can love anyone – race, gender, nationality, are all meaningless. That wasn't a challenge to me, because I believe that with all my heart. It's wonderful to be in a movie where it really happens. I think that's what everyone responded to.

Working with a non-actor

Working with a non-actor is tricky, you know. It's not that they're not talented, it's not that they're not conscientious, but it'd be like a professional footballer working with a non-professional footballer: it doesn't matter how good they are, they're bound to slip out of position. They don't have professional standards; they couldn't have. So what non-actors sometimes do is pick up your tone. Like that scene at the end of *The Crying Game* where I'm tied to the bed and my character says he's sorry. We started doing that, take one, and I started to fill up with tears, right? So take two, Jaye (Davidson) starts to fill up with tears as well. Take three, he's crying more than me, so that's the un-discipline that happens, because you don't just start a scene and go wherever it goes, you go into a scene thinking. You go in with a conscious notion of where you want to go with the scene, and you don't let it knock you about all over the place. That's a football analogy as well; when they talk about the team losing its shape. What happens with a non-actor is that a scene more quickly loses its shape. That doesn't mean they're not brilliant – and Jaye was absolutely brilliant in it – but when they're being brilliant, you have to get it right then. The professional actor will get it, be able to do it again, and develop it. If I was doing a scene with Miranda, the scene would automatically develop, because she's a fine professional actor. It might go in the wrong direction, and then Neil would say 'Well, pull it this way'. But with a non-actor, it doesn't happen like that. You need to tinker a bit more. Not in all cases, but that is one of the dangers with an inexperienced actor.

The physical side of characterisation

You do work on how the character's going to move. I saw *Crime of the Century* (a made-for-cable television movie about the Lindbergh baby kidnapping) for the first time the other night, actually. It works. Bruno Hauptmann was a German, of course, and they are very correct. There's footage of Hauptmann in the courtroom, and he's sitting very erect. Everybody said how cool he was, and they held it against him, but actually, if you look at it, you can see that he's really just holding himself in. He's so scared, he's not cool at all. He's like Lauren Bacall in *To Have and Have Not*; they all said she was so cool, but she says she was terrified, and if you look at it knowing that, all you can see is her fear. She's a young girl of 19. So I was very aware of that for Hauptmann, that he didn't dare relax, otherwise he just would have fallen apart. And I worked from that.

It's a wonderful thing if you're playing a real-life person, and you get a little clue about how they really were. I did a play that Tom Kilroy wrote called *Double Cross*, with Field Day, and it's a great, great play, where I play two real-life Irishmen, both of whom pretended to be English. One worked with Churchill during the war, and was the Minister of Information in Churchill's government, Brandon Bracken, and William Joyce, who was Lord Haw-Haw. He broadcast from Germany; he was an anti-Semite. He was from Galway, he went over and pretended he was English, and then defected to the Germans; he was a really highly-developed racist. But the idea of the play was that these two men were both racists, in a way, but it was against themselves, it was a kind of self-loathing that was a result of the colonial situation here. They despised the Irish, therefore they despised themselves, because they were considered an inferior race for centuries, by the British. So they became British, but that wasn't enough for Joyce. There's some audio tapes of them, so I was able to work with those. It's a wonderful thing to do if you're playing a character, if they really exist.

I do work physically, and I think about that. One of the things I was pleased with was the opening shot of my character in *The Butcher Boy*; you see him walking down the lane, he's pissed, he's an alcoholic – actually, I never thought of him as an alcoholic, but all the reviews say 'the alcoholic father'. But then, maybe I was being more subjective about the character than I thought, because nobody defines themselves as an alcoholic until they reach a certain stage, a certain point of being cured. He wouldn't have defined himself as that, so I didn't. But when you see him walking down the lane, I was pleased with the way that worked, and people said that the opening shot said everything about the guy. He's very drunk but walking, aggressively, but in as controlled a way as he could. I thought about that. Sometimes, physical work is just thinking about it. All acting is thinking, as far as I'm concerned. That's why I like Mitchum: it's all thought. You know, when people say 'research', sometimes research is just thinking about it. The camera likes to watch actors thinking. And I do as much thinking about a part as I do reading or researching it.

Whatever gets a person to the point of performing is entirely up to them. I used to say 'Well, even if it takes six pints of Guinness and a whisky, do it'. That's a highly dangerous thing to say, but whatever gets a person to the point where they can give the performance is acceptable. If they want to go up a mountain, if they want to research for six months, that's fine. If they simply read it, and walk on . . . .Who knows what Spencer Tracy did to arrive at that totally natural acting? Somebody told me he used to go into the desert and scream the lines. I don't know, but I bet he didn't do that invariably, and solely. Somebody can walk on and be very much in touch with their emotions, they don't have to dig them up.

Working with Mike Leigh

I've known Mike a long time and I've done three things with him, and on all occasions, basically, I've provided – without intending it, and without me expecting it – Irish comic relief. That's what I do in *Life is Sweet*. I did a television film for the BBC with him, set in Belfast. It's called *Four Days in July*. The BBC weren't very pleased with it, because it's rather antiestablishment, and pro-nationalist, really. And I did a theatre show with him called *Ecstasy*. It was great.

You don't know what you're going to be doing; all you know is that you meet Mike, you talk, he asks you to focus on a particular character from a particular area, out of maybe eighty people that you've met. He picks one, and says 'Well, we'll work on this as the character'. You might have only met them once. Then you must thoroughly research the character. It's very interesting. You work with it, but you don't know that it's going to end up being a supporting character, you just know you're going to play this character. Then he brings them all together. He doesn't know for sure how the whole thing will finally be structured. What happens after you've selected the real-life person you're gonna work on, you build that up into a character; you work on your own, find information, going back as far as grandparents, the whole family structure and history. Eventually you start meeting other characters, and improvise, maybe just in a room somewhere, maybe in a bar.

You're in character during that time, and you don't come out of character 'til he invites you to. You work for hours and hours on this, and you sometimes improvise for hours at a time. Then, he gradually distills it down into certain episodes, and you can see the scenes emerging. When you're rehearsing, you're improvising on a daily basis. But when you go in front of the camera, it's as tightly scripted as a script of Neil Jordan's. It's minted, and it's like doing Chekhov; you absolutely follow every syllable that has been predetermined. They're all my own lines, but they're not improvised at the moment. It's not improvised in an indulgent way, because improvisation can get loose and people can run away with it. Those rushes of adrenalin actors go on can just mean they talk a lot, whereas Mike's work is very precise.

Where I part company with Mike Leigh, is that he deprives you of objectivity, in order to produce these characters in a particular situation. You're totally subjective the whole time. When you discuss the character with him you describe him as 'he' or 'she', because you have some objective understanding of the character. But you don't have an overall vision of the piece, which I believe you should have, because acting is a conscious art, as well as using areas of instinct and the unconscious.

The concept of the 'jobbing actor'

A lot of these actors may say they're jobbing actors, but they may not mean it. People might say that to deflect questions about their approach, or their commitment. They may feel that it damages their approach to talk about it. I wouldn't talk about lots of things, partly because you don't know what goes on a lot of the time when you're acting. I would never describe myself as a jobbing actor. I would say that I had a vocation to act, which is maybe as pretentious as claiming to be a jobbing actor is mundane. But I always felt I had a vocation, that was what I wanted and needed to do, and I always had a very developed sense of the importance of acting, and of drama, whether it be in film or on stage. Field Day is a very clear expression of how important I thought it was, and I thought we could take big, important national questions, and address them in all sorts of ways, but it was definitely, self-consciously important. We weren't saying 'We're just doing a little show here,' we were saying 'This is something that people need to know about, and want to ask questions about.' So I've always considered it important; I've always considered it an expression of myself. I've done jobs where you could say that certainly didn't happen; on that occasion one was a jobbing actor, because you did a job that wasn't what you thought it might be. It's always a disappointment if you do. In a way, I believe that you're only playing one part, and you're moving towards the ideal statement of that part. You're finding out more and more about yourself, and you're finding out more and more about everybody else while you're doing it. I guess if you're in a soap opera, or something, you could say it was jobbing, but the really good actors like John Lithgow, the Lithgows of this world – who I adore and I've worked with – it would never be just a job for John. He could be in a sitcom and it's not a job. That's a deprecating thing to say 'I'm a jobbing actor'. The ones who say that may be the most serious people in the world.

Judi Dench said she thinks of herself as a jobbing actor? Well, she's one of the most serious artists on the English stage. It is a sort of a British thing, don't draw attention to yourself, don't make a big song and dance about it. But of course, she's completely brilliant! When she does that breakdown scene as Queen Victoria in *Mrs Brown*, she's not thinking, 'Oh, it's just a job'. She's just hugely talented. Don't tell me that it didn't come from some deep personal understanding of what that kind of grief is. But she doesn't want to talk about that, so she says 'I'm a jobbing actress'. (British accent) Thank you deah.

Does acting have the potential to harm the actor?

When I played Creon in *Antigone* for Field Day, there was a mild sense of paranoia because the guy was so unpleasant, and so clearly in the wrong. And I was also running the company. And the paranoia could have crossed over very easily. I've really never had that problem. I do believe that the work we do is not meant to destroy the participants; it's meant to explore and enhance people's lives. And I think that if people are getting into it on a level where it's damaging them, there's something wrong with the process. I understand that any artistic process is a difficult undertaking, and painful in many ways, but art is meant to redefine, and to turn the bad into the good.

But sometimes you can be so much in touch with your personal condition of pain, which we all live in, you can be so close to it that you can't act. It can actually get in the way. Because acting is not just about expressing pain and emotion, it's about a view, it's about an understanding of the piece, it's about having a panoramic vision of a piece as well as having a subjective view.

There are certain roles that I've declined to investigate – I've been asked to do things that relate to child abuse; I wouldn't do it because you have a choice about which areas of life you want to explore. And I don't really care to go down the road of identifying with someone like that. Obviously I'm drawn to certain kinds of roles, and someone said I always play the role of an outsider, and I guess that is true. Even in a film called *Bad Behaviour*, which was an improvised film – it didn't occur to me, but someone said 'That guy was an outsider even in his own family', and I suppose it's true. It was a little unnerving, because it was improvised, so I must embrace that outsider thing. I am drawn to those kind of roles, but I don't know if I have that dark side of myself. I'm not interested in finding out whether I have or not. And I question the purpose of these kind of ventures, and actually the ones I've been asked to do on that subject haven't survived in any way. They've vanished, they've been of little interest. If you look at Fritz Lang's movie *M* with the great Peter Lorre, there was something about that that was really brilliant. But the idea of what he does with the children is not investigated. Nowadays one is so prurient, and everything is so explicit in movies.

The Butcher Boy deals with child abuse, but why is it somehow not a depressing experience? The trouble with that is that the boy seems to be right on top of it, because he's using it to get the chocolates and cream cakes. I think that what Patrick McCabe has done is to lift the experience into something that you can understand. It's creative. Of course there's violence. But that's a regular experience of growing up around that time. That was kind of normal. However McCabe has described it, and created the work, it's a huge comic enterprise. I don't know how anyone can do a comic novel about child sexual abuse.

Handling conflict

I think all actors have problems with directors. Occasionally you have directors who are wonderful, but a lot of the time, they're not. The more experienced you become, the more you're aware of what the process should be. And so often it isn't. That can drive you mad. I worked with a director fairly recently, and I couldn't stand anything he did. And the worst thing about it was that I knew that about him before I went to do the job, but I liked the writer. You know, all movies are an act of faith, theatre also. You don't know what is really going to happen. It could be great, and maybe it isn't. Most actors bring huge commitment and belief in the possibilities of what theatre and movies can do. And so often that belief is betrayed. The saddest part is that a lot of directors are less technically equipped than the actors. I have had problems with directors. But finally, you have absolutely no control – that's the most frustrating thing. You can explain what you believe is important in a scene, and they can do a version that matches what you believe. But in the end, they can use whatever version they want. They can use a version that is absolutely against everything you believe in. They can do that in movies, and the theatre isn't that much more pure in its own way. A director can choose to go down a certain path, and there's not much you can do about it. There's a lot of area of failure in this work. There might be 50 movies on in town, and only 3 that you like, or that have a morality and a vision, and a technical skill that is acceptable. It's very difficult.

On the other hand, when Neil Jordan and I did *Angel* together the crew was completely against him, because it was his first feature, and they didn't think he knew what he was doing. They were immensely skilled people and what they failed to see was that this guy, who was seemingly inept in some areas, had a vision that could actually redefine their technical skills. Both are deeply important, the technical skills and the vision that shapes them – one is nothing without the other. And so it was very foolish of those people at that time to be so ungenerous with their skills. No question. It happens in subtle ways, where people don't quite give their consent. Or they can undermine the energy of a day without it being a confrontational thing. You can sense something from the tone of a script, and with *Angel* you just knew Neil's script was something very special. And there was something about Neil's instinct about how he worked with the camera that was very particular. In the case of conflict, usually it's not that you don't understand the character, it's that your style or your way of working sits with some difficulty with the way the thing is written, where the actor's delivery and the writer's delivery don't come together. If I don't get what's going on, I ask anybody for help – the stage crew, the focus puller, anyone.

But when the creative juices aren't flowing, it's a kind of a nightmare. It's very difficult to know what to do with that. I've been in situations where I thought I was bad in a role, and I couldn't work out why. Usually it's not as deep as you think, and the odd adjustment can make it right. Or it's because you're surrounded by a great deal of incompetence. The right director could assist you just with a slight adjustment. But acting is a very difficult thing, because you're doing it in public, and it apparently has no particular skill. You just walk on and talk. And yet, it's enormously difficult.

I've done things with a group where we used to expand the words of a text incredibly, and that would give you a certain freedom. You threw the whole thing around, and stylised it hugely. Acting is either terribly easy or impossible; the whole thing either comes to you and falls into place, or you can work your ass off and get nowhere. And a lot of things are just down to giving into what the work is. Sometimes it's that you don't see what the work is.

On being faithful to the text

I don't believe in changing the words around too much. I think it depends on the text. I mean, what are you going to do, change Beckett? How can you possibly do that? You can't change Beckett, you can't change Pinter. That alteration is an evasion of what the work is demanding of you. If you can't make it work, then it's your failure. Sometimes you work in other areas and the writers are less strict, and they prefer you to throw things around. But even then, I did a film where the whole idea was that it was a joint experience, the writer, the director, and the actor. But then when I changed something, the writer got miffed. It's

Honor Heffernan and Stephen Rea in *Angel* (1982)

very strange working in this kind of corporate way. Whatever works, works. There's no method, where you can say, 'If you do this, you're going to produce a great work of art'. It doesn't go that way. You just have to use all the means that you can, and sometimes all sorts of things work.

The only thing that's important in all of it is the ideas, in the theatre or in the movies. And sometimes people are faithful to the text because it's safer; it provides a structure. And you have in England an extraordinarily capable theatre, in that you can put on a play in five weeks, and it can look tremendously professional. Maybe the ideas suffer a bit, as they usually do in England. It's not a country that's too terrific about new ideas.

But then no one would be more determinedly serious about text than Beckett. He wrote it and it was meant to sound a certain way. Do people when they're doing a work of Schubert change notes? But in jazz, that's the deal, you do change notes. I don't see why everything has to be the same. I don't see why you can't be on occasion, utterly faithful to the text, and on other occasions utterly faithful to some inner voice that tells you to go anywhere with it. I don't see that those two things are mutually exclusive, because the purpose is to get at the ideas in whatever you're doing. Everyone thought that Charlie Parker was crazy, and if you listen to Charlie Parker now, it's the most structured, clear, absolutely lyrical musical perfection. But people thought he was crazy at the time.

Irish acting: more instinctive?

There's no conflict between doing a text in it's purity and responding to it instinctively, is there? I don't know what it means to say that someone is instinctive. I know that the two countries – Britain and Ireland – have had very different experiences. In terms of the canon of literature available for work by the English actor, it's huge compared to what the Irish actor, who hasn't crossed over to live in England, has on offer. And English society is much more a society which presents itself, and has controlled the world, shall we say. It's a much more structured and organised society, and therefore the people it produces, and its actors, are liable to be more structured and organised. The theatre is probably much more institutionalised than anywhere else in the world. Maybe in Germany, there's as much structure. The English have a national theatre which suddenly becomes the Royal National Theatre. It can't just be the National Theatre; it has to have a doubly institutionalised title.

And in Ireland, one of the best pipers I know is actually a carpenter. He's a piper when he wants to pipe, but he makes his living as a carpenter. So, the attitude toward the arts in Ireland is less formal, and maybe more serious. You're talking about two hugely different cultures. It makes it sound as if the Irish are this kind of natively more spontaneous, less intellectual people. I don't believe that's true. Nobody made more plans and schemes than Cyril Cusack. And was Ralph Richardson not instinctive? I don't like the idea that the Irish are like the black actors who are supposed to have rhythm. I really don't like that. I mean look at Denzel Washington, look at Morgan Freeman. Let's not get into clichés about racial stereotypes, because nowadays the whole world is available to us. I don't mean that people should be cut off from the richness of their own particular culture. I think the agenda here is the old Irish-English-locked-in-a-cultural-struggle-and-cultural-misunderstanding, which was based on the domination of a very formal country over a not-quite emerging, independent country. And it confuses the issue for me.

I've been as much influenced by Americans as I have by anybody. I couldn't say that I feel I'm of a different nationality to the American actors, because I grew up with them. They were in the movie house down the street. All I know is that I identified with the American actors and I didn't identify with the British actors, because I thought they were different.

Ireland is much more of a shambles than England. We have not got a theatre that's really structured in the same way; it barely has any shape at all. It's a reaction to lots of other outside things. It can barely express the important things that are happening in the country; we have not got the equipment to do that. That's what's always made me mad. That's why we developed Field Day, because we were trying to deal with what was happening in the country. But it can only happen if people want it to happen. People have left the theatre in Ireland so they can be in the movies. And a lot of movies that are done in Ireland are simply versions of Irish life that are fed to the outside world, they're not explorations of what is. Not like the French cinema of the '30s, '40s, '50s, nowhere near it. Maybe *The Butcher Boy*; that's better.

What next?

One finds that it's difficult at this stage to find things that are really challenging. I feel I'm at a point of decision about what I'm going to do. I've often been asked to direct, and maybe I will. It's not the process of acting that's boring, but the whole paraphernalia of acting is boring. Having to turn up and wait four hours before you work, and sometimes ten hours before you work, if the director's a jerk, which sometimes they are. Just to spend your day lying around in a trailer is very frustrating. Theatre's more focussed than that; you tend to be working; theatre is like prizefighting, you stand up and get thumped every night. It's very draining and exhausting, and I don't feel any appetite for that either. It's not that I'm making a choice between theatre and movies; I respond to scripts, and if the script is good, I'll do it, whatever medium it's in. But the actual work that I enjoy, the work with the camera, and being with the camera crew – there's so little of that in any day. It's all being lit, and make-up, and tracks being laid, and then by the time you get to the thing you really like to do, it lasts such a short time. So I find it a bit mentally stultifying. I used to enjoy hanging around; I used to love it, I was good at it. But now, I'd rather be at home. It's okay if it's stimulating. It's always stimulating working with Neil, because he works very fast, he can't bear to work slowly. Neil keeps it going, because he loses his creative edge when it slows down, and that's why I love working with him. It's great; all actors love working with him. I think that with maturity and experience, you know what should be happening, so you can't bear it when it isn't.

I would like to have more control – I would like the impossible: control as an actor. Which is not Kevin Costner control, where I can demand another close-up; I don't mean that kind of control. I do sometimes wish that the director was smarter. I only want to work with people who I can learn something from, and that is increasingly rare. Maybe that is because of my arrogance or ignorance, I don't know (laughs).

Ian Richardson

'When you're speaking Shakespeare and it's making sense, you can make it relevant to real life – albeit heightened by poetry. There's only one other level to reach beyond the speaking of Shakespearean verse, and that is singing.'

Ian Richardson was born in Edinburgh in 1934. He began his career at the Birmingham Repertory Theatre Company, playing such parts as Hamlet, John Worthing in *The Importance of Being Earnest* and Adolph in *Creditors*. He went to Stratford and joined the RSC to play numerous roles. Amongst them were: Sir Andrew Aguecheek in *Twelfth Night*, Don John in *Much Ado About Nothing*, Oberon in *A Midsummer Night's Dream*, Antipholus of Ephesus in *The Comedy of Errors*, The Herald in *Marat/Sade*, and the title roles in *Coriolanus* and *Pericles*. He also played Prospero in *The Tempest*, alternated Richard of Bolingbroke and Richard (with Richard Pasco) in *Richard II*, Berowne in *Love's Labour's Lost*, and the title role in *Richard III*. Richardson made his first London appearance at the Aldwych during his tenure with the RSC, playing Count Malatesi in *The Duchess of Malfi* and Edmund in *King Lear*. He toured Europe and the USSR with *Lear* and *The Comedy of Errors*, with which he made his New York debut. This was shortly followed by a New York run as Marat in *Marat/Sade*.

After leaving the RSC, he performed the starring role of Tom Wrench in the musical of *Trelawney of the Wells* at the Bristol Old Vic, which transferred to London. Other theatre credits include a stint as Henry Higgins in a revival of *My Fair Lady* on Broadway, the role of Jack Tanner in *Man and Superman* (played in its entirety at the Canadian Shaw Festival), *The Government Inspector*, *The Miser* and *The Magistrate*.

Richardson's television credits include *Danton's Death*, *Tinker, Tailor, Soldier, Spy*, *Ike*, *Churchill and the Generals*, *Private Shultz*, *The Woman in White*, Sherlock Holmes in *The Sign of Four* and *The Hound of The Baskervilles*, *Mountbatten – The Last Viceroy*, *Blunt*, *Porterhouse Blue*, *The Devil's Disciple*, *The Winslow Boy*, and *House of Cards* (for which he won BAFTA, Royal Television Society, Press Guild, and Variety Club Awards), *To Play the King*, and *The Final Cut*. Amongst his films are *Marat/Sade*, *Brazil*, *The Fourth Protocol*, *Rosencrantz and Guildenstern Are Dead*, *M. Butterfly*, *Dark City*, *Words Upon the Window Pane* and *Savage Play*. Ian Richardson was awarded a C.B.E. in 1989.

I spoke with Ian Richardson in his dressing room at the Richmond Theatre, where he was performing *The Magistrate*, in November, 1997.

Early years in Edinburgh: a seed planted

When I was a boy in Edinburgh, the war was on, and my father was away from home. Just before the outbreak of the war, my father's family who in general, had been in trade, went bankrupt. A lot of people did, except those who made armaments. So things were rather tight, financially, around the house. There wasn't really money available for any kind of cultural excursions, nor do I think my mother, at that time, would have been remotely interested in such things.

I had one champion at school, who taught history, and took an interest in me. He tried to discover why it was I showed absolutely no inclination to any subjects except English and history. Anything like mathematics or geography, were to me, anathema. He wrote to my mother and said that he suspected I was artistically inclined, and was there such an artistic inclination in the family in general? My mother wrote back and said 'Absolutely not'. I was then given special art classes, only to discover that if I had any artistic inclination whatsoever, it was certainly not going to be putting paint on canvas! Then the same history teacher suggested music, and so, at great, great cost to an already strapped household, a piano was purchased, and a tutor. Indeed, I became quite accomplished at the piano, but it was perfectly obvious that I was never going to sit at a Bechstein grand on a concert hall platform, playing a concerto.

So, it went on in this kind of indeterminate way until we had our armistice service. It was my turn, that year, to read the Binyon passage – 'They shall grow not old, as we that are left grow old' – and it's usually recited at every armistice service, it's only a four line piece of verse. I memorised it, and I walked to the centre, in front of the altar, and spoke it to the audience. I can remember to this day, all these years afterwards, I was extremely struck by the silence that followed the reading of it; it was as though they'd all stopped breathing. It's an experience I've had only a few times in my professional life, but it can happen. It's a moment of magic, and this was my first experience of it. The history teacher at once wrote to my mother and said 'I've made an awful mistake. All this time, he's a born *actor*'.

So here begins, if you like, the only cultural activity of my childhood – my mother made inquiries around Edinburgh, and found a rather good amateur theatre company. I say good because they were a cut above the usual church-hall thing; they actually took on a proper theatre, and they did about four plays a year, and good plays at that. The amateur members of this group consisted of rather well-heeled people from Edinburgh – certainly better-heeled than my family was at that point – also people who spoke with a slight Scottish accent, but not as strong as my own must have been at that time. I was fourteen, so there were never any roles for me to play of any size at that age, except for the occasional 'boy' who was required. My voice had just broken, I remember. I did mostly stage managerial things, unseen, setting up the props and pulling the curtain up and down and things like that. But I was mingling with people who seemed to understand whatever artistic inclinations I had, and to sympathise and to encourage, which was the first time such a thing had happened to me. So rather like an unwatered flower in a pot, I suddenly had lots of moisture and began to blossom. They – to a man and a woman in the amateur society – said that I really should consider taking up acting professionally. And of course that was a seed planted.

In those days, unfortunately – or fortunately, depending on how you look at it – it was necessary for one to do one's army service, and so when I was eighteen, I had to go into the army. While I was there, it was perfectly obvious to me that I was a completely hopeless solider; it was fairly obvious to my commanding officer too, and so when I applied for permission to be seconded to the Forces Broadcasting Service, a radio station broadcasting to the troops abroad, it was agreed. I became an announcer and programme presenter with the Forces Broadcasting Service in the Middle East, in Libya. I found artistic freedom and self-confidence through sitting or standing in front of a microphone and producing material for myself. The chief announcer, who had, and still has, a beautiful voice, used to correct my vowel sounds and pronunciation, so that ultimately when I came back home after my military training, I spoke with an English accent, much to my father's dismay and horror. So strongly was it embedded in me, that I could only do a Scottish accent by putting it on.

In *Private Schultz* and as Ramsay MacDonald, the two times I played Scotsmen, I had to work very hard at the accent. It was quite extraordinary; I had to work as hard at my own birthright accent, if you like, as I do when I'm to play a foreigner, like Pandit Nehru, which I did, or a Frenchman, or an Italian. Mind you, when I get angry, or if perhaps I've been rather foolish and had three glasses of wine, or maybe more, and am a bit tipsy, my little vowel sounds go awry and a bit of Scots comes through, so it's still there at heart. I was slightly worried about it, because I went to an extremely good voice teacher who said that people who've completely obliterated their given regional accent, stood in danger of blocking, if you like, the umbilical cord from the emotional centre to the vocal cords. She said that she didn't think that had happened with me, and I said 'Well, I don't suppose it has, because I've been speaking with this accent for quite a long time now. I even dream in the English accent I have never, ever dreamt in Scots'. So that was a danger that I didn't have to face.

Drama education and some thoughts on the Method

The Scottish educational system involves various methods of teaching its students that you don't find in England. At the Glasgow College of Dramatic Art, where I went, I discovered that in order to get into the drama school, I would have to agree to do a course of studies at Glasgow University, and get, not a BA, but a teaching degree. My father agreed to this, because he was actually against my becoming an actor; he suspected that the theatrical population was rather over-full of people of curious sexual habits – which I suppose in some respects, is true, but the same could also be said of long-distance lorry drivers. But, anyway, he advised me to do this, because, he said 'I'm not at all sure that you've made the right decision to become an actor, and if you have a teaching degree, at least you can get a job in a school, teaching dramatic studies.' But another *vital* thing happened to me there; the professor of Shakespearean and Elizabethan studies in general was Peter Alexander, and he, after one of his lectures – in which he'd asked me to recite some Shakespearean passages to the entire class, which I didn't mind doing, being a bit of a show-off like most actors – kept me back after they'd all gone, and he said 'You know, I want to suggest something to you. You're never going to be an academic, that's obvious', and I said 'It's not my intention to be an academic, professor'. He said 'No, I can tell that. But I think that you have the makings of a rather good classical actor.' This did it, and from that point onwards, I was geared towards the possibility of going into the classics.

My idea of the theatre at the time was very much the sort of thing I'm doing right now (Richardson was appearing in *The Magistrate* by Arthur Wing Pinero): a piece of entertainment in three acts. My idea was something like Ibsen, and Strindberg, and Bernard Shaw, and Chekhov, but also the lighter works by Noël Coward and Rattigan. When I was setting my sights on the theatre, it was the time of Binkie Beaumont, and the theatres were crammed with the sort of stuff that you only now see in sitcoms on television. That was the sort of thing I was aiming towards: nice, gentle drawing room comedies, or, alternatively, drawing room tragedies, whichever. So when it was suggested that I should become a classical actor – it was something that completely changed my focus.

The principal of the college was a great exponent of Stanislavsky. So consequently, everything we did, no matter what, was geared towards the Stanislavsky System. Let me make one thing quite clear: there is no connection whatsoever between the Method theatre as we understand it, and the Stanislavsky theatre. They are poles apart, because unlike the Method, Stanislavsky is never overindulgent, which the Method is. Stanislavsky is never incoherent, which the Method is. Stanislavsky is controlled and technically polished, which the Method could never be. So, consequently, I was trained in the very best ways of approaching a role: playing it from a deep emotional centre, with motivations for everything one does, and subtexts to build the character so that it isn't a facile piece of presentation which won't stand on its own feet on a public platform for more than three weeks without falling apart. There's a bedrock of preparation and reality behind it, and that goes for farcical comedy as well as the great tragedies; it's the same for all presentations – they must be based on truth.

The orientation at my drama school was very much more centred on discipline as well. I remember once, I skipped a couple of lectures at university in order to go and see Laurence Olivier in *The Entertainer* at the local theatre. My principal got to hear about this, and discovered that I was not the only one from my year who had skipped the lecture that day – it was a great draw, Olivier in town – and we were punished by having our production of Pinero's *The Schoolmistress*, taken off the advertising for public performance, and we had to do it without an audience. That is discipline of a quite strong nature. That's the way it was in those days; we responded to it, and I think we were all the better for it. Now it's very lax.

The other thing that I remember distinctly was being dressed in leotards, wearing no period costume other than being clothed by our imaginations. Wearing these skintight things, we would be told 'You are now wearing Renaissance costumes. Behave, and sit down, and walk, in the way . . .' or 'You are now in Edwardian dress with a stiff shirtfront and high imperial collar, now walk like that.' We had that, as well as *rigorous* voice training. I remember, having come out of the army, that I'd picked up – as well as losing any trace of a Scottish accent – in the mess, one or two curiosities of army language, and so I came out saying (with clipped, flattened vowels) 'Now look heah', and things like that. I remember the voice man saying 'What are we going to do about your accent?' and I said 'Good heavens, what accent?' and he said (clipped vowels) 'Thet accent'. So I had to do an exercise which went 'Rolling home to Rio', which I had been saying as 'Rayling hame to Riaou'. It was a wonderful three years.

I'm sorry to see the result of the training offered at drama schools now, and I see it in the kind of material that they produce. A lot of young people are exceptionally talented, but totally lacking in any vocal training. They have no strength in their diaphragm, which can only mean that they've never been given any proper breathing exercises. They lack a certain grace onstage, most of them, partly because, even the girls now wear jeans and trainers. So they're at a loss when they put on a crinoline, because underneath their crinoline, in their minds, they are still wearing what they wear every day: jeans and trainers. They're walking in the crinoline as though they're walking in jeans and trainers, and of course it looks ludicrous and ugly. They're not trained.

The other thing, too, that I notice, is that they talk a very different kind of language. There was a young man in this production who said to me 'I won't be comfortable until I've found my space', and I said 'What do you mean, "found your space?" We're going to do it on a stage, that is your space.' He said 'No, no, my personal space.' 'I've never heard such rubbish,' I said.

Of course, I suppose my training must show on stage, although people never mention that, because I have developed a technique, which I put to full use in this farcical comedy that I'm doing at the moment. If that is the stuff of a particular brand of training, then I can only say that training is best. You see, the trouble with doing it for 'the moment' is that you cannot maintain it. There's a complete disregard for the people on the stage with you, which is something that, in my training, was constantly being dinned into us: you must be aware that you are onstage with other people. They are saying dialogue as well, to which you must listen. The whole art of working as an ensemble is the art of listening as well as speaking your own dialogue. Now, I maintain that if you're the product of a school that teaches you about this business of 'your space' and all the rest of it, they are instilling in their students an utter selfishness, which means that they're out there 'doing their thing', and to hell with anybody else. That's not what it's about! If they do present their performance in that way, there is no guarantee that it's going to be the same the next night, or the night after that; it'll be different every night, because they've got no bedrock of preparation at all!

I think some actors are just born being able to act, and in that case their training, whether classical or Method; is probably irrelevant. They may be great actors in spite of their training. It's not that the Method is all bad, indeed, in its essence it is simply what actors of any sense or sensitivity would do anyway. What is wrong with it is that it ignores the technical tools such as projection and clarity of diction, and however truthfully you may be feeling something, if nobody can hear or understand what you're saying, it's a total waste of time. Brando at his best is splendid, and he is quite capable of giving up the grunt and mumble when he chooses, as witness his Fletcher Christian in *Mutiny on the Bounty*, with an English accent, no less!

The reps and the RSC

By a curious coincidence, and an enormous piece of good fortune, near the end of my time at Glasgow Drama School, I was seen by Bernard Hepton, who, as well as being a very fine character actor in England, was, at that time, artistic director of the Birmingham Repertory Theatre. He'd just lost Albert Finney to grander things, and so there was a vacancy for a young actor, not necessarily a matinée idol, who could play youth and character roles. I fitted very much into that slot, and I got a contract to the Birmingham Rep. I actually had to leave drama school before the end of the term. During my time there, I was asked to play Hamlet, which I did, with reasonable success, and it was seen by no less a person than Peter Hall, who was forming his new company, to be called the Royal Shakespeare Company, in 1960. He wrote to me and asked me to meet him, and he suggested a minor role at Stratford-upon-Avon that I might be quite willing to play, and indeed I was. The upshot was that, after eighteen months, I left the Birmingham Rep, and went the thirty miles down the road to Stratford-upon-Avon, and I was in the classical theatre.

Anyway, there I was at Stratford-upon-Avon, and there I stayed, gradually being promoted up through the ranks, over the years. It was a decade before I thought of casting my eyes elsewhere. When Peter Hall resigned, I wanted to leave too. Trevor Nunn, who took over, begged me not to go, he said 'Don't leave me, because I'm going to need you' – and Alan Howard, and Ian Holm, and Judi Dench and the little group of us who had formed the nucleus – 'Don't leave me'. I have always had a great sense of loyalty, and I believe in doing the honourable thing, and so, against my better judgement – and the judgement, indeed, of my agent – I agreed to stay for another two years at least. In fact I stayed for another four! The other thing, too, was purely domestic. I met my wife in 1960, when I first joined Peter Hall's company, and we married before the new year, and the year after that – or, more accurately, nine months after that – my first son was born, and then my second son came along another year later, and it was jolly nice to have a reliable source of income, when I was embarking on the biggest adventure that any human being can undertake: being married and bringing up a family. For that reason, too, I stayed on. Ultimately the time came when I fell out of love, not with Shakespeare – I shall never, ever do that – but fell out of love with what was happening within the Royal Shakespeare Company.

What was remarkable about the Royal Shakespeare Company at the beginning, under Peter Hall's directorship, was that he did one quite, if you like, radical thing – he established the three year contract. It was something that had never been, ever, in any theatre company, and it meant you stayed. You signed the next three years of your life away, and you dedicated your entire efforts to what the company was doing. Also, you put your entire career into the hands of the artistic director, and he would promote you when he felt you were ready. But perhaps the most important thing, was that Peter Hall established an ensemble style. He brought back the observations of the iambic pentameter in Shakespeare; we were all given training, and voice exercises. When you're speaking Shakespeare and it's making sense, you can make it relevant to real life – albeit heightened by poetry. There's only one other level to reach beyond the speaking of Shakespearean verse, and that is singing.

Before, there was a tendency, with Shakespeare, (in deep, highly theatrical voice) you've got to have a Shakespearean voice. Not a bit of it. My little favourite piece, which I've heard absolutely ruined, comes from *Two Gentlemen of Verona*, 'Oh, how this spring of love resembleth/ the uncertain glory of an April day/ which now shows all the beauty of the sun/ and by-and-by a cloud takes all away'. Now, by saying it perfectly naturally but with upward inflections until the last bit, you're speaking Shakespeare. You're also not declaiming. It's coming from your heart. When you throw out an acknowledgement of the iambic pentameter, you throw out the heart of the text. That's why, when things began to change, under new directorships – 'We don't want any of this poetry crap, let's play it with a bit more balls!' – that was not for me. So I left, and went to Broadway and did Henry Higgins for a year! Crazy.

Peter Brook and *Marat/Sade*

What was it like working with Peter Brook? Frightening to begin with, and then absolutely marvellous thereafter. He and I got on famously. In *Marat*, we were all, first and foremost, lunatics in an institution. We had a rehearsal period, unheard of outside Russia, of sixteen weeks. For the first eight weeks, we never looked at the text. We were invited to bring to each day's rehearsal, actual case histories of lunatics that people had observed, or had managed to get to see. I myself got an introduction to the director of Tooting Bec Mental Institute, who agreed, very reluctantly, to escort me around his mental institute in south London, which he did, and which was enormously interesting, but frightening too. But more important was that he talked to me for about two hours, about mental illness, and in general, the things that can go wrong inside people's heads. We were all doing this kind of thing, the whole cast, and we all contributed. So we had, if you like, a dossier of case histories. At the end of the first eight weeks, Brook said 'Right. Now, you have all been given roles to play, and it's perfectly obvious that you cannot be someone who has speaking problems if you have one of the larger speaking roles. So you have got to choose a case history, or an amalgam of case histories, which will enable you to perform, although at the same time, remain faithful to your established illness, in its reality'. So that's how we did it. Before I played Marat, I played The Herald, who was a kind of master of ceremonies. I found that the best thing to do with him was that as long as everything was ordered and going smoothly, he was fine. But the moment anything unexpected or untoward happened, he became exceptionally violent. When I played Marat in the bath, I could only find the case history of extreme schizophrenia to be my case history for Marat. I regretted that shift in the casting terribly. I was not entirely right, nor was I particularly happy, playing Marat. I build my characters sometimes, not just from the heart out, but from the feet up as well. I enjoy physical characterisation, as well as mental and emotional characterisation, and to put me in a boot-shaped bath meant that I was reduced to the animation of a glove puppet. Whereas when I was playing The Herald, I had the full scope and the languidity of Jean-Louis Barrault's clown in *Les Enfants du Paradis*; I played it very much along those lines. *Marat* was not a happy experience.

But working with Brook was stimulating. Constantly he makes demands. You will give your heart and soul to it in rehearsal, and you will do something that you think is positively the most extraordinary contribution you could have made, and he will sit, and very quietly say 'Very interesting. I think there's more to it than that; think again, and come and try again tomorrow'. In the final analysis, when you get it right, he's your champion for life. Once you get on his wavelength and you understand his discipline, you respect it and obey.

Marat was a very, very exciting experience, but very tiring and very disturbing to do. A lot of people in the cast actually got ill, mentally disturbed. Not lastingly so – one musician had to be put away. One night I was sitting in the bath, at the Martin Beck Theater (in New

York), and the musicians were in the boxes on either side of the proscenium arch. He, the drummer, was in the box above my position in the bath, and he suddenly threw out a handful of dimes, which landed all over my naked upper torso, and quite hurt, and shouted out at the top of his voice 'Three cheers for good old Dixie'. Now the audience, not knowing, just accepted this as part of the craziness of the lunatics. I got the company manager to put through a transatlantic call to Peter Brook after the performance, and I told him about it, thinking he would say 'Well, sack him and get an American musician to take over', but instead, he said 'I think that's wonderful'. The only stable person of the cast seemed to be Glenda Jackson, who couldn't be shaken in any direction.

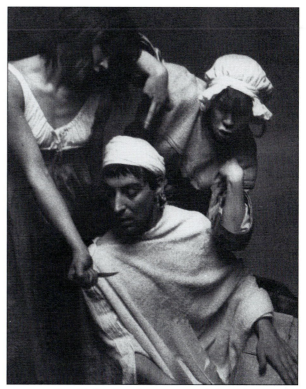

Ian Richardson in *Marat/Sade* (1965)

Francis Urquhart and *House of Cards*

I'd never read the novel *House of Cards*; I was told by Andrew Davis, the script writer, not to read the novel until afterwards. He presented me with a script that leapt – to use the old cliché – off the page at me. However, to have just played, at any time, what leaps off the page, is not enough. There is a typical kind of establishment Englishman, who still exists today in the same way that he existed in Victorian times. They have a code of behaviour, and I knew such a diplomat very well indeed, and when I started off on my search – not just for character, but for character idiosyncrasies: the way he holds a teacup, how he drinks, how he sits, whatever he does – I brought back to mind the body language of this charming diplomat, who was also hard as iron in his dealings. But he did it in the established diplomatic way.

I then decided that I needed to invent a kind of sexual orientation for the character, simply because it was going to be necessary to do so, because of the demands of the character's sexual behaviour in the piece. I studied a book about people in power, and how they needn't necessarily be like the film stars that the girls swoon over, but they have this incredible aura of power about them. I thought 'How do I establish this aura, so that when I'm on camera, it is a measurable chemistry?' Stanislavsky talks about the circle of concentration; you imagine a band around your head, which you expand outward and outward until it touches the audience. I wanted to create that same band, but create it with an aura of power. I realised that the most essential ingredient in achieving that was self-confidence, enormous self-confidence, and this was an aspect that was amply filled by my director, and indeed by Andrew Davis, who actually said on one occasion, that when I walked onto the film set to do a scene, I brought this particular aura already with me. So I was winning, I was getting there. Don't ask me *how* I achieved it; it's like asking me how I make love: I can't tell you because I don't want to tell you, and if I did tell you I might spoil it for myself. I don't know quite how I got there, but I did, and it was just through digging deep, deep, deep.

Now, the other thing is, how do you play a man who is so incredibly ruthless and cruel to the point of pathologically murdering? Fear is the next thing. The man has, inside him, a terrible fear, or a guilt, which goes back to his youth, and a burning, burning ambition, fed in the same way as Macbeth's ambition is fed, by his wife. As I said to the director at the time 'If Collingwood had kept his promise, and promoted Francis Urquhart from being the Chief Whip, to being the Home Secretary, Urquhart would never have gone on a path of blood.' He comes back, from having been told he's to stay exactly where he is, and his wife says 'Well, why don't you do something about it? Why don't you bring him down?' and that begins it. There's a wonderful line that Macbeth has: 'I am in blood, steeped in so far that, should I wade no more, Returning were as tedious as go o'er.' That's what happens with Urquhart. First of all, that drug-sodden press agent has to go, then poor Matty has to go, then before you know it there's another girl in the next series and somebody else; the newspaper editor has to go, and then even his aide has to go, and it becomes almost Jacobean.

The other thing that I decided was that the only way to make this monster acceptable to a viewing audience was to give him what my diplomat friend had, which was enormous urbanity, wit, and charm, exquisite manners, beautiful dress – always Savile Row – and a cultured kind of knowledge which left you breathless. So I prepared all those things, because I'm not like that at all. And I built the character up steadily until it all began to fall into place. I did most of this on my own, because things now have pitiful budgets; there isn't the luxury of rehearsal time, although we did have two weeks. I did most of the research and the preparation in my own study in London, with the result, too, that I came to it knowing exactly what I was going to do, but more than that, I came to it knowing every single word of every single episode in the series. It was a lesson I learned from no less a person that Alec Guinness, when we were doing *Tinker, Tailor, Soldier, Spy* together. He said that he learns the whole thing because it's the only way to place each scene – shot out of sequence as they always are in the movies, and in television – in its position on the graph of your entire performance. So knowing every word of it helped the self-confidence required to establish this aura. I remember, too, outside my dressing room at Ealing studios, there was a great mirror. The dresser used to put me into my Savile Row suit, and just as I opened the door, I would suddenly see Francis Urquhart in the reflection, and not me any more. I had changed.

There are very, very strong similarities between the Urquhart and Richard III, whom I had played. Curiously enough, when Richard achieves his ambition, which is the crown, the part, and the play itself, are on a downward course from there on, and the same is true of Francis Urquhart. That's why the first episode was such a strong one compared with the second. In the second one, he is Richard III maintaining his grasp on the throne, and the third one, he's Richard III facing his Bosworth.

After doing two series, I didn't want to do a third one, and the producer persuaded me to have a very neat little package, a trilogy, as opposed to just two series, so I said 'Oh well, all right, I suppose'. And then I thought 'I wouldn't be at all surprised if they went for a fourth and a fifth', and I could see the whole thing just getting worse, because already it wasn't so good. So, the next morning I went into the filming, and said 'By the way, I've been thinking a great deal about this, and I will agree for a third one, but only on one condition, and that is that Francis Urquhart is assassinated at the end, and I leave it to you to work it out.' I also said 'I want it to be as bloody as possible. If

Ian Richardson in *House of Cards* (1990)

it's going to be a question that he actually commits suicide or something, then up on the roof, please, so that I go the same way as the kid did.' But they didn't want that. I was rather disappointed; if you read the novel, Urquhart sends the father of the two boys that he shot as a young man, an invitation to the unveiling of Thatcher's statue, and in the invitation are the two crucifixes that he took from the boys' necks. That is the invitation to come to the event, and to kill him. So Urquhart does it himself. Andrew thought that was wrong, and wanted Mrs Urquhart to blossom forth into the real murderous demon that she is, and *she* did it. *I* thought *that* was wrong. I felt that Urquhart was not the kind of man who would back away from a decision to engineer his own demise, and I was deeply disappointed with that decision.

The quite astonishing success of the *House of Cards* brought me a recognition that I had not hitherto enjoyed, and stamped me in a strong way on people's imaginings of what I am like. I think very often that I come over as cold, and I would like to be able to get more of the common touch, hence *The Magistrate*. But, I sense, going out there each evening onto the stage, that it's quite a little way into the first act before the people realise that I am expecting them to find me amusing; that I am not Francis Urquhart. *House of Cards* has unquestionably opened doors for me in terms of international film roles, but they wanted more of the same. I have been purposely looking for something totally different, unless of course, greed gets in the way, and they offer so much money that I would be out of my mind to say no.

On working with the camera

I always asked to be told what lens they were using, so that I knew the size. I've always found, particularly of television, cameramen very forthcoming. They realise that you need to know how close they're going to be – because the camera doesn't always move physically towards you, but the lens does. In close-up, the blink of an eye is as big as a wide, policeman-like street gesture, halting traffic or waving them on. So the first thing you have to train yourself to do is hold your eyes open during the take. Not permanently, otherwise it becomes a bit of a worry, but not to blink too much. The other thing is to keep your eyebrows steady, because, again, the eyebrows are like extravagant gestures, especially if they're dark, and of course, after you've been in the make-up chair, they are dark, and they can distract. And stillness, utter, utter stillness. No gestures whatsoever, so that the performance is all coming from behind the eyeballs. The only thing I used to find a bit scary and off-putting, was if they put a filter into the matte box – and as I'm talking to the camera, I was able to see my own reflection. So I used to get them to put just a little mark on the underside of the matte box, because I didn't want to look at my own face speaking. I played it all to that little spot. It makes me very cross, incidentally, because people think that I probably had an autocue for Urquhart's speeches – that I read them – not a bit of it!

I was told at the outset that they thought I might be rather worried and frightened by the business of speaking directly to the audience through the camera. I said 'You mustn't think that for a moment', because one of the things that Peter Hall established in Shakespeare playing all those years ago, was instead of the soliloquy being addressed vaguely towards an exit light in the back of the first circle, or to a place just by the proscenium arch, he established the pattern of saying a Shakespearean soliloquy *to* the audience, taking the audience *into* your confidence. So I said 'I'm not at all frightened of doing it to the camera.' In fact, I enjoy it, it's rather nice because it's a tremendous feeling of power. There's no other actor around me, there's just me, the camera, and the audience, and I loved it. It goes right back to 'They shall grow not old, as we that are left grow old', I had the prospect of holding the audience, metaphorically, in the palm of my hand, and that's wonderful, especially if you're playing someone who has this enormous sense of power.

Also, there was something else. I said to Andrew Davis that the only way that the television audience is going to believe that a beautiful young girl is actually going to invite me to take her to bed is if they have seen for themselves, through their contact with me in close-up, talking to them, the kind of bolts, charges, of chemistry that are hitting the girl. The audience must feel that too, and he agreed, and he wrote some more soliloquies for me as a result of that, so that the audience could see for themselves that it would be perfectly easy for an impressionable young girl to fall into the trap.

The intention was to make you, the audience, as guilty as he is, partners in crime with him. I remember there was one scene in particular where I say 'Oh, come along now, you know very well . . .' and I was thinking of all those poor unfortunate people in their drawing rooms and sitting rooms at home, with their televisions, and this guy is actually turning round and saying 'You're just as guilty as I am', in a big close-up. It must have been quite a shock! But that was one of the reasons for the device – appearing to take the audience into your confidence, and not giving anything away. I remember during *Tinker, Tailor, Soldier, Spy*, a very clever director, John Irvin, took me to one side and said 'I haven't got a great deal to say to you about the playing of the role, except to say that when we see your eyes as you're speaking to us, if we look carefully, we should realise that you're thinking about something else. Although you're saying one thing, your eyes are actually doing something different; in other words, you're hiding something.' Which sounds like a vague and rather difficult instruction to give an actor, but it's actually pure gold, and I used that very much with Urquhart. The eyes would be there, and I would say something, and I used to shoot my eyebrow up, because I expected them not to believe me, and I quite enjoyed the fact that they didn't. It was a wonderful challenge, that.

It sounds very basic, but the first thing you have to learn is which camera is actually photographing you, if there is more than one. A helpful little red light comes on. It is important to make friends with the camera, and still more with the camera operator. And you *must* be truthful, and let your soul show through your eyes.

Researching non-fictional characters

I sat through six hours of documentary footage on Nehru (for the series *Lord Mountbatten – The Last Viceroy*), I sat through about an hour and a half on Montgomery (in *Churchill and The Generals*). I saw very little of Blunt (*Blunt*), because I wasn't allowed to. This was the presentation of a play *about* Blunt, not an interpretation of the real man himself. But certainly, with Montgomery, and more particularly with Nehru, because I'd never played an Asiatic before – nowadays, one wouldn't be allowed to, for goodness sake – I studied endlessly. I'd never been to India before, and so I insisted, before I said yes to the part, that I be flown out there for a week of research, visiting the places where he lived, the parliament buildings, and the residential palace, so I could get a feel of it. All of that was tremendously valuable. Also, I spoke to people who knew him, and I brought back recordings of his speeches, and practised.

It didn't seem to trouble anyone in India that I was playing an Asiatic, but in England, yes. We did one scene before we went out to India, in the Islington County Hall, which has a rotunda that is exactly like the rotunda in the Indian Parliament in Delhi, and we did the 'Freedom at midnight' speech. I only did one take, because at the end of the one take, not Indians, but West Indians, came in with placards saying 'No white actors with black faces', and so we had to abandon filming for that day. In India, on the contrary, the people who were the extras actually thought I was a reincarnation of the man himself. They had to be physically stopped from bending down and kissing my sandals; it was quite, quite bizarre. It's typical of England and of Islington in particular.

In actual fact, for the record, I was not initially considered for Pandit Nehru at all. My photograph was submitted, with my height, my weight, my CV, as a contender for the role of Mountbatten. I was not considered right for that, so I was turned down, but they kept my photograph and my details, because there were so many English establishment figures going to be in it, that there'd got to be something for me to play. The producer, said to her office staff 'Run these photographs through the copying machine, so that we can put them up on the wall.' My photograph was the first one to go through the copying machine, and it came out rather dark, but they pinned it up on the wall anyway. I wasn't there, but the story goes that the producer looked at it, and then she got some of that white type-correcting fluid, and painted a little congress cap on the top of my head, and then took her pencil and darkened the eyes a bit, and then she said to the girls 'Who's that?', and they said 'Oh, it's Nehru', and she said 'No, it's Ian Richardson', and that's how I got the part. She'd come that day from having sat through four hundred auditions among the Asian community of actors. *Four hundred*, and not one of them was right. Now, unfortunately, since they're obliged to cast within the Asian community, or, indeed within the black community, only now and again, will one get a really wonderful performance. I know this is a cruel thing to say, but I rather suspect that we're in for several decades of rather disappointing Othellos.

The amount of research you do all depends on the script. There are some texts, some scripts – fictional or non-fictional – that you get, where the characterisation or the basis of the character, is so incredibly sketchy that you have to invent an enormous amount of background before you can even begin to understand, and thereby interpret, ultimately, the way that character behaves. There exist very small parts which are jewel-like in their construction, where you know all about the character from what he has to say, and it would be pointless to make any kind of sub-plot for oneself. General Burgoyne in *The Devil's Disciple* and Sir Robert Morton in *The Winslow Boy* are such examples; they are known in the trade as *actor-proof*. There are other scripts where the characters are so cardboard that it is essential to make up some kind of background, which will not be known to the audience, but will help the actor breathe some life into the part. There are yet other parts which are historical characters and there, of course, you want to find out as much as possible that may help. In the end the useful details may be trivial. For example Pandit Nehru always wore his watch with the face to the inside of his wrist, but these are the details that convince people you really know all about the man. There is absolutely no point in doing historical research for Shakespearean plays, because the history is very often quite different from what is presented in the play and what you want to do is to follow Shakespeare's vision and not give a history lesson.

Dealing with temperament

I've never had a bad time with an actor, other than the usual temperamental things; you can nearly always trust. Once I had a slightly worrying time with an actress who's ego I was obviously puncturing severely. There have been cases where it was desperately important that my relationship with other actors should be warm and I have, in fact, disliked them. I would then make a point of being particularly nice to them off stage so as to preserve that warmth when playing.

There was one director who, I think, because of the nature of what I'm going to say, must remain nameless. Again, it's a question of ego. He was a man with a tremendous ego – totally unjustified, his conceit, *totally* unjustified. We were doing a film in Ireland, and he behaved so badly; he behaved like the world's worst sergeant-major – a sergeant-major with a posh accent, if you can imagine such a thing. So martinettish, and dictatorial, and I don't work that way. With your director, as with the rest of the cast, it's a question of sharing, of an input of effort, not standing in line with your heels together like some squaddy on a parade ground, being shouted at and told your number. That's not the way that an actor responds to a director. There was one occasion when I was kept waiting for a stills photograph, for about three hours. It was all I was being kept there for, in this freezing castle in County Sligo. Eventually, I heard the director say 'Oh, well, he can do it tomorrow, never mind, it doesn't matter, send him home', and I exploded. I said 'How dare you keep me waiting for three hours and then, in this cavalier fashion, tell me it *doesn't matter*. It matters a great deal, and don't you ever do it again!!!' From then onwards, he was like a dog coming and licking my hand.

It shouldn't be necessary to do that. But he was like that with everybody. There was one shot he needed to get from the middle of the river, so that the camera would see the water flowing by, and the house way, way in the background, with me coming down steps with ten or twelve dogs, to the river. So the camera was placed on an anchored raft in the middle of the river. It was hauled in for the camera people to get on, and then pushed out. He did the classic thing; he stepped with one foot on the raft, and it moved out, and he went in. It was quite a deep, fast-flowing river, and he disappeared into the water. Standing around were all the camera crew, all the electricians, the dressers, the makeup people, the actors, me, and twelve dogs, and nobody moved!

Sometimes I find myself out of sympathy with a director – we don't see eye to eye about anything, or he is of no help to me. In this situation – after trying very hard to co-operate – I usually think out what I want to do, agree with everything he says, and do it my way all the same. It is amazing how many directors just don't notice that you have, in fact, defied their instructions. Sometimes it is because the script is poor – usually in some part which has been accepted only because one's been out of work a long time and needs both the occupation and the money. I try reworking the script, if I'm allowed to, and if I'm not, I just do it loud and fast and hope not too many people see the film.

Theatre vs. film

Preparing for a film is very different from preparing for a play. If I have the script in good time I try to make myself *au fait* with it, without being dead letter perfect, so that I can find the graph of the whole performance and know where I am, and in what emotional state at any given moment, because, of course, films are shot out of sequence. For actual rehearsal, there is really always plenty of time on the shooting day as there are huge *longueurs* while lights are set and cameras are moved about, as well as the official camera rehearsal which immediately precedes the shot. At this point one is at liberty to ask if you can alter awkward moves and try out one or two alternatives.

Although I usually do a lot of preparation beforehand, when it comes to actual performance I rely heavily on my instinct and try not to remember all the preceding thought. There is nothing worse than watching an actor and 'seeing the wheels going round'. I never watch rushes. They would either depress me or imbue me with false confidence, and either would be bad for me or for the rest of the film.

Jazzing up Shakespeare

I have a gut feeling against revamping Shakespeare, but I wouldn't condemn it wholesale. There have been some very exciting productions where in that unpindownable way, it has all felt right. I think anything that gets people interested in Shakespeare has to be good, but I would hate to see it degenerate into a kind of Reader's Digest or Disney version, of which there is a real danger.

I think it is a mistake to try and bend the plays of Shakespeare to any particular psychological angle. We are dealing with genius here, and all you really have to do is understand the lines, and say them. He's done all the psychology in the format of the verse, so that some comes out jerky and disjointed, some smooth, some hysterical, some flowing and limpid, and to fight against what is contained in the structure of the verse is a fruitless exercise. The man's *done* all that you need. Chekhov, of course, is a very different story, where absolutely nobody says what they really mean, and that requires a totally different approach and can be open to very different interpretations.

English actors and FU money

Most English actors are jobbing actors, that is to say they are ready to take on anything and are not ashamed of playing small parts. This is partly to do with money – even established actors can have long periods of inactivity, when they rapidly run out of funds – it being a sad truism that the better and more interesting the work, the poorer it is paid, so that if you want to play, for example Medea, you have to go and do it for tuppence. And you do, because it's a part you want to play. The jobs that pay the most are usually the pits as far as artistic satisfaction is concerned, but we do them so that we can afford to do the good work. This is known in the trade as FU money, meaning that we will be able to afford to turn down the next truly ghastly part that comes along, and finance ourselves through the next bit of artistic satisfaction. English 'stars' are not paid as much as their American counterparts, but I was interested to learn that our supporting actors are much better paid, which I think is a good thing. On the whole, we're quite humble, recognising how much is due to luck, at least when starting out.

I for one find the amount of money paid to American film stars quite grotesque. It means that there is correspondingly less money for everything else involved in a film, or it means that the film costs so much to make that it is almost impossible to make a profit. If you make a nice cheap little film, nobody's going to be ruined if it's not a huge success, and therefore the film gets made. It also seems to me that many of the trappings of American stardom are out of all proportion to the talent involved: my Winnebago has to be bigger than yours; I want a personal gym hitched onto my trailer; I can only eat Peruvian Broccoli so please ship it in for me; if any lowly actor or extra gets into my eyeline, he's to be fired. That last one's true, by the way. What is all that to do with acting? There are many honourable exceptions, of course – Paul Newman and Richard Dreyfuss spring to mind.

On the whole, English acting tends to be understated and depends heavily on nuance and irony, which is why Chekhov has always been so popular here – much more popular than in Russia, by the way. Of course there are many styles and they are constantly changing. There has been a heavy upsurge of raw realism lately which has produced some remarkable actors, most of them with heavy regional accents and therefore probably not all that versatile, and I don't think they can be deemed typical. Back to irony. If one has to make comparisons I would say that to the British, Americans in general seem to suffer from a serious irony deficiency, which is strange given that Russians and Jews are wonderfully ironic – I should know, I'm married to that mixture – and that they form a large part of the US population. Perhaps, that's why we can't quite believe our own publicity, and the *stars* can.

Final musings

Alec Guinness is one of my heroes, it was he who first taught me about acting for the camera, and how to simplify things, because I tend to over-elaborate. Sir John Gielgud, the greatest exponent of Shakespeare and the classics in general. Ralph Richardson as an object lesson of how to go over the top convincingly. Interestingly enough he was capable of really appalling performances, especially in his youth, but he seemed to have had no fear and I admired him for that. Paul Scofield, as an actor who is never less than mesmerising. Shakespeare, of course, is the God of my idolatry.

In my own career, I'm sorry not to have played Cyrano in the Anthony Burgess version, and I'm too old for it now. I would like to have had another go at Prospero and I would have loved to have played my favourite Berowne, from *Love's Labour's Lost*, as many times as possible, but he's one that's gone now. Lear, I suppose, but *everyone* does Lear.

Miranda Richardson

'Sometimes the equation is, if there is no apparent effort, then it can't be registering, which is ridiculous, because if you see effort, you know something isn't right. It's excruciating to watch.'

Miranda Richardson was born in Southport, Merseyside, England in 1958. Her work in provincial theatre includes *Who's Afraid of Virginia Woolf, Insignificance*, and *Einstein* at the Bristol Old Vic, the title role in *Educating Rita* at the Leicester Haymarket and the lead in Robert Wilson's production of *Orlando* at the Edinburgh Festival. In London, Richardson has been seen at the National Theatre in *The Changeling, Mountain Language* and *The Designated Mourner* (which was also filmed). For the Royal Court, she has appeared in *Edmond, Lie of the Mind* and the title role in *Etta Jenks*.

Amongst Richardson's films are *Empire of the Sun, Dance With a Stranger, Enchanted April, The Crying Game, Damage, Century, Tom and Viv, Kansas City, Evening Star, The Apostle, The Big Brass Ring* and *Sleepy Hollow*. For television, she has starred in *After Pilkington, The Master Builder, Sweet As You Are, Secret Friends, Old Times, Redemption, Fatherland, Saint X, Dance To The Music of Time, Merlin, Alice, Ted and Ralph* and *Jacob Two Two Meets the Hooded Fang*. She has also appeared in several instalments of *Blackadder*.

I spoke to Miranda Richardson in Edinburgh in August, 1996, where she was performing in *Orlando* at the Edinburgh Festival.

Early cultural influences

My parents are very into music, and so we went to a lot of concerts when I was growing up. Drama-wise, it was only television, the same as anybody else. There was a cinema a hundred yards away from where we were living, so I'd go and see matinées, and things like that. We had occasional visits to our school – Adrian Henri (a Liverpool poet), I remember that; at that time I was very into poetry, so I found all that very interesting. Between the ages of 14 and 17, I had a great English teacher. There were certain books I was really into. We were studying *The Spire* by William Golding. Of course Shakespeare. There were always set texts, which we would perform in class. It was a very academic school. I went to a state school for my secondary education, and then to a private junior from which I remember nothing except stupid rules, really. I have to say that it's an enormous relief not to be going to school.

I went to the cinema a lot, and what I liked best were the guys, because the guys had the best parts. I liked westerns a lot – John Wayne westerns, I'd go and watch those all the time, and be able to practically recite the whole movie. I had tremendous recall for things like that, or anything that was on the television that I really liked. I'd go and see movies several times, whatever your obsession is at the time, whatever excites the imagination. I was extremely into T.E. Lawrence. I don't mean Peter O'Toole, although I saw the film and I loved it. At the same time I was reading all about Lawrence's time in the desert, and the kind of a guy he was. The women came later; I wasn't too enamoured of many actresses, I can't remember many at that time. I remember Irene Worth very strongly. I went to see her in *King Lear,* and she was wonderful in that. It was a mixed bag of people, really.

Drama school at the Bristol Old Vic

I took my exams early and then had a year out – during which most people travel the world, but I didn't – I just did various jobs. I moved to Bristol and worked there because it was the only opportunity of getting a grant for drama school. I wasn't going to get a grant from the council where I was from, near Liverpool, which is partly why I don't go back. They're cretins, really. This discretionary grant system was constantly raising its head. I get so many letters every week from students now, saying 'I'm doing six jobs, and I've got to pay my fees, and I don't know how'. There's a perverse romance about it at the time, you've got energy to do certain things. At drama school I remember at the end of the day, looking at my watch because I had a cleaning job to go to. Nat Brenner, who was running the school then, knew immediately if your attention wasn't completely there, noticed me looking uneasy. I said 'I'm really sorry, I'm going to have to go now because I'll be late for my cleaning job', and he said 'Well, cleanliness is next to godliness, so please go ahead.' He was very understanding, very good about that. All these silly prizes that have names to them, grants given to the school; he would deal them out to the people who were the most needy.

I knew I wanted to be an actor at around 17. My parents didn't discourage me from going to drama school, but they were worried, like anyone would be. I did this ridiculous secretarial course for something to fall back on. It actually got me a job before I went to drama school, which meant I could earn some money. But there was never any intention of that being a career. Actors are always saying: 'Got a job? When's your next job? Anything in the pipeline?' No one ever takes anything for granted, because it might stop.

I still thought at that point that I would go to university and study either English or drama. As the practical became more important to me, I didn't see why I was going to university. So many people, if they have the education, go on to university almost automatically. I woke up to that and thought 'Why am I doing it?' I think that it can work against you. They have a post-graduate course now at the Bristol Old Vic where people can come for a year after university, and they have to unlearn everything, because they've got into habits; they're so academic about texts that they deny their instincts. They have to learn to play again.

I did an interview for the drama department of a university, and I enjoyed the practical day enormously, and didn't enjoy the interview very much at all. I felt even then that one's instincts were going to be quashed, or channelled in certain directions. I'm sure that was just my perception of it, that's not the fault of the interviewer; it's just the sense that I got.

All they're doing is inviting discussion, but I suddenly got a very strong feeling that it wasn't quite the place for me. I was asked what my decision would be if I got a place at both the university and the drama school, because I had declared my intention of applying to the Old Vic. I was so pissed off after the interview, that I said 'I'd go to drama school'. And that's what I did. I've always taken it as a compliment that the university didn't offer me a place, an indication they thought I would get in at the Vic.

I got into the Vic, and I remember being excited to go in every day, and learn something. That's the best of being a student really. There's speech training, there's movement training. The Vic has a tradition for being quite a workmanlike school, a classical school. You work from the Greeks, and on history plays, and upwards. We didn't do really any modern stuff; anything like that was extra-curricular, and of course, that's what you wanted to do, because it was like a breath of fresh air. Quite a number of plays were done: I remember we did *Three Women* about Sylvia Plath, some Albee, things like that. You have the energy to do that outside of the class hours. I enjoyed the speech training although, perversely, I remember that I became so conscious of how to produce a sound that I actually lost my voice for a time. It was very strange, and made me think that actually what I wanted was to do it by myself – bedroom ranting, as I call it – and I had no business being at drama school. To be a performer, you have to be out there. It was a very strange experience.

Movement was great, because I'd never really done anything like that. I remember doing Laban-based movement. And yoga-based stuff, mad Greek dancing, in the heat of the midday sun. It's very good for co-ordination and form. We also put routines together, in case we were ever called to be in a musical – how to put something across, even if you're not a naturally wonderful dancer. They're concentrating more on that now that there are so many musicals around.

They're very strong on imagination at the Vic. Whatever your text is, it should offer you all the answers if you study it well enough. And it's not only what's in the lines, but what's between the lines. If there's a silence, why is there a silence? What might be happening in that silence, what might you be thinking in that silence? But it's not until you leave drama school and start applying things that you really find out what you've learnt. There were many times where you didn't see how you were going to apply what you were being taught. There were some rather good disciplines – we would spend ten minutes doing an arm gesture, while saying one speech. It's very good if you're extremely young and full of energy, and liable to fling your arms, or snatch at sentences. It's something I still do. In texts you have to follow the line through. It's very good for concentration and focus, calming you down and making you think and listen, particularly if you're at the age most people are when they go to drama school – eighteen, nineteen. You're in such a hurry to get things across, to get things done, so I think that was very useful.

At that time, representatives would come to the end of the year shows from the various repertory companies, because they had a couple of cards to offer, usually acting/stage management posts. Decisions wouldn't be made then, they'd just do their preliminary scouting, and you'd still have to write the letters, and audition. If you were offered an audition, it was usually in London, sometimes in the town where the company was. It's excruciating, really, presenting yourself. I haven't had to do a reading for quite a while, which is a relief. Because there is a bit of you that feels like the person's made up their mind as soon as you walk through the door anyway, and unless they see exactly what they're looking for, you have to second-guess what somebody might be wanting. I find that a very tough process. I don't get defensive in those situations, but it's kind of a no-win situation.

The beginning of a film career/*Dance with a Stranger*

I was doing a play, *Insignificance*, back in Bristol, having a great time, and somebody came to see that production, and they'd been looking for somebody for the lead role in *Dance with a Stranger*. I had no idea about film. When you're doing theatre, you don't really think about film, and when you're doing film you don't really think about theatre, or I don't. They saw me and thought that I might be worth seeing in an audition situation.

They'd been looking for quite some time. They didn't know what they wanted, somebody who was already known, which means that people might have preconceived ideas about them, or someone nobody had seen before. I don't know how many people they saw. My agent said to me afterwards – he was rather confused – that when he set me up to read for the part, he thought that my situation was somewhat similar to that of Ruth Ellis, not that I was a hostess in a drinking club, but that I had somehow reinvented myself, lost my accent, to do this job in *Insignificance*. But that wasn't my story. However, it did work out eventually. Not on the first reading. I remember rather spectacularly meeting Mike Newell, the director, on the way out as I was going in to read; I was furious. I'd travelled all the way down from Lancaster Rep, and I thought 'Some people just think the whole world stops for them'. I didn't read with other actors, but I knew Rupert Everett was going to do the part. I didn't know at that point that Ian Holm was going to be in it. When I heard that Ian Holm was going to be in it, I thought to myself 'Oh God, I've got to take this seriously now'.

I didn't know what I was in for, and they said 'Well, you're going to get very, very tired, go away for a week'. They sent me away for a week just to prepare for the fatigue. And they were right. It was nine weeks of being on every day. I had no resources, really. I didn't feel protected, but I wasn't expecting to be protected. In retrospect, I felt very well looked-after cinematically. I thought they did a brilliant job. But I was thrown in the deep end with a million props, and the continuity lady saying 'I'm going to bug you. You did this on this take, and that on this take; if you could do that again that would be wonderful.' I was concentrating so much about getting that right, I didn't have time to worry about the big pressures; I just did it.

Things like hitting your marks for the camera just comes to you, but you also have to practise. If the technical stuff is really a problem you can work something else out, physically. Or if it's really difficult for you to bear down emotionally, intensely, at that time, then something can be worked out. But when you're shooting every day for nine weeks, you get into it quite fast. And Ian was so great, very supportive, no ego-trip going on there.

I didn't work with a dialogue coach, but I heard one little bit of tape of Ruth Ellis talking to Desmond, Ian Holm's character, and they're very drunk. She's very hyper, very highly strung. That's where that voice came from, really. And the pretension, somebody who's trying to make herself other than she is. And I also had to understand the time the film is set in; I thought the film captured the '50s very well. I didn't know much about the real person;

there's only a couple of books written about her. There's one very salubrious book which I read, and one that concentrated more on the events leading up to the trial. I looked at pictures of her, how she comes across in photographs. That's very helpful when you're doing something very physical.

The script was good; the backstory is implicit in the script. I think that kind of work goes somewhere here (points to head). Though I did read stuff beforehand so I could have an awareness of where she came from, what she was escaping from. But you can't play that all the time. I remember talking to someone who worked at the Royal Shakespeare Company with one particular director, and the director was finding it hard to articulate what he meant, and eventually an actor said 'You mean you want us to invest that line with the sixteenth century?' And he said 'Yes!' But you can't do that. You can do as much research as you like into the manners of the time; you can try and disclaim all knowledge of the twentieth century, but you have to always remember these are people that you're playing.

With film you come in with a sort of broad landscape in your mind, and a familiarity with the words, rather than knowing the script and the character so well that you can't discard something, or find them for yourself while filming. I don't know if I knew that at the time. It's kind of instinctive, really. We talked and read through scenes for about ten days beforehand, but that's only to make everybody feel at ease. You don't end up playing what you did in rehearsal, because once you're shooting, your playing arena is completely different. The confines of the set, and what's around you, paints the picture as much as anything else. It's the day to day processes: who you're playing with, and what they offer you at the time in that situation.

It's very unusual in the British film industry to get 10 days rehearsal, normally you just get a few days. It depends on the nature of the piece. If it's improvisational, you probably just do it straight off. Mike talked about the '50s a bit: what people were looking for after the war. He said everybody wanted a party, which I found a very useful note. So Ruth Ellis was providing a party atmosphere for a lot of people. She was a very small fish, really, but a big fish in that very tiny pond. I felt sorry for her. Her death sentence was horrific, just horrific. She's made an example of. She didn't make any attempt to save herself, either; she said 'I intended to kill him'. So it sounds like premeditated murder. I think she was very self-dramatising, and this was the most famous she was going to get. She bleached her hair specially, so she would look nice in court, and they wouldn't think she was a fleabag. She made no attempt to come in looking ghastly, and sorry for herself and out of it, if she had then there might have been mitigating circumstances. 'Crimes of passion' didn't apply in England, just on the Continent. We're not supposed to have those here.

I also thought she was funny, sometimes unintentionally, sometimes intentionally. I do think you have to find some enjoyment in the characters you play. You don't have to love them, but you have to understand them.

Seeing myself for the first time on screen was awkward, but I almost didn't recognise myself. I remember seeing a rough cut; I was terrified, because I knew so little about filming, and the soundtrack was not ready, the levels hadn't been balanced, and I was horrified. I saw this scene where there was this enormous sound of a hoover going on in the club, and I thought 'They can't be going to leave it like that'. That's how naïve I was; I just thought this was awful; how can they hear anything? I saw the finished thing, and it was very different.

Just this funny little person. I thought 'How can she have caused such a scandal?' I hardly recognised myself on screen.

I wasn't very well after the film; I'd just got completely run down. I was in a daze, really, that's the best way to describe it – not a glorious daze. It was a lot of hot air, a lot of inter-viewers asking the same things, again and again, photoshoots, not feeling up to it, and not knowing what would come next, and not ready for it either. There was a big thing about the resurgent new British film industry. I think it was a very good film, but there wasn't an obvious follow-up to it in British film.

On technique and film acting

The only time I've sat through a lot of rushes was for *Kansas City*, which I did with Robert Altman. It was really like a party. Jenny (Jennifer) Jason-Leigh is very practical about that kind of thing. No matter how tired she is, she goes to rushes. She says 'You must come! You missed a great scene yesterday'. She shamed me into going, and when I went, I had a good time. But I was in very capable hands in that movie, so there wasn't too much reason to feel worried. When you feel in less capable hands, those are the times when you should go to rushes more, and say 'God, I really hated that, I'd like an opportunity to do that again, if it's at all possible', or 'What are you going to do with this?' or 'Are you going to use that shot? Because that other shot seems much better to me'.

But there isn't enough money and enough time, and there have been a couple of times when I've come into conflict with people on a film, almost always in Britain. Having the pressure of knowing that you have to move on, and you only have two takes, is very diffi-cult. If you're not happy with it, you either get so you don't care, and say, 'Oh, fuck it', which is dangerous, or you get angry. So, there have been times when I've thought 'Oh, okay, I've got to save myself, because I'm the one who's up there in the end'. It's very aggravating and frustrating. Although there is something to be said for not doing too many takes. I don't necessarily think that take fifty-four is going to be better than take one. It might be slightly different, but to keep on slogging is not necessarily the best way of achieving a performance.

I think the kitchen scene in *Damage* was good, and we did it in one take, really. I thought it was so well-written, it didn't really need to be directed. We knew what the physical confines of it were; it had a natural arc to make, and we knew it was the emotional high point in the film. I didn't analyse how I was going to do it, I just did it. There's a bit of you watching what's going on at the same time at it is happening, and you feel that some-thing is right. That's the only way I can describe it. The only other way I've described acting on film, or what it feels like, is a sort of moment-to-moment combustion, like an engine firing. It's partly to do with preparation, partly to do with the atmosphere in the room, and giving more or less energy, depending on whether you're performing in a close-up or in a really wide shot.

I'm not always as aware as I should be of exactly where the camera is. Unless you're in a big close-up, then you can't help know it's there. I always feel like I'm being pulled into the camera when it's near, like ectoplasm or something. It happens even when I'm playing a scene where the other actor is right there, it's really strange. The same is true on stage; it doesn't mean you're not focusing on the person you're playing with, but the audience is out there, and you're aware of that.

I think some things about acting for the camera can be an instinct, but they can also be learned, and hopefully one learns more the more you do it. I'm sure Jack Nicholson is past master at that. But I also don't want to be so caught up in technique that I can't just play, so I haven't made it my business to learn all about that. I want to be free; I want to be able to trust that those people know what they're doing.

A need for variety

Quite soon after *Dance with a Stranger*, I went back to the theatre, because I need that variety. There is an unreality about the film world. With theatre you can feel the process much more clearly. If you're going from point A to point B, you know how you got there, and there's a lot more dialogue, more interaction. I did Mamet plays at the Royal Court, I did a film and some television. Things that I was quite drawn to.

I don't really see a pattern in the things that attract me, other people do. I don't take roles for the reasons you might suppose. I don't think 'Oh, here's another dark person.' I did *The Crying Game* because I wanted to work with Neil Jordan, and I thought it was a great script. It was like being in a circus troupe – and there was a sort of a lack of responsibility about it as well. It had something to do with the way he films. Another reason for doing *The Crying Game* was because there was a chance to do something with more action in it, be quite physical onscreen, which is a relief. A bit of gun-toting, and running, and sort of roughness. I really relished the opportunity in that particular instance. I had to be persuaded to do *Enchanted April*, but actually it was rather nice. I liked the idea of the English personality being transported somewhere else, and something else happening – broadly speaking – to the English psyche. I thought 'Oh, well let's try this, let's see if it happens', and of course what happened was that it rained in Italy all the time. We left brilliant sunshine in England. It was perverse.

I also feel a lot luckier than people who have to work in America, because they are made to play the same thing again and again, 'You did that well, here's another one, do this, and then you can move on to something else', but you end up playing four or five parts which seem to me very, very similar before you can break out of it. Then it seems like a major move, and 'Gosh, we never dreamt that this person could do this! Wow! Because we're used to seeing them doing X.' It's very strange, and frustrating, I would think. It's all about money. Terrible, really.

It's a complete world for that amount of time that you're working on a film. It's like a big family; everybody's focused on that one thing. In theatre, to a greater extent, people have their lives, they go back to their house during the day; you do the thing and you go home. There are other things happening. On location for a film, when you're removed from most of the things that normally surround you, different things come into play. Myths are built up around actors, which I think are very damaging, because people start to believe what's said about them, or think they're gods, or that they can do anything they like. Everybody needs to be given confidence to be able to work, but I think the hype actually works against people; they get less secure, because in the end, people are frightened to direct them, they're frightened to make any demands on them at all. You get more left alone, and it would be terrifying if somebody felt that they were so in awe of you that they didn't direct you. I couldn't handle it.

On the mysterious process of acting

You should use whatever works for you, bits of anything. The only book I actually enjoyed reading was Uta Hagen's *Respect for Acting*. I thought there was a lot of sense in that. One of the most important things is just to try and keep open, and observe. Hopefully you have to be curious, otherwise you just end up playing an aspect of yourself all the time. Some people do very well with that; it's limited, but comfortable for the public, because they know what they're going to get.

Most people think of Jennifer Jason Leigh as a Method actor, but Jenny works in a pretty similar way to me, except that she does more research. She's extremely practical, and she gets as much information as possible about anything pertaining to the part beforehand. I rely on the script a lot more; what's actually there on the page. I might subsequently find that what I'm actually supposed to say doesn't completely do it for me. Continual discoveries happen when you're filming. When you're there, you flesh it out more, even if you're not working in chronological order, which is what usually happens. Jenny doesn't have any problems shedding the character at the end of the day. She's tired – we're all tired – but we go out and play. It's good to spend time with somebody that you have a lot of screen time with, just so you can trust each other. You feel like 'Whatever I'm going to be thrown, or throw at this person, they'll be fine.' It's character-based, or your instinct says, 'do this'. If you stop and say 'Actually, that was crap', or 'I don't think that was really very truthful', you can do that comfortably. You're not going to spoil anything. It's partly a practical process. I'm not trying to completely demystify acting, because I don't think you can. No matter how much you try and analyse it, it is a mysterious process. It's actually difficult to talk about, because when you get up there something might just come in from left field. You don't know where it comes from, but it feels right, or it's interesting.

Of course, the story affects you while you're doing it. You're concentrating on it, and focusing on how your character reacts in this situation. But I don't have to wear the same clothing the person wears when I finish shooting for the day. That's one way of doing it. It's a superstition with certain people who feel they have to hang on to that, or nothing's going to happen. I don't do that; I don't have a problem leaving things behind at the end of the day. That doesn't mean that I'm not thinking about the next day, it means that I don't have to be in character when I'm off-screeen.

Sometimes I improvise, but just for myself. Jenny and I would do it to free up energy sometimes. We'd do what our characters would be doing before and after a take, and then we'd drop it. We'd rush around vaguely in character, and then be in the scene and then come out of it. Bob (Altman) often encourages that anyway, and sometimes he specifically wanted text that wasn't scripted – there's a scene in Union Station where he wanted us to improvise some stuff before we ever shot it. The night before, we sat in his caravan and drew out some things about the Lindbergh baby kidnapping. I was very grateful to Jenny in that instance, because she came in with that already researched and had information about what was going on at the time. So we were just two women talking about something sensational that was happening in the papers on a daily basis. That was great fun. I would never stop a set to do that, though.

I saw Holly Hunter giving a master class, a Q and A, and say that because she wanted to feel a certain way before a scene, she actually got the extras to push her around. She said anger was something she had trouble getting in touch with, and she wanted to feel really, really pissed off, so she got them to physically push her. I've never asked that; I think I'm too self-sufficient, I always feel that I should be able to generate it for myself. It doesn't always work if you can't generate the sad feeling about a scene you're in, to think of some other situation in which something similar happened to you. I think what you do is you remember that emotion, sort of a sense memory, part mimicry, part instinct, and part relaxation.

On a film script, particularly, you can't work in a vacuum, you have to work in tandem with the people you're working with. You can see what the text says, but until you get there and find out what the situation is, and whether indeed you are going to say those things, or whether it's going to be changed, which quite often happens, it's more a question of thinking around it, saying 'What is truthful to my character?' It's like boxers in a ring, because you come in from each side and you play it out – not necessarily so that one wins and one loses, but what kind of action you take and when.

Tom and Viv

I remember when shooting *Tom and Viv*, I'd do a take and I think, 'That can't be all there is to it. I must have missed something'. I don't know how often I articulated it. I'd think, 'But I just sort of did that.' I'm often amazed in that way; I feel I got away with something. Sometimes the equation is, if there is no apparent effort, then it can't be registering, which is ridiculous, because if you *see* effort, you know something isn't right. It's excruciating to watch. But sometimes, it's like 'Why was that so easy?' I don't trust myself then, I feel I shouldn't be doing the job because it's that easy. But of course, the goal is ease – apparent ease; that's why a lot of fabulous actors don't really get as much attention as they deserve because what they do is so effortless, it's so right, it's so zen! They don't get the notices, but their work is just wonderful. Brian (Gilbert, director of *Tom and Viv*) was very supportive and actually very confident in what he saw and what he wanted. Oftentimes, he would just say 'I'm very happy. Do you want to do another one? Are you happy? Well, if you're happy, okay, fine!' You have to trust that, you can't go on forever, wanking. Maybe the reason that felt easy was because here's somebody, Viv, who was actually expressing herself, while everybody else was much more cramped and stolid around her, and not saying what they really thought. She was refreshingly honest; it was a relief. So I felt fine, and full of energy. I didn't have a problem, and wasn't emotionally brought down, but I occasionally distrusted that.

I read a lot of accounts of the relationship between T.S. Eliot and Vivien, but they're all

Willem Dafoe and Miranda Richardson *Tom and Viv* (1994)

biased, that's the trouble. I'm not saying that just to defend her, but it's everybody bolstering Tom, and saying she's dragging him down. I've been reading a lot of Woolf, for *Orlando*, and being swept away by it (I spoke with Richardson at the Edinburgh Festival where she was performing in avant-garde director Robert Wilson's production of *Orlando*). There are mentions of Viv in Woolf's writing, very kind mentions. It's not at all one-sided. You can see that here's somebody who's actually being encouraged to write, and who apparently thought very highly of Virginia, and Virginia had obviously given her enough encouragement to continue her writing. She was using it almost medicinally; she was writing just to express. I didn't feel I had to read *all* of Eliot's stuff to understand. I read quite a lot of his stuff, and listened to his tapes as well. I found him quite mad, really. I mean he's the one who's nuts; he's stuck, that's what we try to show in the film.

What Vivien had was basically a hormonal imbalance. They talk vaguely about the endocrine system. It's something that still can be troublesome to diagnose. I turned on the telly quite by accident and saw a re-enactment of a case history of a teenage girl who'd been a model child and a really great, happy-go-lucky free spirit, and at the age of 13, she shaved all her hair off, cut herself, set fire to the curtains in her room. She became an idiot, a delin-quent, and her parents didn't understand. They took her to the doctor, and he didn't know what to make of it. But because her parents cared enough, her father did his own research and found a case history which completely matched his daughter's and it was to do with her menstrual cycle, and this imbalance was making her apparently mad. The girl said 'Had it not been for him, I'd have been locked up in Borstal.' It's quite easy to rectify once it's diagnosed. For Viv, it was basically appalling P.M.S. Her periods were very erratic – she would have a period for three days, and then a gap of a week, and then it would come on again, so she was all over the place emotionally. She was diagnosed as being morally insane, which really means bad behaviour. If she had been allowed to have a child – had they not been so terrified that this was a genetic malady that would be passed on – it might have rectified itself anyway.

But her tragedy was living in the time she did, the lack of understanding about this specifically women's problem, the concerns of the family for respectability, and the right form of behaviour for the class they were in. She's not pukkah, they're upper middle-class, merchant class, not top-drawer. I think had she been upper-class, with a great deal of money she could have done what the fuck she liked. She wouldn't have been locked in a tower in the east wing; she'd have just been allowed to roam the property and be eccentric. The requirements of that class and that family at that time were other. And then she met Tom, who was incapable of rising to the occasion in any manner. She became the cross he had to bear, part of what informed his work, instead of it being a marriage. The intellectual spark was there, but then he was so lionised and applauded, and so needed and wanted, that I think she felt shut out. I think it diminished her. Her writing is extremely personal. In the characters that she does manage to get down, there's always a central woman, an aspect of her; you can feel it very strongly. But she wasn't supported. Everybody tread very carefully around her, and nobody said what they really thought or felt.

She suffered from an appalling lack of self-esteem, because she's let the side down from the moment she reached puberty. It's a shameful thing, and I think there are times when she reacts with rage against that, and times when she just feels guilty and extremely depressed, and is at the mercy of her body, and can't see anything clearly. Towards the end of her life, it really was quite moving, in her diaries, she's bought something and like any of us who are impulse buyers, or hormonal buyers, you get it home and say, 'It's awful, I look like shit, what am I going to do now? I have to take it back'. She tried to make herself better by doing it externally, by making extravagant purchases. Yet she looked more and more wretched and ragged and worn. In photographs she looks sort of ravaged, really, at the end of her life. She also looks like a different person from photograph to photograph. It's quite uncanny. There are an awful lot of photographs in which she's blurred, because she's always moving. There's an energy; she's on all the time. The camera's caught this sort of languid group of people, while Viv's always in motion, looking at something else. So the photographs, again, were extremely useful.

I don't think Tom would have written the books he wrote if he hadn't met Viv. She's threaded through his work. She's also tremendously supportive to him, and expected and wanted him to be championed, but not to the exclusion of her personality. Tom was the star; nobody wanted her outpourings, certainly not the Bloomsbury Group. They wanted carefully considered, reworked expression.

Tom never visited her in all the time she was in the institution. There wouldn't have been any conversation between them; can you imagine? It would have been excruciating. Tom couldn't cope, emotionally, at all, with the guilt. He was free, in one sense, once she was institutionalised, to get on with his work, but bearing that enormously important burden out of which came his work. I think that eventually the institution was a sort of sanctuary, and I think Viv would have been more lonely out on her own. Her mother died when she was in there. She didn't have the resources anymore to start again, and say, 'Right then, let's discover the world now'. And she wouldn't have had the money; she's not landed gentry.

Avant-Garde theatre: performing in Robert Wilson's *Orlando*

It was different from anything else I'd done before, which I knew it would be, and which I wanted. It was very physically based, which I also wanted. I loved the idea of being part of the architecture and this enormously luscious, magical text which was being spoken at the same time. The play allows your imagination to do the work. I think audiences want that. I don't mind if they come in not knowing what the hell they're going to

Miranda Richardson in *Orlando* (1996)

see. You're guiding them through the story, telling them the story, and the movement score is abstracted from the text somewhat. Sometimes it illustrates, sometimes it just underpins. Movement is like memory, there are reverberations of the movement, there are different interpretations of similar movements which appear later on, so somewhere in your brain you're going 'I've seen that', or 'I think I've seen that'. You make your own connections, and I find that very fascinating.

There is a movement score, but because it's me doing it rather than somebody else doing it, like a dancer doing a classical piece, the interpretation is going to be different. It's the first time it was heard in English, and it's partly about Englishness and England, rejoicing in that. It was very important to hear it in English. I saw it in French (Isabelle Huppert enacted the role in Paris), and without understanding a lot, I still made my own story, but it became as much a sound piece and a dance piece as a text piece.

The career arc: fusing instinct and technique

When you're 19, you feel like you can do anything, and you do, instinctually. Later on there's a sort of fusion of instinct and technique. The more you think you know, the less you know. It happened in this production; there was one night when I got practically suicidal coming off, and the first thing I said to Bob (Wilson) was 'Sorry', and he said 'I hate you. You were too good tonight', and I thought 'All right, I know nothing, I know nothing'. The audience was doing half the work, and you can't manipulate that, you can't control the connections people are making, and what they're feeling, and how something is coming across. So I don't know anything really.

Perhaps it's more to do with a sort of compulsion in the beginning. I don't know what it is now. I often think I'm not always going to act; I don't know quite what else I would do. I think you get more fearful, but then it's something that you have to work through. At times when I say to myself: 'You're mad, you're mad. What makes you think you can do this?' It's partly an act of will, trying to move on in some way, to different challenges. The physicality of it is very important to me, because this is your instrument, and a lot of the time, it's concentrated up here (points from neck up). And it's a relief to feel everything working at once.

I do a lot of yoga, which is marvellous. The movement that you do at drama school is all supposedly gearing you towards ease and freedom of the voice as much as anything, because if the body is free, the voice is free. A lot of that stuff that people take the piss out of all the time is actually useful. You know that 'Uh!', and people shaking forward and throwing out their arms, all that stuff is designed to loosen everything.

Take from everything

I think one takes from myriad things, whatever makes you feel wonderful about the creative process, about art, the visual arts and music. There are a number of people I admire greatly, and it's something to do with an honesty about what they do. I think Francis Bacon's stuff is wonderful, because I find it very honest, not because I'm morbid, or like to see something flayed. I find it very honest. There are writers who I love to read because I feel the honesty in their writing, and it's something to do with 'Yes, that's how I would want to say it if I had chosen that form'. There are actors who are wonderful in specific things; some people who you like to watch all the time. I love Paul Scofield, oh God . . . too much, too many. Sometimes people affect you at a particular time in your life, I'm sure that's true. Some people say you can't listen to Mozart before you're 30, I don't know if that's true. But maybe Oasis means more to you at a certain age than Haydn. Take from everything.

Fiona Shaw

'... *all actors have a fantastic sense of mortality. Particularly stage actors, because to choose a way of life where you give your life's blood to concentrating and perfecting events that pass in a second, and only live in the memories of those people who are watching it, is an incredible throw-away relationship to eternity.*'

Fiona Shaw was born in Cork, Ireland in 1958. Her work for the RSC includes leading roles in *As You Like It*, *Philistines*, *Les Liaisons Dangereuses*, *Mephisto*, *The Taming of the Shrew*, *Much Ado About Nothing* and *Electra*, for which she was won the Olivier Award for Best Actress. She has played the title role in *Hedda Gabler* both at the Abbey Theatre in Dublin, and in London, where she received the London Critics Award. Shaw also starred in Samuel Beckett's *Footfalls*, and performed the title role in *Mary Stuart*. At the National Theatre, she has played in *The Rivals*, *The Good Person of Setzuan* (London Critics Award for Best Actress), *Machinal* (Olivier and Evening Standard Awards for Best Actress), the title roles in *Richard II* and *The Prime of Miss Jean Brodie*, and Millament in *The Way of the World*. She toured North America and Europe, and played both London and New York in Deborah Warner's production of T.S. Eliot's *The Wasteland* (N.Y. Critics Circle Award).

Shaw's television appearances include *Fireworks for Elspeth*, *Maria's Child*, *Hedda Gabler* and *Persuasion*. Her films include *Mountains of the Moon*, *My Left Foot*, *Three Men and a Little Lady*, *London Kills Me*, *Jane Eyre*, *The Avengers*, *Anna Karenina*, *The Butcher Boy* and *The Last September*. She has been awarded an honorary degree from the National University of Ireland and is Honorary Professor of Drama at Trinity College, Dublin.

I spoke with Fiona Shaw in her Primrose Hill flat in October, 1997.

Childhood, school and family

I come from Ireland, so the cultural life is very palpable, but it isn't necessarily formalised. There was actually very little theatre while I was growing up. There was no professional theatre in my town. I don't know when I saw my first professional play; I might have been 18 or something. There were amateur plays at the school, and of course, there were student dramas. But, in my early childhood, there was performing in that the family was always rehearsing something. I came from a family delighted by literature and music, so there was always reading. Now reading seems to have gone. The American style isn't it? Reading – who reads reviews? Reading went out with the dinosaurs. It's a terrifying notion that we make our living by the word, and yet don't read the word. I always read lots of novels. My mother is a singer, my uncle is a pianist/doctor, as it were. And my elder brother is now a big double-bass player. And of my other brothers, one played the violin, and one played the flute, and I play the cello. So, music and performing within the family was very big.

I'm the only daughter in the family. I had three brothers: one elder and two younger. The youngest was killed in a car accident. There were lots of stories, lots of story-telling. But not much in terms of official culture.

The school I went to was a small house on a street, and a kind of hopeless school, which was why I liked it. And a lay-school, not a nun-run school – which is unusual in Ireland – but the result was, it had a slightly more liberal feel; small classes, and because it was in a house, it was like being at home. It was full of madness in terms of imagination: eccentric teachers, and eccentric pupils. So, it was a very contained, delightful, provincial upbringing.

This lay-school was more Catholic than you can imagine. (Laughing) It was completely full of prayers, and religious classes. So, there was no lack of Christianity or Catholicism, but I think my mother had that little germ of liberalism. It was also a smart, socially-right school. All my parents' friends' children went there. So, one's family life and school life and leisure were completely intertwined. We rarely went to the cinema. We weren't allowed to watch television. And we weren't allowed really to go to the cinema very much because, in general, it was thought that the films were unsuitable. I did at 6, see *Mary Poppins* six times, and I saw *The Sound of Music* three times. But I don't think I saw another film for maybe four years. Julie Andrews was *it* as far as I was concerned, the very ultimate. I couldn't wait to get to Salzburg, and see that hill. I knew all the songs by heart. I got the song book. So that was my relationship with cinema, a complete involvement, but with less films. But I wasn't hankering for the cinema. Also, we weren't given much money. My parents were very well off, but we weren't given that kind of money for going to the movies all the time. We must've gone as treats. Performing and doing poems is much nearer the heart of my excitement.

I was a big performer at the school. A lot of the school remembered me mimicking the teacher. And I think that must've become an enormous fixation for a while. I don't want to be so self-focussing, but it is remarkable that the germ of your life occurs very early on, isn't it? I never knew I was going to be an actress, but I was doing it before I even knew I was doing it. It's quite moving about humanity, actually, that we already know where we want to be by the age of eight, don't we? I thought I wanted to be a doctor, but I actually wanted to be an actress. But I didn't know what that meant; I had never seen a play.

We did do things in school, lots of Shakespeare, so I would always be the one reading aloud Bassanio or Portia. And then, later at school, I went to classes, to a woman named Abbey Scott, who'd been to RADA. She was the first person to put RADA in my head. I never knew there was any such place, that there was a sort of paradise or promised land for those who wanted to become actors. I entered these competitions called a *Feis*, which is festival, really. And it's now one of the biggest festivals in Europe, where you could do poetry under 10 poetry under 12, or dramatic scenes. I was always pairing myself off with some unfortunate, unwilling actor to act with me, and I won lots of prizes. I was Miss Prize-winning Actress; I adored it. But I had no clue, I just couldn't stop doing it. I could stop doing it now, very happily. It's funny, the need to do it at a certain time, the need to be in that state of heightened imaginative reality. The excitement of being Gwendolyn, or Cecily, or Lady Bracknell or Lady Wishfort. I was obsessed. And I was very interested in people from other periods, which I think is quite telling. I wasn't very modern. It has something to do with the slightly exotic nature of my upbringing in an otherwise incredibly parochial world. But there was an excitement about language that existed in centuries other than the one I was in, and maybe my mother's heightened relationship to history. Somehow, all history seemed exotic.

That, I think, stood me in incredibly good stead later, because when I went to RADA, I was absolutely back of the class when it came to Barry Keefe plays about the East End and people fighting. But as soon as we went into Restoration, I was at home. Suddenly the 18th Century came along, and everybody else was floundering, and I was completely there. I discovered one could learn about history through the emotional investigation of plays. And when it came to do *Hedda Gabler*, I found that I learned something about my grandmother by doing the play. It wasn't that I used my grandmother through the play, it was the opposite: by doing the play, I felt I learned about my grandmother. I haven't analysed this, really – when I write my autobiography, then I'll think about it.

I was a very shy little girl, but at 10 or 12, I became an extrovert. My mother was great at parties, and I think I borrowed that behaviour. But, I have subsequently become much more like my father. I think people do that, shift from one parent to the other. My mimetic behaviour was my mother's; she was very extroverted. I suppose I was full of the need to show off. If you took away the moral unattractiveness of the desire to show off, I would say it was a need to experience life at a heightened frequency, and I don't regret that at all. I think that you can either live intensely, or you can live half-asleep. And I think I was always excited by intensity.

I went to Cork University and studied philosophy, and I suppose my parents anticipated that I would become either a philosophy teacher, or I'd go into medicine. My father was a surgeon, my uncles were all doctors. By the time I reached that phase, I don't think my father's expectation was that I'd go into medicine. I showed no interest in it. A professional education, that's all that any parent can offer. But drama school – it just had no meaning. It's like saying you want to be an astronaut. It doesn't mean anything there. 'What are you going to do, starve? You don't need to go to drama school just to starve.'

My family felt very forcibly that I was making a mistake. Not so much with my mother, she – like other mothers – was keen to live vicariously through her daughter, and would've been thrilled. I think my mother's view of becoming an actress was glamour: the world of Maria Callas. To end up in these strange, difficult experiments I do, is not what she intended. She thought it'd be all about furs and little foxes, you know. She was very encouraging and very protective of my choice. The choice is done and I don't question the choice. I just chose it and wanted it very deeply.

Royal Academy of Dramatic Arts

When I went down to RADA, it was run by an absolute genius of a man, Hugh Crutwell. Very old, very wise, remarkably moral. He's Geraldine McEwen's husband – an incredibly well-spoken, passionate man, whose only interest was in getting you better, and who didn't talk about the profession in any way that had to do with an orientation for work. In fact, it was one of the criticisms of him, that we weren't ready for work at all. We were good at acting, but nobody had an eye on a career, which of course, was perfect, because it was the way of preparing you for your art rather than preparing you for a job. There was an emphasis on poetry and classics.

So, initially, upon first beginning theatre school, I lost an enormous amount of weight. I'd been a student drinking Guinness and eating toasted ham sandwiches, and suddenly at RADA, we were doing four classes of movement before lunch-time. I think it went: movement/voice/movement/voice, all morning. By the afternoon you did some rehearsing, and then singing, and then you did some dialect, and finally, private tutoring. You went home jaded, and this whole thing began again the following day. It was a very, very disciplined, fantastically high-powered, very intense course. It made an enormous schism between the life I led before, which was as an idling, dawdling, reluctant stone-kicking student avoiding writing my philosophy essay, and doing plays. Instead, I was being used to the pitch of my ability. And every day you were facing other people whose abilities were as good as your own and greater. And you were discovering the grammar of the theatre – so that you could see why somebody was good. What they were good at, why it was good, how you could help yourself to that place.

The Americans have a whole language about: 'How do you get to your character?' The culture in this country – and the teaching at RADA – isn't toward characterisation. The problem about character is that character then drives the narrative. Of course, in film it can; you are fascinated by a character, and you see what he does. The tradition from Shakespeare on, is that character is the combustion of yourself with events. So, put yourself in the situation, and you'll discover your character. You don't have a character that walks into the situation. You can't know your character, in fact. You're just you.

If I do Portia for you now, you'll tell me something about Portia that may say something about Fiona, or it may tell you something about Portia. But if I try to think up a Portia without the situation, I won't know what I'm doing: does Portia take sugar, when I don't? It's irrelevant. Portia's the person who says: 'You see me, Lord Bassanio, where I stand such as I am/ Though for myself alone, I would not be ambitious . . .' What is the point of my saying: 'Well, I think that Portia has a high voice, and she's got red hair, she's got ten rings'. I'm not saying that to decry the way other people approach character; you could do all that to ground the character. So, we didn't do character in that way, though you were exposed to a series of writers, some of whom demanded that style of characterisation. But it wasn't all Stanislavsky, not at all.

It's very easy to talk about character after the event. The discovery is what works at that moment, and what doesn't work. Afterwards, you can look back and say: 'I think it must've been that'. But you can't plan ahead what's going to happen with these people. You don't know who they are. You find out by doing it, and, subsequently, my main body of work, my life, really started after the RSC, when I started to work with Deborah Warner, who doesn't speak at all. She wouldn't know what you are talking about, if you talk about character. It's to do with the fact that if you are conscious of the pros and cons of character, then you are *describing* the event, when in fact you should be *experiencing* the event. The experience of the event is the greater totality. So, you plunge in.

It is much nearer imagination and intellect than an act of painting a description. It is about harnessing things you know and things you don't know. So, if you say: 'Well, I'd like to see you act Fiona Shaw sitting at a desk and giving an interview', I wouldn't know where to begin. If I can get involved in the interview, then you'll find that one hand is beneath my knee. I didn't know that, but that may be of importance, or it may have no significance at all. If you plan it, then somehow you signal it. If you signal it, then one bit of your brain is being used to signal instead of being as concerned with the crisis of thought as the character is. Any energy left for decorating is a diffusion of the energy. So really, the best actors in the world are those who are often rather simple about what they do: they just do it, they don't plan it or organise it or manipulate it, they just *are* it. It's very near what Peter Brook says about language, it's to find out *what it does to you*, and not *what you do to it*. It's just a matter of exercising the imagination. At RADA, we were put in these enormous productions where everybody's absolutely terrified, where you have to hold the house using your thought, and the imagined world around you. And those whose imaginations were expanding – literally like a muscle – were able to be dexterous in the moment, and those who weren't, weren't.

I mean, what is acting? It's walking and talking. But it isn't. It's about seeing the possibility or significance of those moments. What's poetry? It's only a few words put together on a page, but the significance is greater than anybody else putting those words on the page. So, it's a very hard thing to name, which is why I suppose people think actors are born, rather than made. You can make good actors better, but you can't start people from nowhere. They have to have a fundamental ability to be in a binary state, in permanent dialogue with their own imaginations, so that when they utter forth something, people hear them. Very few people in the profession have that gift, you know. Maybe in film, you don't need to have that gift. In film, the camera goes in chasing you. In the theatre, you have to be able to communicate.

I would say that all actors have a fantastic sense of mortality. Particularly stage actors, because to choose a way of life where you give your life's blood to concentrating and perfecting events that pass in a second, and only live in the memories of those people who are watching it, is an incredible throw-away relationship to eternity. If we put as much effort into sculpting something or painting something, at least we know it will live after us. But acting is the most throw-away of all the arts. It takes enormous man-power, will-power, imaginative power and dedication. And for what? Where's my Shrew now? Gone. Where's my Hedda Gabler now? Gone. Except for these little television things that capture bits of it, but not really. So, gone. Those moments where you have the play and atmosphere singing. And actors are very good at playing with atmosphere, and this thrilling, heightened relationship to reality. Somehow, this is the redemption for the actor, and they tend to be pretty hopeless at anything else.

On styles of acting, the Method and Shakespeare

I've nothing against Method acting, I believe in whatever produces the event that occurs in front of my eyes. Except where it's not totally achieved, and that's usually the luck of the person who is applying it. So, for instance, who are the great Method actors we've got? You've got Brando or De Niro, obviously, Harvey Keitel. They're very similar, all three of them, you see. It suits their personality. But I don't think they represent an enormous spectrum of mankind. There are tricks with all styles of acting. And the Method was a moment of reaction against what was seen as an untrue style. You see, the great French style of acting was about pretense, because it came from the court. It was about dressing up, and masks and pretending. So, somebody who was in the court of Louis XIV, trying to be the beggar, would do some sort of gesture toward pretending to be a beggar. Now, this was seen as false, but its nature was false, and it was meant to be false. I am the courtier, so I could never be a beggar. It was about the dance of falseness, about disguise: underneath this beggar is in fact a courtier. The Shakespearean style in England was much more robust, really. It was for Henry V, 'O for a muse of fire . . .', it was people coming and saying: 'I won't give you a whole biography about me, but picture this: "O for a muse of fire . . . "' Othello would come out and talk to you. Much nearer to what was later to be called Method. It was about being. It was about the fusion of emotional consequence with intellectual thought, fabulous intellectual thought due to a particular quirk of Elizabethan language.

By the time we hit the 20th Century, you have a country, America. I'm now going to precís into something very unworthy of America. You have a culture that, due to its multinational mix – which is why it was called a melting-pot when it was formed – had a tendency towards the noun. People stopped using the filigree language of the 18th or 19th Century, because people would come from all over the world going: 'coffee', or 'pizza', or 'work', 'car', 'money'. (Laughs) The fineries of the inherited courtier behaviour: 'Would it be possible for me to interest you in a cup of coffee?' just had no place for a moment. This produced an imagination of an immense sad loss, of distant inheritance, which is captured fantastically in the 20th Century film world of people unable to reply, unable to speak. So, instead they used these tiny words, and they broke up what they were saying. They invented this thing of broken thought. And broken thought is often what is mistaken for Method acting; which is, you are speaking, and half-way through your thought, another thought comes in, which is hidden from the listener. Now, this has subsequently bubbled up into the biggest trick of Method acting. So that anybody who . . . stops . . . halfway through a line . . . .

The style of the Elizabethan language is merely that while you said, 'To be or not to be, that is the question', you were genuinely trying to communicate, 'To be or not to be, that is the question', not 'To be . . . or not to be . . . that is the question'. You weren't trying to say: 'I am more important than what I am saying', you were saying, 'What I am saying is more important than me'.

I don't believe the rather school-marmish reply to Shakespeare, I don't believe that when Hamlet says: 'To be or not to be. That is the question', he's really thinking about how to go to bed with his mother or something. Because the energy needed to communicate to the audience, 'To be or not to be' should take the entire concentration of that actor to really make you hear it – the actual force of intellectual power to be able to thread that thought right through to the end of that speech. There is no energy left to be going, 'But what I really want to say is, how am I going to kill Claudius?'

When you deconstruct language as we have done – I would say that when God died, the end of God by Nietzsche at the end of the 19th Century, resulted in the preoccupation of drama changing from being about describing or coming to terms with the world outside you, to being about the *inability* to come to terms with the world inside you. By lowering language, by using much fewer words: our books are smaller, our vocabulary's smaller; by losing faith in the fact that we were in dialogue with the universe/God/audience, we're suddenly thrown back into a world where there is no God/audience/universe, so we've begun to implode into our inner world of chaos. And because of that, a few little dribbles that come out of our mouths: 'The horror, the horror . . .' in *Apocalypse Now* replaces the great text of *Macbeth*. Now they just say, 'the horror, the horror', and that is full of what's called subtext, because of the enormous gaps between these tiny utterances and our emotional experience. This new language we've developed, is a sort of debris language. It's a language of: 'Did you go to the movie?' 'Yeah.' 'How was it?' 'Great!' You sense that the person really wants to go up to bed, or wants a coffee, or a drink. You sense other things because what's being delivered to you is not valuable. I do believe that we are trying to apply these subtextual discoveries – this notion that when people speak, they're thinking about something else – to earlier plays. But as soon as you get back before the 19th Century, it doesn't really function in that way. This is not to mean that there isn't psychology in Shakespeare. It's full of psychology because we're full of psychological baggage. But it's very hard to name your own. I find more and more the people in the rehearsal room who tell each other about their psychological baggage, are missing the entire point. The point is you can't see your own. You can talk about it, but don't see your own.

I think psychology is a tool. I think learning iambic pentameter is a tool. None of these things need be oppressions or totalities. They're so evidently not. But, again, maybe this is a bit like what Sartre would say: 'Destiny is history', isn't it? You could look back at the moment before you die, and say: 'I see, so that's the way my life went'. But how can we describe that in advance? In fact, it becomes very obvious why your life went like this when you look back. When you look forward, it could be anything. So, when you say: 'Well, because I'm doing this, I'm sure my character would do this', is to reduce the possibility of that person, because we are built in contradiction. The really fantastic thing about Shakespeare is his obsession with antithesis – the antithesis being so total – that even 'the cat is dead, or the cat is not dead', you get it within the line: 'To be, or not to be', I mean, that's only half a line. 'That is the question.' Three separate thoughts, two of them opposites, all in the same verse line, before you even get: 'Whether 'tis nobler in the mind to suffer the slings and arrows of outrageous fortune/ or take arms against a sea of troubles, and by opposing, end them/ To die. To sleep'. This endless balance – we live somewhere in that, I think. I just did *Richard II*, two years ago, and you get this fantastic sense in Richard II of somebody – again, now I'm standing over the play, and I hope this isn't an interpretation – who is both loved and is destroyed by his cousin; and who both loves and wishes to destroy his cousin. Well, you'd think: either you want to destroy him or you don't, but no, people are like that. How many of us love our mothers more than anyone else in the world, and the person you most want to murder in the world is your mother? It is precisely this contradiction in which I think we all really live, and I think the great healing power of theatre – or the potential of theatre – is that by looking at other people's troubles and contradictions, you don't feel so bad about your own. It has a fantastic healing power to see other people making mistakes, to watch Macbeth get steeped so deep in blood that he goes on. To watch him do that, to watch him go on murdering, to know that it could be you, allows you to forgive other people's sins and your own. A bit Catholic, isn't? (Laughs)

An Irish view of being an artist in Britain

It just isn't good form to be seen to be an artist in this country. People don't take art seriously. People don't take actors seriously, and that might not be a bad thing! So, actors are never allowed to turn into the sort of demi-gods that they are in other places. The great unity of characteristics that are attractive to the English psyche are: clarity of thought, humour, self-deprecation, irony, modesty and power. All of these qualities are quite in combination with England as it would wish itself to be. A lot of the Shakespearean heroines have that mixture. The other side of that, is that it's a perfect combination for building empires, because power becomes ruthlessness, et cetera.

We have a fantastic cultural inheritance and tradition here – and I speak about this as an Irish person – that you absorb before you even begin. This is a funny, dusty little corner that was for a long time the language-Renaissance-Merchant Bank of Europe, so anybody who hangs around it gets it under their skin for nothing. Most kids here know who Henry V was. They don't have to work out who he might've been; they have a sense of it. They might not know the history, but they absorb it. So, the moment they start speaking as Henry V, they've already got immediate rights. When you go to America, you find the students are really struggling with who Henry V might be, because they haven't inherited that. It's a cultural gift. The British call themselves 'jobbing actors' because they are waiting to be asked to be in somebody's play. And, when they are offered a play that they like, they are in it. They don't necessarily initiate the work on their own. And they are not necessarily trying to use the theatre to move it forward. It would sound very grand to say 'move modern thought forward', but something like an attempt to get to the heart of something. Acting is only a cog in a wheel. Each actor only carries a bit of the play, but sometimes the great leading actors and the play, or the experience of the play, become one thing; where the play and the experience of the play is absolutely bound in with the person you're seeing. That doesn't mean that they push everybody off the side. Greek tragedy, for instance, often takes that form: where the actual production and the person playing it are carrying the entire emotional darkness of what you're experiencing for the hour and a half. It's embodied in them. Jobbing actors – maybe it's a way of not taking responsibility for the event. But it's an inability we have to name our jobs as in any way important. And perhaps it's terribly important that actors aren't important. The other thing is that people think of actors as vagabonds and thieves; that's the big tradition. They're not respectable people.

I landed myself in quite a difficult role, because I didn't really want to just keep doing jobs. I didn't become an actress to do a television series here, and a play there. That's not what I want. I want something more from it, and often get less. It's not a rewarding profession in many ways, it's a very cruel mistress or master. I take a long time between each thing, not because I don't want to be doing it, but because the choice is so enormous. I did mainly comedies at the RSC, and I was described (in an ironic tone) as 'the comic jewel in the RCS's crown'. I used to be completely orientated towards comedy. I found that laughter caused by the actor the ultimate relationship. I did one tragedy, *Electra*, that changed my entire relationship to theatre, and changed the entire theatre relationship to me. People completely stopped using me to do comedy.

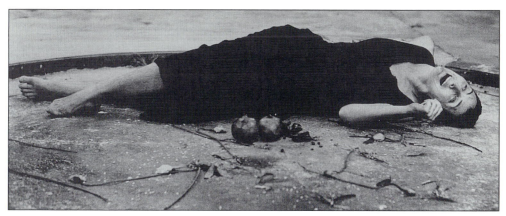

Fiona Shaw in *Electra* (1991)

Connecting life and art: *Electra*

What happened with *Electra* was that by trying to vault the cost of doing it, making it so much higher – completely masochistic thing to do, I'm not sure I approve of it – I'd never done that before; I'd never turned myself really inside-out. I damaged myself with it, but the reward was enormous. It made me nearly suicidal. But I got somewhere. I don't know if I can explain it without boring you rigid, but somehow the effect of it was that people were queuing up all night to see this play. Not to blow my trumpet about it, but it meant something happened, and I could sense it; there was some kind of chemical reaction to it.

This is so profound an area, I don't know if I can talk about it. I'm not sure I can glibly tell you what I learned about this, but *Electra* was very connected to the death of my brother. I didn't know that at the time, really, and I didn't realise that was the right play. I'm sure that there are always things at work, and when I say I'm on a hunt for a play, it's sort of a mania to complete something. And it's very difficult. I would say that sometimes you have to be very true to the desert in order to get to the water well. It's quite humiliating in the desert. You're waiting for this feeling because you can't say: 'A really clever move to do next would be this. . . .' Well, that's really not what's at play. You're waiting for the thing to come to you.

I have no doubt that *Electra* was the thing I needed to do after my poor brother Peter died. It's not because of Peter – I won't say too much about that because it's too hard, or too multifarious, really – but the death of a brother is the death of a close family member, who is not your primary member: not your father, your mother, or your child, but it's the death of your childhood, of my childhood. It's the death of innocence in a way. It heralded such a wedge in the family unit, in the family expectations. I don't know if all families are like this, but it was like Kennedyitis; it's the sense that your family is this fantastically strong unit. When the youngest is killed in that way, the whole thing breaks open. In a way, I suppose it was the beginning of my growing up. I was 26. It separates you from many people, because if people haven't experienced death at all, and a city like London is very anti-death, there's not much death-talk here. So, I don't want to diminish my poor brother's death, but it's more than the death of my brother. The death of the brother becomes the death of all sorts of things. It's a herald of one's own death. *Electra* certainly chimed with that, and afterwards I was changed. *Hedda Gabler* was also a really enormous experience. It not only told me about my grandmother's life, but about my mother's life, because I put enormous mannerisms of my mother into Hedda Gabler. And my mother's alive, so there's not much I can say about that; my mother's very alive (Laughs).

Hedda Gabler in Ireland

Snatches of songs and moving the furniture in *Hedda Gabler*, came from my mother. It was a very central part of the experience. I can't tell you what I discovered, but by enacting it, I became rhythmically like my mother – and you know rhythm is a great key to the uncon- scious. If you pick up somebody's rhythm, if you mimic them physically – you get a feel of what they're feeling. It's an old drama exercise. I think that changed me in how I began to look at family. It's hard to talk about this because it's not conscious at the time. You discover these pools of unreleased potential, because they ring true to you, because they are about you; it's all about you. There's no doubt that the more interesting actors are people who are in touch with the interior in a way that is interesting.

The best thing I've done, really, *Hedda Gabler*. I've told you how you get a feeling about something. A play becomes like an island, and you say: 'I think I want to go to that island'. So, you get in your boat, and you go. In terms of *Hedda Gabler*, the play was to take place on an island, and it happened to be my home island. I went to Dublin in a car packed with this designer, and this director, so I was taking them on a journey they've never been, myth- ically, very Ulyssian. And then we get to Dublin, so of course, you say: 'Whatever is going to happen in that play is going to combust with this town'. You cast it with all Irish actors, so the imagination would be Irish.

My idea for *Hedda Gabler* was that the place should be full of furniture that was too big, and that it was very crowded, so that you always had to stand on top of somebody to get past them. A sense of bodily claustrophobia. Hildegard Bechtler who designed it, took that idea and did the opposite of it, which is often how you get to an idea: she had the idea that there was a big extension to the house, a huge room, a cold room, with floorboards and no carpets, that had all these tables, glass, chairs, sash windows never before built by the Abbey Theatre, giant, extended. She had taken for her reference, some of those American Southern houses, which are a bit like the Anglo-Irish great houses, but with icanthus leaves, enor- mous doors, so that if you were to take out all the realistic elements, all the detail away from the set, you'd be left with a Classical Greek set, with the icanthus leaf arch and the big window. It was full of furniture, which as the show went on – you can't really get this in television because they shot it wide – the furniture gets moved, and finally it's an empty space. It's just a sofa, and finally even that goes, and she's just in an empty room. It was inevitable.

It took a lot of rehearsing. Always fixing the furniture, never at ease. It has to do with your spirit, not being able to settle in a place until you have a seeming order. Your order could be anything, but you never get your order right, because you're never at home. I wanted to capture boredom through not-boredom, through the opposite. You see, boredom is not something you can act. If you act bored, it has no energy, and plays have to have energy. Boredom is a much more serious thing: boredom is not knowing what to do next, but trying very hard to go up an alley, down an alley, up another alley. I know piles of people who are like that.

I think Hedda says exactly who she is, when she says, 'I am a coward'. Once you say: 'I'm a coward', you opt out of the ability to cope with all sorts of things in the world. You opt out of being able to say, 'Would you like to have a cup of coffee?'; you'd say 'I'd like to make some coffee, but I'm a coward', and 'I'd like you to take me, but I'm a coward'. So, you disengage. I felt terribly moved by Hedda saying she's a coward, and I used it for every beat of the play after that, or even before that, I used as the centre of the play: coward. She married this man. She married the last man in the town. I think the received history of the play is incredibly destructive and unhelpful to discovering anything about the play, because if Hedda was such a vamp, she would've married someone extraordinary. She didn't. Nobody left to marry, so she can't have been this great shakes that everybody says, 'Oh, you're the great Hedda Gabler'. She so clearly isn't the Great Hedda Gabler. That's fascinating. She long since stopped being, or she never was the Great Hedda Gabler. I thought we got that rather well: this vulnerable, helpless, potentially wonderful person. That's what's moving. That's why I didn't want the first entrance to be somebody saying 'Good morning', and she says, 'Good morning'; 'Has the bride slept well in her new home?', 'Oh yes, thank you'. She didn't, she never will. How could she? The play's about the last forty-eight hours of somebody's life. It's unlikely that they are having a great time two days earlier. She's already on the way to her death. Say, two days before Princess Diana died, you'd say, 'Did you sleep well?' and she would've said, 'Yes'. Massive turmoil was going on in her life; it's unlikely that it's nothing.

I wouldn't draw any elaborate theory from Hedda's pregnancy, except I felt very strongly that she was pregnant, she absolutely didn't want to be, and she certainly didn't want to be pregnant with Tesman. I'm only the actress, you've got to take the meaning from it – my memory was that she was mortified that the aunt would think she was pregnant because then she was going to be owned by this cozy family. That has meaning beyond itself – the stifling panic of being owned by a family that you don't even like.

I also didn't want to make a big emblematic scene about the father, and I feel that was right. I think sometimes you get caught in a crass psychology of an inherited history, a very important point that Ibsen was making for the time, that has long since worn thin. Hedda being the daughter of a great general, was a very important admission point for the play then, but it isn't now. Other details of it are much more interesting now. We've flogged daughters and fathers since, so it's much more interesting to be in the 'panic' areas of women's lives in the generations before us, and maybe our own.

I began thinking during the play, that you could set it in a high-rise block. This notion that women are now free is erroneous; there are different things that trap them. But the panic of her imagination! Hedda is no great brain, but she has an imagination, and because of that, she falls into a series of traps. She says to Judge Brack, '(Tesman) . . . was tying himself in knots because he didn't know how to find anything to talk about . . . And so, to help him out of his misery, I just said – quite casually – that I should like to live here, in this villa.' I don't know if moments like that happen in your life, but it's happened in mine. You casually say something to someone, and you realise it's the biggest thing you've ever said, and you didn't even mean it. So, you have the ironies of her pitiful existence, and what I think makes her tragic, is that she's aware of it. If she wasn't aware if it, she'd just be an annoying woman, who made a lot of mistakes, and died. The fact that she watches her own demise, and goes, 'Oh, my God. I can see what I've just done!' is what gives her this ennobling or tragic quality. Her tragedy is being aware of the series of mistakes that she makes and goes on making. Her tragic heroism lies in the fact that she finally does something about it. Though it's possible that that was a mistake too: that the gun goes off, and she just dies by accident, which would be the most pitiful thing of all. She's a very moving creature, I think.

She's living in this house. There are no neighbours, and they don't seem to have any real friends. Her husband hasn't even got the job, they've got no money, they're going to be in debt shortly, they can't entertain, and she's threatened by Judge Brack because of the gun she gave to Lövborg, and she says to Brack: 'In your power . . . at the mercy of your will and demands. And so a slave!' So, she's blackmailed, and I don't know whether she loses feeling, or because of her situation, she begins to retreat. I don't want to describe it to you, but my feeling on it at that time, was that every beat of it – that's why it's such a brilliant play, and why you can't cut it – is that every line is a stage in her defeat. Brack says 'Every single evening . . . we shall have a pleasant time together here, you and I', and rising panic when he says, '. . . one usually manages to tolerate the inevitable'. Bigger panic, because he can sleep with her or not sleep with her. He was the man who was the custodian of her secrets, and he's become a complete nightmare. I mean, daily mental rape. He has her, and he knows he has her, and he has absolutely no love for her because it's about owning her, and Tesman owns her, and the aunt wants to own her. Everybody wants to own her, and she doesn't own herself. And she has only one way out. I think those themes are enormously well-drawn in the play. There's nothing grand about her at all; she's just ordinary, but like all ordinary people, has this need for a group of intimates around her that has a significance beyond herself.

People ask why Hedda burns the manuscript, but I wouldn't do the play if I could answer that. She burnt it in that moment because of what happened in that moment and the moment before. She found it and just burnt it, because as she says to Brack before about Miss Tesman's hat, '. . . that kind of thing comes over me – just like that. And then I can't stop myself'. Rather than solve it and say, (in a professorial voice) 'I think I did it because of psychology', she says, 'I don't know why I do that kind of thing'. Well, I think I did know why she does it. She does it because every now and then, she gets a burst of energy to change the reality. The aunt's hat drove her mad where it was on the chair, 'Take that terrible hat off the chair'. It's a terribly cruel thing to do to the aunt, but she's already in a panic. She comes into the room, and can't bear that she's not in control of anything in the room. With the manuscript, it's not that you plan it; it's like all of our sins. You murder someone, and they say, 'Why did you murder him?' You say, 'I murdered him because . . .', 'But did you plan it that morning?', 'No'. You do it, and then you realise why you've done it. I remember waking up one morning realising what it was. It had no rhythmical connection to what I, Fiona, was; if I did that, I would be just acting a stage direction. It was that impetuous entire child. She sees what she's done at that moment; I doubt she knows the moment before what she's doing.

But it's shocking that she should do it, and she shocks herself by the doing of it. She does change the reality by doing it.

But people do live like that. People behave appallingly. People wilfully destroy one another. In Hedda's case, she can't bear the fact – it's thought-by-thought, really, rather than fact-by-fact – Lövborg has written this book with somebody else. She should've written it; she hasn't written it, so she destroys it. She can't breathe because she hasn't written it. She hasn't helped with it.

It's like at the end when Tesman says, 'Let me have the manuscript, Hedda . . . .' She says, 'I have burnt it.' It's a potent line. 'Burnt! But, good God! No! . . .', he says. She says, 'Well, it's true, all the same.' It's as if up 'til that moment, she doesn't know she's burnt it; it's like, 'I've killed the baby. I've killed it'. Well, people get into those states all the time. It's almost Dionysian, when we do these terrible

Fiona Shaw in *Hedda Gabler* (1993)

negative acts; we do them, and then you see the consequences of them. But in a way, there's something very honest about saying, 'I burnt it. I burnt it'. She keeps repeating it. I think that was wonderful – she's pregnant with his baby, but he can't fucking believe it. It's fabulous stuff, really, because it is how people are out there, really. It's not waving, but drowning. She's drowning.

It's so uninteresting to judge her as a hard-hearted woman who has all the power. She's powerless, and has all the danger of the powerless, as we know. Often, I think in family dramas, the mother is blamed for destroying the family. But of course, this edifice of marriage is built which is so unequal in relation to the potential for the wife to develop, that the wife's power is often exercised on the children or on the family, both creatively and destructively. I think there's a crack in the plate of creation, or in the institution. It's so flawed that in the notion of marriage, one member of it can continue to work and develop, and the other has to freeze their development. And to allow for that with what would seem to be the compensation of children – but that isn't the experience of the woman. It's an incredible problem for the organisation of society. Hedda is, in a way, the carrion call for the 19th Century marriage. She is the death rattle of early tribal civilisations, and she is the herald for the new world, none of which she knows. And that also makes it very sad. Whoever Hedda Gabler might have been based on, or all those women who'd lived lives a bit like that, or all those strange suicides that occurred at that time, that may have been fragments of that lifestyle. All of them, the unsung, unknowing, and unknowable heroines of a new generation.

To film or not to film

I made a decision at a certain point that I was not going to concentrate on acting in films. I wanted the dynamic between the actor and the audience of stage performance, what you and I are doing now. I adore talking and being talked to, and at and with. It's a dialogue, really. And you don't really have that in film. I might regret that now, because you might say that a great film is in dialogue with a massive audience, and the potential is sort of main-lining audiences. You get millions of people in dialogue with you, but do you? Now, it may be that if you're not a great beauty, you're unlikely to communicate internationally. And the difficulty is that if you are a great beauty, you can only communicate for a short time. I think that maybe I made a decision thinking my gift is language. Not my face, it's fine, I wouldn't change anything of it. But, if the price to appear in these films is to change the happy, sham-bolic way I am, then I wasn't willing to pay that price.

Last year, I did *The Butcher Boy* with Neil Jordan. It's a fantastic film. Working with Neil Jordan on that film was heaven. Just as good as being in the best of the plays I was in, because I'm with somebody whose mind makes you believe what you're offering him day-to-day is changing his relationship to the aesthetic of the film. But if I'm a hired hand, like a baddie in a film, where you have come full of ideas, and they don't need any of them – this isn't to be cross with film – it's just that chemically, I have no place there, 'Okay, so what would you like me to wear?' That's not why I am an actor.

But I have nothing against popular culture. There's no point in doing a play in a room because it's perfection. The problem about doing things in this vast market, is that it's another job. It's another completely different world. And when it distracts you from the focus of what it is you thought you wanted to do, it would be far more pertinent to ask 'what is it doing to me?' There's a bit of a merry-go-round: doing the National and the RSC, and then the National and the RSC, and the Royal Court. I mean, life is life, and there are bigger canvases, maybe, to paint. I do these films completely because they release me from this agonising about what play to do next. I can just pop off and do a film and not worry about it.

On the working atmosphere

I haven't had a personality clash for many years, and completely don't need one to release the action. I function much better in a benign atmosphere. Maybe it's also because I have a good eye for who I work with. I suspect, although this is out my brief, that there are actors – you may hear that I am one of them, but I don't think I am – who need to suck the entire energy of the room before they create. They're very good actors, but it's an incredibly expen-sive way for everybody else. What's terrifying is that they make themselves very uncomfortable in the process, of course. I am so not like that. I'm so excited by other people. I get dazzled, I fall in love with anybody who offers me a reality that takes me somewhere else. I might be inventing a thing as I go along, and I'm excited, and somebody comes along and goes 'Bong', and I go: 'Great! Now we're going this way!' I genuinely get excited. It may be, of course, that if you are as forceful as I am, that you sometimes knock out somebody else's rather poor idea. So, it might be that one appears more dominant. Also, this is a tricky area of leading actors, and particularly leading actresses. As a leading actress, if you are famous, then the cast are often already intimidated, which is a terrible thing, because you want to be with a group of equals. So, you spend all your time trying to encourage them. This is why in some of the great plays, like *Electra*, we had a chorus that was the most fantastic group, the entire cast of ten or eleven of us were all friends. And it was marvellous! Nobody had a status higher than the other. You're in a very thorny area that's hard to describe, but in my experience, I've had one clash. The clash I had was when somebody told me what the play was about. Plays don't function like that. You can't find the play, and then take the actors and say, 'Look, this is the shape of the play'. That's just dead truth. You say, 'Here are two actors. What is the play about?' And then you find to your surprise, 'Wow. I didn't think it was about that. Goodness, it goes like this.' Because the play in the moment is the confrontation of actors and text.

On directors and rehearsal

I find acting all one cry for help, I mean I haven't a clue. I have no idea when we start, no idea. And I like not knowing. I like that line of Picasso: 'Why paint the picture you know how to paint. Paint the one you don't know how.' That's why I don't like things that are the line of least resistance. I prefer the things I haven't a clue how to play; I'm waiting for that. In fact, when I read a play – and I get sent lots of plays, I think, 'That just needs to be rehearsed and played'. That's done. It's only when you get a mountain of a play, that you want to go in there. It's a daily, long search for help. What I do is jump in and try things, and of course, the true one is the one that rings true. There is no other way of saying that. It's a very instinctive process. It's not intellectual. We're having to talk intellectually about it now, but I don't experience it like that.

I find in rehearsal that I tell piles of anecdotes about my childhood, so I'm always relating back to: 'that reminds me of the time when . . .' This thing is a way of my connecting tiny moments of the play with things that I remember. So, what I'm doing is fusing the experience with my entire history. It's boring and banal, but that's what I do. I don't even notice it, they think I'm stopping for a coffee break, but in fact I'm rehearsing, because I'm always stopping and saying, 'once I did . . .' I can't stop this thing. I babble away with jokes, memories, and fragments of memories. Funny incidents, or contradictions, or strange things that we use to make sense of the world.

Help can come in may ways. Stephen Daldry directed me in *Machinal*, a most peculiar, physically astonishing production, on an enormous stage – the Lyttleton at the National – and the terrible death of this woman, and he'd say, 'Fiona look out! Out! Out!' He was absolutely like that, and I adored him because he left the other stuff for me to do. His help was in helping me present it. But he couldn't, or didn't need to help me discover it. That was one way of doing it. Deborah (Warner) doesn't really talk about it, but she lets me talk about it. Her fundamental belief being that the moment of cognition, or the moment of inspiration or the impetus has to come from the actor. You can't excite the actor – you can prompt them, you can garden them once they are growing. The word 'director' is a very peculiar word. It implies directing, but in fact, all you're doing is directing the actor's thought. You're not directing their action. If you're directing their action, you're doomed. The action is a fusion between the text and the actor, if they're good actors. Good actors are inventive, and no director can invent reality quick enough. They're working on seeing, and trying to capture what the actor offers. Yes, I'm permanently looking for help, and what you find with a director you like working with, is you get someone who is in reply to you.

I'm a mad rehearser. I rehearse in many different ways! I can't name a method at all. For instance, when we did *The Wasteland*, we were given a house to rehearse in. We rehearsed in a house, on the edge of Brussels, with all different stories to do with the house. Deborah and I would go in there, nobody to play with, nobody to talk to, except each other. We had this text, and we'd make up stories, and suddenly I'd go up to a room, and she'd sit in the sitting room, waiting for me to come up with something. If you saw it, you'd die of boredom wondering what's going on. But something's going on; and it's her job to capture that. Nobody stopped me if I wanted to go for a run, I'd go for a run, and she'd read the play. We'd do another two hours, break for lunch, we'd go off and come back. It can be different horses for courses. I'm like a child, I think. I just play.

The imaginative game

In *Richard II*, I'm standing there, facing the audience, saying, 'I'm pretending to be Richard II, and you're going to pretend that I'm Richard II, okay? That's what we're going to play. So I'm pretending starting now!' That's all your doing. It's an incredible indulgence that the world is willing to pay money to watch you be something you're not, or be more truly something you are. That really is the wonderful tension between the imaginative game, that if you can do it well enough, you can get people to come with you. It's an immense privilege, but it's so near play, and so near totality. It's about being sure that you won't make an inappropriate decision because you're imaginatively in it. You can't do foolish things. You can't do things that break the form – they don't break the form, they actually expand the form if you're in it. It's both very difficult, and incredibly simple at the same time. That's why on the nights that it's good, it's because for some reason there's nothing interrupting your imagination. When you get a good night's sleep, or you're fresh, or you're preoccupied and escaping, you can go like a turbo engine with it. Not to get too romantic about it, but I think when actors are too comfortable, they lose their edge. I heard Neil Jordan say that about filmmaking, that on the set, if there's too many jokes and laughs, and everybody thinks it's a great film, then in fact it's not; it needs an edge of discomfort. So, often it's encouraged by him, hard work and a slight pressure that keeps the thing heightened. I don't really enjoy the acting bit of it. I find it quite hard because the pressure of only being awake to the imaginative reality is really tiring. There is an element of escape. You're escaping life, because you're so totally in this other one that you've invented. I want to live like George Bernard Shaw said he did, which was to be exhausted by the time he died.

Antony Sher

'I find that the good performing artists – not just actors, but singers, dancers – have an element of danger about them. It is a dangerous business, standing in front of several hundred of your fellow human beings and saying "I am interesting enough to watch". The good ones keep danger in the air.'

Antony Sher was born in Capetown, South Africa in 1949. He has appeared extensively with the RSC, notably as the Fool in Adrian Noble's production of *King Lear*, the title roles in *Tartuffe*, *Molière* (both filmed for the BBC), *Richard III*, *Tamburlaine the Great*, *Singer* and *Cyrano de Bergerac*. Sher also played Jean Cocteau in Pete Postlethwaite's production of *Astonish Me*, Shylock in *The Merchant of Venice*, Vindice in *The Revenger's Tragedy*, Henry Carr in Tom Stoppard's *Travesties* and Leontes in *The Winter's Tale* at Stratford and the Barbican. He portrayed Johnny in Athol Fugard's *Hello and Goodbye* at the Almeida. For the National Theatre Sher has played Austin in Sam Shepard's *True West*, Joseph K. in *The Trial*, the eponymous role in Steven Berkoff's production of *The Resistable Rise of Arturo Ui*, Astrov in *Uncle Vanya*, and the title role in Pam Gem's *Stanley*, which transferred to New York. At the Royal Court, he has played in *A Flea in Her Ear*, David Hare's *Teeth and Smiles*, *The Glad Hand* and *Shades of Brown*. Other roles have included Arnold in *Torch Song Trilogy*, Muhammad in Mike Leigh's *Goosepimples* at the Albery, and Clive/Cathy in Caryl Churchill's *Cloud Nine* at the Hampstead and later in the West End. Sher received the Olivier Best Actor Award for *Stanley*, *Torch Song Trilogy* and *Richard III*, for which he also won The Evening Standard, City Limits and Drama Magazine Best Actor Awards.

The actor's film work includes *Shakespeare in Love*, *Mrs Brown* (for which he won the Evening Standard Film Award as Best Supporting Actor), *Alive and Kicking*, *The Young Poisoner's Handbook* and *Genghis Cohn*. For television, Sher has performed in numerous productions, including *The Moonstone*, *Mark Gertler*, *The History Man* and *The Sheikh of Pickersgill*. Antony Sher is the author of five books, both fiction and non-fiction, and a prolific visual artist.

I spoke with Antony Sher in December of 1997, in his dressing room at the Lyric Shaftsbury Theatre, where he was appearing in *Cyrano de Bergerac*.

Growing up artistic and gay in South Africa

I had a sense, when I was growing up in South Africa in the '50s and '60s, that it was sort of the wrong place for me. There was not much sense of a cultural life; the white South African society was very sports-orientated. All my instincts were towards the arts, and they were just instincts, because they weren't able to find expression in much except drawing and painting, which I did. So, I had a sense of discomfort as a child and youth. I'm sure, this was to do with a lot of other things, like being gay. When I go back to South Africa now, I'm incredibly comfortable there, I'm in love with the place. Maybe it's like any place that you're growing up in, and which you want to escape from – you only value it properly when you go back.

There were teachers who encouraged me at school. An art teacher, called Mr McCabe, a Scot, who had moved to South Africa, communicated a kind of excitement about my skills as an artist. And there was a drama teacher – it was called elocution in those days – called Esther Caplan, who became very enthused about my possible acting skills. So the two of them almost ended up having a tug-of-war over me. Mr McCabe and my parents had always talked about me going to art school when I finished ordinary school. And then I developed this other talent towards acting.

I was very shy, very withdrawn as a kid, and my parents sent me to these elocution/acting classes as a way of drawing me out of myself. I really began to like the fact that I could deal with my shyness by becoming other people, so there was that first delight in discovering that you could escape. I wasn't very comfortable with myself, and I could escape by becoming other selves. I remember we did a play at school, a farce, and I played one of the main parts, and got laughs from the audience. I remember that sense of power that you experience, in your first taste of what it's like being on a stage, and working for an audience. There's a strange contradiction in being shy and withdrawn, and suddenly standing centre stage with a lot of people watching you, and signalling their approval with – in that case – laughter. It's a very exhilarating experience, particularly if you've been someone who has hidden away in their lives.

I was quite keen on the cinema, and went a lot. But again, we're talking about South Africa in the '50s and '60s, so many films were banned, and many films were heavily cut and censored in a completely insensitive way. I remember jump cuts within sequences, because it was a heavily censored society. But, I grew up with it, so it just seemed natural. My family weren't in any way a political family. No one drew my attention to the outrage of others, it just was how things were. One play, a theatre event, did make a huge impression. It was shortly before I left. One of the early Athol Fugard plays *Hello and Goodbye*, had its premier, with Fugard himself playing. It's a two-hander, and he played the man's part. I remember being knocked out by that. It was so different to the little theatre that I'd seen, which were all just imitations of British or American theatre. Suddenly there was this authentic, disturbing, powerful South African voice speaking from the stage. He was writing, in that play, about the poor whites of South Africa, which are a very distinctive group. It was very shocking, very powerful; it's the only really powerful theatre memory I have before I left South Africa.

Going *overseas* to drama school

My family were very supportive about my going to drama school. My mother has always been a great theatre goer. Both my parents used to travel *overseas*, they used to come to London a lot, and see all the shows in the West End, and bring back the programmes. My father just tagged along; he was a businessman, he didn't have any great enthusiasm for it. Once it was decided that that's what I was going to do, he was very supportive in whatever way he could be, although it didn't excite him. We were a business family, and didn't have that book-reading intellectual side, so there were no great ambitions about university, which I regret now. I wish I'd gone to university. I find I'm not a reader; I'd love to be more of a reader. I find reading quite difficult.

My parents had always had the ambition for me to train overseas. When it was going to be art, they always talked about art school, and then it changed to drama, and London was the obvious place to come for drama schools. Having finished school and the army – I had to do compulsory military service – I came over here to try and get into drama school. At that time, 1968, Central was *the* place to go, probably because they had just had a few successful graduates, or people who'd made a few movies. So Central was trendy. But Central and RADA were the two schools I applied to, and they both turned me down very smartishly! Strangely enough, in the film *Mrs Brown*, in which I play Disraeli – the scene in Parliament, where Disraeli's making a speech – the man playing the Speaker in Parliament was the principal of Central School, who had in fact been the principal at that time, so I guess he must have been sitting out in that dark auditorium. I didn't dare go to him and say 'Look, here I am now playing Disraeli'. Maybe I wasn't very good in that 1968 audition. The system was very cruel then, it was very fast. You went in, you did two pieces, and you were out. They take much more care now, at drama schools.

But I'd just come over from South Africa, I was terrified. God knows what I was like, maybe I was awful. It's perfectly feasible, even for good actors to be very bad in auditions. Auditions are a ridiculous way of judging someone, really. I'm not bitter about it, but it was very shocking at the time, because I'd travelled across the world, and at that time it seemed like I'd made the wrong decision, and what was I going to do now? My parents had to go back to South Africa, and I was left in London, and was very miserable for six months or so, but then I did get into one of the top drama schools, Webber Douglas.

They didn't have a particular theory or philosophy, which is probably just as well. Quite luckily at the time, Steve Berkoff was giving some classes. He did a production with us, and I found him very inspiring. His work is very physical, and I responded to that a lot. And there was a mime teacher called Ben Bennison, and, again, I responded to his improvisation. He did mime in a very modern, quite anarchic way, not like Marcel Marceau. Those were the two teachers I remember being very inspired by. I regard drama school, in a way, as a place to learn some technique, and spend a bit of time growing up. I think I really started to learn about acting once I started doing it, and yet you can't do it too soon. Acting is a hard thing to learn. I think people go to drama schools much too young, because they're not formed as people, and yet they have to start interpreting human behaviour. It's something that older people who are more mature, are better at. You're too young at 18 or 19, like I was.

I suppose because I grew up with movies, I imagined actors were like those Hollywood stars. I don't know if I ever thought I'd be that, but that was where the childhood fantasy started. Once I got to London I used to go to the RSC a lot and see all the plays at the National, when Olivier was running it. Then, my ambition became the work. What those two companies were doing seemed like the standard of excellence, and that became my ambition. I got more excited by the possibility of achieving that kind of excellence than fame.

I think I was more ambitious then than I am now. In a way, I have achieved what I wanted. When I look back at it, the journey surprises me; it's quite a big journey from Capetown, South Africa, to being a leading actor in both companies, as I have been. That's very satisfying. I feel quite content with how life has worked out. People are always saying to me 'But you don't do movies, doesn't that drive you crazy?', and it doesn't really. I suppose one would have to still be itchy and ambitious about conquering movies, which is not how I feel, because I don't find the work I see in films as exciting as I did when I was a child.

I'm more a workaholic than ambitious. I do have a restlessness and an itchiness, but that's to do with being a workaholic. I'm not very happy unless I'm working. Now, doing this run of *Cyrano de Bergerac*, I'm writing a novel at the same time, and if I didn't have that novel, I'd be going crazy, because doing the show isn't enough for me. That's something different from ambition.

On good acting: danger, truthfulness and the Method

I'd certainly say that, as an audience member, I find that the good performing artists – not just actors, but singers, dancers – have an element of danger about them. It *is* a dangerous business, standing in front of several hundred of your fellow human beings and saying '*I am interesting enough to watch*'. The good ones keep danger in the air. I've worked with a few of them. Jonathan Pryce, Helen Mirren, Ian McKellen – and it's very exciting watching them from night to night, the way they change things, yet always deliver the essence of a scene. It keeps the audience on their toes.

I think that actors generally divide into two groups: Personality Actors and Character Actors. The first, who are just *naturally watchable*, pull a role towards them and fit it to themselves, the second travel away from themselves to the role. Neither is better or worse than the other. Most American film actors are Personality Actors, and very fine actors too – Paul Newman springs to mind. But I am, or I used to be, exclusively a Character Actor. Nowadays I like to experiment with the other kind too, and when the experiment pays off, as I think it does in the gay movie *Alive and Kicking*, it's very satisfying. I think you mustn't create too many boundaries for yourself as an actor. Critics, casting directors, other people will do that for you all the time! Your job is to keep growing.

I don't really pretend to know the theories of acting. I wasn't taught them, so I don't know how to talk about them. I can only talk about what I feel instinctively. I've come to be more and more interested in so-called Method acting. There was a documentary on Lee Strasberg a few months ago, and I really did like a lot of what he was saying, and what his students were describing. In *Woza Shakespeare!* I write that, instead of Method acting, you could just call it good acting, in that it's utterly truthful; it's got to come from within. I do believe in digging deep into yourself to make the emotional moments of a role as truthful as possible.

That sounds simple, but it's certainly taken me a long, long time to realise the value of that, as opposed to the kind of flashiness, or showmanship, or disguise of, say, a Laurence Olivier. Because he was a big hero in South Africa; I'd only seen him in films, and then I arrived here and saw him on stage several times, all of his last great performances: Shylock, *Long Day's Journey into Night*, and *Dance of Death*. I remember being profoundly disappointed

Antony Sher in *Cyrano de Bergerac* (1997)

each time, because although what he was doing on stage was very impressive, it never touched me, it never moved me. There was something cold about it. It's taken me a long time to come around to realising that what I actually like when I'm sitting in a theatre watching actors, is complete truthfulness. Cyrano talks about his 'visible soul' in the play. That's what I want when I go to the theatre: to see an actor's visible soul. I always find that very moving. It's actresses in this country who tend to do that more. I'm thinking of Judi Dench, Fiona Shaw. Watching Fiona work in the last few years has really made quite an extraordinary impact on me. Her commitment, the absolute exposing of herself that she does on stage is really quite remarkable, and almost goes further than anyone else I know. So I've really come round to believing in that kind of acting as being the most essential element, but it's only an element.

Again, *Cyrano* is a really good example – without the technique, you can't play the part, you simply couldn't, and yet without putting your heart in it, you can't play the part. *Cyrano* only works if it's played from the heart, which is, let's say, Method acting, and yet, it also only works if you're able to do it technically, and that's what's called the classical tradition of acting. It's a rather good example of needing both things. At its best, British theatre acting combines superb technical skills with complete truthfulness. Judi Dench is an excellent example, as is McKellen, Gambon, and a few others. At its worst it can be very unfelt.

Text and spectacle in British theatre

I think British theatre at its best does find a middle ground. The exciting Shakespeare productions I've seen in this country achieve both things, they have to. Shakespeare is an epic writer, a very theatrical writer – in other words, a writer of spectacle. And when the productions work very well – and it will only work if brilliantly spoken, beautifully spoken, and I don't mean beautifully in an old-fashioned sense; I mean in the sense of clarity and being really exhilarating by going through the text. I think we do achieve that, I think both at the National and the RSC, one does. Or something like *An Inspector Calls* is another very good example of both the text being served by people who can really do it, and at the same time, there's a tremendous production mounted round it. I'm less keen on theatre which is exclusively one or the other, and you do see that in this country, where it is just the text served up in a rather bland way. There's a production recently – I mustn't be rude, so I won't say what it was – which has been very acclaimed, a Shakespeare production, that I found far too empty for me, because it was simply serving the text. Nor would I want theatre simply to be spectacle; it becomes completely empty. After playing on Broadway this year, I briefly visited Las Vegas, and that's what that kind of theatre will be – as empty and as boring as that. So I think that British theatre at its best does achieve something in between those two, and that is when it works for me.

On excess and naturalism in performance

When I look at human beings, I think we're much more fantastical and grotesque – and I use the word as a compliment, because I love the grotesque – I think we're much more excessive, extreme people than the kind of mutual conspiracy we hold about how human beings behave and what we look like, and what we seem like. As far as I'm concerned, when I write characters, or paint them, or act them, that is how I see people. I don't see it as excessive or extreme. But it is said about my work sometimes, and I can only say that I can't identify with that interpretation. Because it does seem to me naturalistic. I think we are very extraordinary creations, and people are quite bizarre, all of us.

> 'Excess is necessary to approach the essential and the true, that which is hidden by what men ordinarily call reality, as by a curtain'.
>
> Peter Brooks, in *The Melodramatic Imagination*

That's coming close to what I feel, except I think it's holding up the mirror to nature. What actors do is show you, the audience, how they see human beings. That's all you can do as an actor, and I guess that's how I see human beings. I'm not setting out to in any way exaggerate; it's how I see people. But then, someone like Fellini for me, is one of the most truthful, one of the most exciting artists, certainly of this century. His work is very meaningful to me. Maybe that explains what I mean.

Working on a role: *Stanley*

Obviously, with a famous work, like a Shakespeare or *Cyrano*, you tend to have seen it beforehand, you'll know the piece, which is a drastically different experience from, say, *Stanley*, which comes as a new script through the letterbox one morning, and which you experience without any preconceptions about how other people have played the part, or what the piece is. So they're two separate things. And the classics, of course, carry with them that tradition of famous people who've played the part, and are you prepared to deal with that?

It's easier to talk about a new script like *Stanley*. The thing that has got to happen is that it's got to move me in some way when I read it. *Stanley* is a good example because it was quite unfinished when I got it first. I hope Pam Gems won't mind me saying that, but she rewrote it quite considerably several times after the version that I first saw.

She had done a very excellent translation of *Uncle Vanya* at the National a few years ago, which I did with Ian McKellen; I was Astrov, McKellen was Vanya, and Janet McTeer was Yelena. It was a very, very strong production by Sean Matthias. Pam had worked on that, and she knew that I could draw and paint, so she wrote *Stanley* with me in mind, as a result. Anyway, the script that arrived was far from perfect, but nevertheless there was something at its heart that moved me greatly, and that made me want to attach myself to the project and see it through the rewrites, the casting and everything.

I don't have a set way of working, except to remain flexible. It will depend on the director that I'm working with, and the other actors. In *Stanley*, for example, I luckily hit off the most terrific chemistry with Deborah Findlay, who was playing Hilda. I knew her from before, she'd played Portia in the production of *Merchant of Venice* in which I was Shylock. But in that play, of course, we obviously had very little to do with one another, and now we had to have this almost symbiotic relationship, and we were like that from the start. We even started learning the lines together. Normally, you'd sit alone in a room learning; we'd learn the scenes together until we could virtually breathe together. And we did slightly improvise around some areas from night to night, and kept it very fresh. It needed to be like that for the story, for the peculiar relationship that Stanley and Hilda had. So, that's an example of how a particular actress, and the particular way we were doing it, affected the direction we went in, which is not remotely how I worked on *Cyrano*.

I love researching, and I do a lot of research for most things, although I end up throwing away a lot of it. It's again – this word keeps coming back – a flexibility. For example, with Stanley Spencer, there is film of the real man, so you've got that, and Pam Gems, myself and the director looked at it and decided not to play him like he really was. In the play I used a Berkshire accent, because Pam's angle on the whole thing was that he was very much the outsider of the art establishment, just this village boy who happened to be gifted. And so it helped, in a way, to give him this country accent and to make him different from the sort of London artists that you saw in the play. Now, in real life, the man, although he was from that little place, Cookham, had lost his accent rather like I have, and spoke rather like I'm speaking now, in a *received pronunciation* way. But it was dramatically more interesting not to do that, so again, it's the flexibility, of saying 'Oh, this is very interesting, that's the real man, but no, we're not going to do it like that'. And Pam had very imaginatively sprung off the historicalness of the material, and we wanted to do the same thing, because Pam in that play has written as much about herself as about Stanley Spencer. That play is quite deeply autobiographical, and I like that about it. I don't like biopics, generally. So we wanted to do something similar with the way that we played it, an imaginative version of the artist.

His philosophy is quite chaotic, and I like that. It's part of him being a child-man, and that essential naïveté that he retained, which is what makes his painting great. He really did maintain a kind of child's view of the adult world, and I think you see that most clearly in his relationship with Patricia (Preece), and the famous double paintings of the two. 'The Leg of Mutton' where he's crouching over her; he could almost be a little boy with this very sensuous adult woman. There's this boy crouching above her, not actually making sexual contact, just staring, unable to really participate. There's another painting from behind the back of his head; she's spread out very sensuously on the bed, and he's again, looking, perhaps touching but no more than that. So it really is like the little boy, the child with the adult sexuality, fascinating and yet out of reach; there's nothing that he can actually do. Particularly 'The Leg of Mutton', I think, is one of his masterpieces, and in a way he needed to go through that very confusing, crazy, almost inexplicable relationship with Patricia to have produced that extraordinary work. It doesn't add up fully, it doesn't make complete sense. I like it when art does that, when there aren't clear answers, yet the thing works somehow.

Making judgments about people is probably something to do with coming from the background I do. One of the great lessons of my life has been coming to terms with what me and my family, as white South Africans, have been part of. The first novel that I wrote, *Middlepost*, is about the journey of a Lithuanian Jew from a small shtetl in Lithuania to South Africa at the turn of the century, a journey that changes him from persecuted, to persecutor. And it's the journey that a lot of the Jewish population of South Africa made, fleeing the pogroms at the turn of the century, or later, fleeing the Nazi threat in Europe, and coming to South Africa and finding by an extraordinary chance of fate, that the boot could be on the other foot, and that they could be the bosses, the rulers. And a lot of them went along with that, not recognising what they were doing. Now, I think that is something you have to come to terms with, because it is, on face value, very shocking, and I was really quite judgmental about that in my early years in this country, as I gradually discovered more and more about the society that I'd been part of. I condemned it, and once I was apart from it, over here, and seeing how evil apartheid was, I became very

Antony Sher and Deborah Findlay in *Stanley* (1996)

critical of my family, saying 'How could you possibly support this system, you who all talk about how your parents and your forefathers suffered? How can you not draw the obvious comparison about what's going on here?' But they didn't, and they couldn't, and life was too good and comfortable. My partner, Greg Doran, who directed this production of *Cyrano*, said to me when I was writing *Middlepost* – and it's one of the most important lessons I've learned – 'You must stop talking about *them* and start saying *we*, because it is human, it is totally human what the Jews of South Africa represent'. I'm generalising, of course; there were famous Jewish figures like Janet Suzman's aunt, Helen Suzman, who fought the system, but I'm talking generally, about people who bought into the system. It has taught me that human beings are very complicated, and that we are very vulnerable, and we are mixtures of things. There is Richard III inside me, and there is Stanley, and there is Cyrano, and there are other characters, and being judgmental about people or about characters doesn't seem to be a realistic way of approaching humanity. Because they're not strangers, these people who do awful things, they're just us, they're aspects of ourselves.

Do you have to like the character? Take someone like Richard III, I mean, you're not going to *like* him or find him sympathetic in the way that one might like a Stanley or a Cyrano, because he is obviously quite monstrous. But there is something about his energy that is attractive. And the audience will find Richard III attractive despite their own moral objections to what he's doing, and that's what's successful about that play. In the same way, as an actor, you've got to be excited by this man who's breaking the rules, who's living on the dark side, on the wild side. What I wouldn't be able to do is play a character that I couldn't in any way understand, or be in a play where it was representing, perhaps, political sympathies or a view of life that were very opposite to my own. I do have to be committed. I am going to put a lot of work into a project; it's got to be meaningful to me. I don't see it just as a job, I don't see myself just as a sort of service for hire.

The uses of psychology in acting

Psychology is an essential part of approaching any part, for me. Let's take *Cyrano* again. There's a tradition of playing the part with less anger, I suppose, than what we've done in this, and I think it's why some people have objected to this production. It's not as romantic, in an old-fashioned sense, as the play sometimes is, performed. Now that's precisely because once Greg and I started talking about the part, we talked about what it's like to feel ugly, to feel like an outsider, and the amount of anger and pain that is involved in that. There are lines to support that. We have certainly slanted things in that direction. Freud's work was known by the time Rostand wrote *Cyrano* (1897). I remember when we were talking about casting, we said how we didn't quite understand why Roxanne and Christian were often played quite soppily, as your ingénue leads, your pretty girl and your pretty chap. They both seemed to us, from reading the play, much more spirited characters, and with more energy and comedy in both of them. We just couldn't understand why people didn't see that. These funny traditions come up in classical plays. You have it with Shakespeare constantly, there's a way of playing Falstaff, or Hamlet, or whatever, that can quite fix these characterisations. I think one of the challenges of doing the classics, is while being aware of what came before you, to really think of it as a *Stanley*, by Pam Gems, that has come fresh from her word-processor printer to your doormat through the letterbox. What would it be like if you got *Cyrano* for the first time, and you read it? I think what Alexandra Galbreath does, seems to be very truthful to what is written, that she's this *précieuse*, this socialite, who's sort of in love with the idea of the artifice of beauty, who's very flighty and funny. And she goes on a journey of learning about love being about what is inside, rather than outside. In a way, that's not as radical, but it's more truthful to the writing. Maybe the previous actresses who've made the part a bit soppier and less colourful, have been more radical, have more drastically changed what the writer intended.

With Shakespeare, people sometimes argue 'But he was writing before Freud', yet I think good writing can always take a layer of what we now know about psychology, and when I watch theatre, I'm only interested when there are those other levels working. It's just got to be there for me.

It's also got to do with film acting. Acting has developed in this century by people being able to act on camera, where it can be very enigmatic, because the camera can go in and read people's thoughts, and all those complicated things that go on when you and I are having a conversation, the things we're thinking about at the same time, and the currents that go on in any human contact. Then, we can feed that back into the theatre.

Acting for film and theatre

What is great film acting? It's only the same as great theatre acting. It's the combination of truth and imagination that an actor has. Two of my favourite film performances are Brando in *The Godfather*, and Meryl Streep in *Sophie's Choice*. In both cases, the actors have created completely successful characterisations, that are quite different from how those two actors actually are as people. They've both travelled quite a distance away from themselves, transforming themselves into these other people in a way that I find utterly convincing, and yet, they have put their own hearts and souls into those two characterisations. Both Don Corleone in *The Godfather* and the character of Sophie are filled with those actors' visible souls. They've invested those two characters with enormously complicated feelings and compassion. We were talking about being judgmental; look how compassionate Brando is to that character of the Godfather. In someone else's hands, another actor might be trying to say 'Look what a bastard this man is, look what a monster he is'. Brando plays that, but he also plays him with this kind of weariness, and this sense almost of failure. This man has spent his life washing his hands in blood, and it has left him with his spirit scarred and mauled about. And he animates that, at the same time as having all the power and status of the man. It's astonishing. It's really the element of tragedy that he brings into the centre of that film which, I think, transports it way beyond what it could have been, to the level of something quite Shakespearean. The part is actually quite underwritten, but he brings such enormous vulnerability and melancholy to the part, that it takes the whole film onto quite another level.

Onstage, the responsibility for telling the story of a scene lies with the actors who are in it, and their storytelling powers have to reach the back of the auditorium. This often means they're going to be slightly larger, and simpler, than life. If they're good, you probably won't notice. On screen, the storytelling responsibility lies in other hands – the director, the cameraman, the editor, even the musical composer – so the actor can be far more complicated and enigmatic, like people are in real life. The actor can think instead of stating.

When I played Disraeli in *Mrs Brown*, I did all the research, and there are some very specific descriptions about his style, but in the end, you've got to find your own way of doing it, and find what the film needs him to be, rather than what he was. It's a dead thing simply to try and do some impersonation that is divorced from the rest of the story. The way *Mrs Brown* is written, Disraeli has a very specific function, because there's this curious, sort of ambivalent love affair going on between Queen Victoria and John Brown. Disraeli's function in the film is that of the master politician sorting it out, eventually, but also observing it throughout the film, becoming increasingly worried, juggling the various things, while being very fond of Victoria, as Disraeli was. It's said that after Albert died, the two people that she was closest to, certainly the two men, were John Brown and Disraeli. There's enormous mutual affection there. And so that's what was required of that part.

Again, you've got to be flexible about it, and interesting though it is to read about his early life, and his travels in Europe, and the anti-Semitism that he encountered, none cropped up in the film. So you can take some of this knowledge, and hopefully it adds a layer somewhere along the way. Disraeli's Jewishness was one of the most interesting things to research, because without knowing a great deal about him, I'd simply thought of him as Britain's one Jewish Prime Minister. So it was a huge surprise, as I started reading about him, to discover that in fact, his father had a row with his synagogue when he was growing up, and fell out with the synagogue, and, as a result converted the whole family to Christianity. In fact, at the age of 13, the very coming of age time for a Jewish boy, Disraeli was converted to Christianity and was a practising Christian for the rest of his life. I found that extraordinary, really, it was not something that I knew about.

But I think I was able to bring personal insight to the situation. When I came to this country, I remember one of the various closets I was in, was the Jewish closet. I felt I couldn't make it in British theatre, as a Jew; I felt it was some kind of disadvantage to me. In a way, learning to lose my South African accent, I was also losing a kind of Jewishness, the Jewish intonations that I'd been brought up with. I sublimated all of that, I hid all of that for a while, and now I'm happily out of that closet, like my other closets. Reading about Disraeli, similar things cropped up in his life; he was very determined to be *the Englishman*, the upper class Englishman in strict terms. He wasn't, and the establishment weren't completely comfortable with him, so he was bent on infiltrating it. And yet, there was an outrageous side to him, because he always dressed in this very dandified way, and had a peculiar kiss curl, and this strange, very un-English look, that he cultivated; he deliberately made himself look quite exotic. He's rather like Cyrano, who is absolutely mortified by his nose, and it's the source of all his pain and angst, yet he comes on stage at the beginning of the play, and the first thing he does is have a ten-minute speech about his big nose, flaunting it in everyone's face. Those contradictions are very interesting to play, as an actor.

On critics

A difficult topic. We're exceptionally lucky here in London, where we get about two dozen heavyweight opinions everytime a show opens, as opposed to New York, where there's basically only one. Most London shows end up getting mixed reviews, which seems a very healthy state of affairs.

To read or not to read them? I've gone back and forth with this over the years. With film, or the books I've published, it can be joyous or painful to read reviews, but the work itself is safe from them, it's completed. With theatre, it's different, and dangerous. It's not advisable to perform a show with phrases from the reviews, good or bad, echoing in your head. On the other hand, people will rush to tell you what the critics said, so it's difficult to protect yourself from them completely. My latest solution is to get a *temperature reading* of the reviews. I ask someone, Greg, or my agent, to read them for me and mark each out of ten. That way I get a feel of how a show's been received without being exposed to those phrases, those echoing phrases.

Acting: change and growth

I do find that I'm constantly changing as I 'grow up' as a person; I constantly change my feelings about acting, and I like that, that it's not fixed. It seems to me just like we, as human beings, change and grow up and learn more and mature, that acting should, as well. One of the best lessons I had as an actor was right at the beginning of my career, at the Liverpool Everyman Theatre. Alan Dossor, the director there said 'What do you have to say as an actor, and what do you want to say?' And I didn't know what he meant, because I thought acting was just an interpretive art, that the writer was *saying* something, the director was *saying* something, and we were simply some sort of a cypher. He impressed upon us, that as actors, we *could* say something. Which goes back to what I was saying about my belief that acting needs to involve the actor's visible soul. You're talking about human beings, you're talking about people, so it becomes part of your life experience, and yes, it is going to change you, because you're going to learn. What I love about theatre and acting is that I'm constantly learning new things, and of course that changes me. I didn't know about Disraeli, I didn't know much about Stanley Spencer, and now I know more about them, and they're both extraordinary lives. Learning about them has enriched my life. It seems to me acting is a constantly changing experience, in the way life is. It's perhaps summed up by two phrases from Cyrano – 'the casual dress of the flesh', that is beauty or ugliness, your looks, and the 'visible soul', or the inner life. When I began as an actor, I was enchanted by the casual-dress-of-the-flesh aspect, by the opportunity to change myself, to hide away. Now, while the disguise can still be diverting, fun to do, it's no more than that. The visible soul has to be present, *it* is the most important.

David Suchet

'If I had a prayer that I would pray every single night for myself, as an actor, it would be: "Please, give me more and more everyday, courage, courage, courage, to enter into and display the truth."'

David Suchet was born in London in 1946. For the RSC, he has played in *Romeo and Juliet, As You Like It, King Lear, King John, Love's Labour's Lost, The Tempest, The Merchant of Venice, The Taming of the Shrew, Othello, Richard II,* and *Measure for Measure.* The actor portrayed Salieri in Peter Hall's production of *Amadeus* at the Old Vic. Suchet's performance in *Timon of Athens* at the Young Vic earned him an Evening Standard Best Actor Award. His role in *Oleanna* at the Royal Court and Duke of York's garnered a Best Actor Award from the Royal Variety Club. Suchet played George in *Who's Afraid of Virginia Woolf?* at the Aldwych, and won the Critics Circle Award for Best Actor. He has also acted extensively in regional theatres including Liverpool, Birmingham, Chester, Exeter, the Edinburgh Festival and the Chichester Theatre Festival.

His television work includes Agatha Christie's *Poirot, The Life of Freud,* and *Blott on the Landscape* (the latter two roles winning Suchet the Royal Television Society Best Actor Award), *The Muse, Once in a Lifetime, Bingo, Separation, Secret Agent* – all for the BBC. He has also appeared in *Playing Shakespeare, Ulysses, Seesaw, Song For Europe* (Best Actor, Royal Television Society Awards), *The Last Innocent Man* (Best Actor, Ace Awards), *Cause Célèbre* and *Moses and Solomon.* Amongst Suchet's films are *A World Apart, Red Monarch* (Best Comedy Actor, Marseilles Film Festival), *The Falcon and the Snowman, Gulag, Iron Eagle, When the Whales Came, Bigfoot and the Hendersons, Executive Decision, Deadly Voyage, Sunday, A Perfect Murder, Wing Commander* and *RKO 281.*

I spoke with David Suchet in September, 1997, at my home in Teddington.

The early years: regimentation and authority

I was born in 1946, and I was sent to boarding school in Birchington, Kent at the age of seven. During the '50s and thereafter, the only London that I saw was during holidays. So I'm not fully knowledgable about the London atmosphere at that time. I was not really aware of any hardship or change because I had not experienced what it was like before, or during the Second World War. Looking back, I have more of an idea of what it was like than when I was actually living at the time. I suppose that my first boarding school – which was from 1954 to 1959 – was pretty tough. Presumably, boarding schools at that time were tough anyway. But we were still in the decade after the war, so the first thing that comes to my mind is the lack of food, and how sweets were a luxury. We were allowed, every Sunday, to be given six ounces of sweets to last a week. And when we were visited by our parents, they gave us goodies for our locker, and if these were discovered, we were punished with six strokes of the cane. Looking back, and making comparisons to today, I grew up in a fairly disciplinarian way.

My father was beginning to make good head-way in his career as a gynaecologist and obstetrician. When I was eight, we moved out of a rented apartment in the centre of London, and he bought a very big house in Hampstead, and started doing private medicine.

London in the '50s was experiencing great changes in the worlds of music and fashion. Not a change for me, but as far as my parents were concerned, a huge change because we had the Teddy boys. There was a reaction against the military authority – presumably, that's what it was – of the '40s. But my own existence was pretty rigid. We enjoyed our holidays, we went away for the summers. I don't have much recollection of '50s London, or '50s politics. But I remember the fashion. I remember the disciplined life of the boarding school. It has to have effected me. Those years, from 7 to the time you leave school at 18, boarding school has a huge influence on your life, even more so than your parents. Home was warm, and fun and holiday-time. And Dad was very busy, so I hardly saw him. And school was really regimented and tough.

I didn't come from a family who liked going to the theatre much. If we did go to the theatre, it was mainly musicals and light relief, because that's what Dad needed for his relaxation. We would go to variety shows. We would see comedy groups like the Crazy Gang, and that sort of thing. My father, in the 1940s, went to see comedians like Sid Field in the variety houses. I actually played Sid Field here about two years ago. We weren't allowed in the cinema, and the only theatre we did was school plays! The first play I was in was *Alice Through the Looking Glass*. I played an oyster. There were four of us, if I remember correctly, and we were wearing our school uniform, with huge shells on our backs. We would come in, facing the audience with the shell, and I remember coming in facing the audience with my front during the performance. The director of the show shouted out, 'Suchet, turn around!' That was my first venture onto the stage. For me, theatre and cinema was an escape from the regimented and the authoritarian attitude of the school.

Theatre: a sense of freedom

Theatre represented a certain sense of freedom for me at that time, even at such a young age. And that continued, so that even when I went on to Wellington, my public school, and we were doing the school plays there, I found one had a completely different relationship with the schoolmaster who was directing as opposed to the same master who was teaching English in the classroom. It was far more relaxed, far more friendly and open. So it was a real release. The first time I ever really got sucked into the art of what I was doing, was when I was offered *Macbeth* at Wellington. I was so flattered, and so thrilled to be asked, because I was never considered academic. I was very sporty, I played a lot of rugby, football, and tennis, and I was in all the teams. So, when I was asked to be in *Macbeth* by this very young and very go-ahead teacher, I was so flattered and so frightened of failing, and I wanted to do it so well, that I started reading about acting and actors and Shakespeare as much as I could.

I was about 16 when that happened. I started reading *An Actor Prepares* by Stanislavsky. I became absolutely fascinated with the concept of working in depth. The art of being able to change oneself into a different thought pattern, into a different physical life, and in so doing, serving a play and a playwright who chose to write for performance, rather than just to be read. That became an utter fascination for me. Why would somebody write to have their work exposed on a platform by people playing all the parts, and telling us the story that the playwright wants told, rather than putting that story in between two covers of a novel? Why? I've never fully understood, even to this day. But it's still a fascinating concept. The difference is also interesting, because a novelist, although he or she has some control over the reading public, can direct the public far more, in a way, to let their own imaginations fly. The reader can put it down and pick it up, and it might take up to six months to read one novel. A play is very concentrated, and in a sense more manipulative, I would imagine, from a writer's point of view. The whole story's told in front of you, at that time.

The Stanislavskian approach became a fascination. All of a sudden, one was into a whole different concept, a whole different attitude of acting. What I believe Stanislavsky was doing was changing the attitude of the performer, changing the attitude of the artist. That meant a great deal to me and I've retained that attitude even today. As well as the idea of being the servant of the text, yet having independence and control over what I'm doing, and having the right to my interpretation as well.

London Academy of Music and Dramatic Arts

I didn't choose that school, they chose me. I was going to be a doctor. Probably because that's what my father did. It was fairly clear pretty early on in my examinations, that I wasn't going to make it. I decided to give just two drama schools a try, because I thought: 'If I'm no good, then I'm not going to continue'. I was never an actor or a person who said: 'If I can't do this, then there's nothing else in my life'. If I did have a talent that was given to me, then I could use it to get on, and that would be wonderful. But I could only discover that by trying to get into drama school. I didn't want to try RADA, purely and simply because I didn't want that pressure of going into the Royal Academy of Dramatic Art. I'd read so many books about the RADA, and, although I probably knew it was the best at that time, and probably often is considered the best since that time, I was against it precisely because of the label 'best'. So I applied to LAMDA, and I applied to Central. I had a very nice try-out day at Central, only to be told: 'No'. My first letter was from Central, saying that they couldn't really assess my acting ability. They didn't really rate it very high, and I was definitely a no-no on the singing front: 'Thank you for coming'. Dorothy Black was a voice coach and a teacher at that time, and I contacted her, and got some coaching. I went for my audition, and Norman Ayrton, who was adjudicating, and the principal of LAMDA, also interviewed me. He told me immediately that they would like to have me.

How did I find LAMDA? Well, how did they find me is the big question. Being a public school-regimented boy, growing up since 1953 in the school system of England, I naturally turned up on my first day in a suit. So, anybody who looks at that little scene as if it were in a play, and says there's no subtext, is very wrong. Pretty early on, I was a laughing stock, really, because I could not turn up in any form of a relaxed manner at all. I just could not do it. My first movement class, I thought was circuit-training! So, I turned up in my rugby kit, in order to be confronted with girls in leotard and tights, and men in the same. I didn't know what sort of world I was entering. Yes, I'd read Stanislavsky and others, but I didn't know what I was entering.

I found the classes boring, and over-analytical. In a sense, it seemed to me to have more to do with one or two teachers' own pet theories on how to approach a role, than any sweep like Stanislavsky, or any other person who was really knowledgable. But there was one teacher who really, really challenged me, that I sort of did and didn't get on with. I never knew whether he rated me or not. To be quite honest with you, I don't think he did. But he made me realise the seriousness of the profession I was going into, and that was Michael Alfreds who, of course, since then has had his own company, and has done a lot of direction for the National Theatre. I've still never worked with him. I did some work with a professional director called Vivian Matalon, and he said to me something that I'll never forget. He said, 'You know, I think that you have a very, very happy future ahead of you as an actor. But your greatest problem is your talent.' I said, 'Would you explain?' And he said, 'I don't know how to explain it, just that I know it.' He said, 'Every single thing I tell you to do, you're able to do. I don't know where that's going to take you.' You worry about comments like that when you're in drama school, and you're being assessed all the time. But in my final year, I did a play by Christopher Fry called *This Lady's Not For Burning*, and I was cast, of all things, as Hebble Tyson, the old mayor. It was the most ridiculous casting. I think one of the things an actor has to come to terms with very early on in his career is his physical limitations. Of course, at that time, I saw myself as a leading man. To be cast as an old man was a great blow to the ego, as well as not knowing how to approach the role at all. Strangely enough, there was a young man teaching at that time, an English actor who I've never heard of since, called Jeremy Spencer. He was very into *action*. 'What is an actor actually *doing* with that line? What is the *action*? Not the physical action, the action, the verb.' You had to define what you were doing. He would challenge me all the time to be specific. Then in rehearsal, he would challenge me about my psychology in terms of the character. At first, I didn't know what he was talking about at all. What it means, if the character says 'Are you having a nice day today?', don't colour it with any attitude until you've really realised that I'm *asking* you a simple question. Then on top of that, is my objective, et cetera, et cetera.

We also talked in terms of obstacles, what I want, and what gets in the way of achieving that objective. I decided to really buckle down and take this very seriously. That was the first time I had ever really got involved in language relating to character. I began reading the play, and noticing that everybody has different ways of speaking. Then I got interested in the physicality of the character, about becoming this old man. I remember buying a book on make-up by Richard Corson. I bought some make-up, and I would practise at home. I would try to find out what was right for this character. I worked and worked, not only on the lines, but outside the lines. Then, I got into Stanislavsky's 'magic if'. That got my imagination really working.

The end result of all this work was *fun*. For the first time, I was having real fun, and I was being released into an area that was so freeing for me. After we'd done our three performances, at the end of the term, I was told that I'd won the Best Student prize. I remember Norman Ayrton saying, 'I don't know why, but everybody thought it was so amazing, that you have won the Best Student prize for your three-year course.' I couldn't believe it. I was asked what book I would like, and I chose *World Drama* by Allardyce Nichol.

Another huge influence on me as an actor at that time was a professional actor who came in to teach us. He was the late Ron Lacey. We did a play, a Gorky, *Lower Depths,* and I played Kletsch, the key-maker. But Ronald Lacey was insistent on my physical gestures being absolutely precise, nothing extraneous. It was about that time also that I saw Vivian Matalon's production, *After the Rain,* and Paul Scofield became a hero for me in terms of acting, because of his attention to detail. I enjoyed watching him very, very much. I used to go to the theatre when I could afford to go. At that time, I saw Olivier's *Othello,* and lots of things at the National Theatre, the Royal Shakespeare Theatre and the Royal Court. None of it had a huge impact on me, I have to say, except watching Scofield. Anyway, that was LAMDA.

Beyond LAMDA: discovery

I left LAMDA knowing that I had a place in the theatre in England. I determined to hone my craft. I was very fortunate in being accepted, very soon after LAMDA, into the English repertory system, and went around England from 1969 to 1973, before I joined the Royal Shakespeare Company, doing virtually a new play every other week. That's about five years' worth. During that time, I studied my acting. I studied my voice. I studied my movement. I studied my approach to roles, and developed something during my early years at the Royal Shakespeare Company, that has helped me ever since. I was more concerned than anything to find why I was written into the play. I was reading *Othello,* and I didn't know how to play Iago at all. I didn't know what to do, until I read the play without him in it. Now, when I get a play, any play, and I want to do the play, my first way of studying the character is to *remove* him from the play. Because a play, I discovered, is rather like a stew or a soup: lots of different ingredients that make up the whole, but the whole would not be complete unless every ingredient is in there. If you take out this particular spice, or a particular vegetable you can tell what is missing. You can't have minestrone soup without tomatoes. If you're a leading vegetable, if you're one of the little vegetables, you try to find out what you're there for. But by removing your character from a play, you can often see why the playwright has written it. Anyway, when I read *Othello* without Iago in the play, there was no real jealousy; Iago is jealousy personified. It was only by removing him that I realised that *Othello* is a very happy love story, and would have ended in Cyprus, on honeymoon, and Desdemona and her husband would've lived happily ever after.

Shakespeare and subtext

I don't think for one moment, looking at Shakespeare's plays, and having been in the majority of Shakespeare's plays, and the majority of my acting life spent in the classical theatre, that one can say that Shakespeare wrote on the surface. He was a very dark, confused man. His sonnets reveal a personality that is very subtextual, and in his plays, there are kings who are not kings, and lovers who are not lovers. 'What a smiling face falsehood hath.' He knew people and he wrote about them. He knew that people had a public face and a private face. The most famous, probably, is Iago with his 'motiveless malignity'.

You cannot play Iago just on surface. To say that Shakespeare is without subtext is absolute nonsense. To say that Sheridan and people later, wrote without subtext is, however, quite possible. They wrote comedy or satire, and were aping and mocking the gentry to a great extent. Also, the language in England became more theatrical. But one must be very careful in the theatre not to make generalisations. You have to look at each individual playwright. Because they reveal more of themselves through their writing than anything else. As a doctor, Chekhov knew that people have a public face and a private face. We all do. But certainly, psychoanalysis or psychological understanding in the 20th Century, has really opened up the inner nature of human beings. I don't think one can say we are going too far. We may be going too far when the playwright hasn't written a deeply psychological play, and we try to invent a subtext. But for those playwrights who demand that we play the subtext, thank goodness, then, that we do live in an age where we've experienced this development.

Freud for the BBC

My study of *Freud* was as detailed as any part I've ever played in my life. When I was offered the role, I decided that he was such an important figure in history, that I had to get as near as possible to what I believed Freud was actually like. That was my *raison d'être*, it became my obsession. So apart from reading his authorised biographies, which I did in detail, and made notes on every page, I read every single thing he wrote: every paper, every article. I immersed myself in his writing. And then, I immersed myself in his biographies, and dated the writings with his life. I realised that Freud's own concepts relating to the subconscious actually stemmed from his own experiences. I did not, and I still don't, go so far as taking drugs if my character takes drugs. So I certainly did not take cocaine, and certainly not in the way Freud took it – he drank it! But one of the most revealing things about Freud taking cocaine, was not the fact that he took cocaine, because there was nothing shocking about that, it was used in surgery at the time, and it was not illegal. What he said about it was that it made him feel *normal*. Those words, as you can realise, come right in front of my mind when I think of Freud now. So, I had to find out from his birth, from his father, from his mother, from what he tells of his early childhood – in what areas of his life did he feel abnormal, and why. So, I went into his psychology. I started psychoanalysing Freud. I then went to Freud's flat in Bergasse in Vienna. I took two weeks in Vienna at my own expense, because the BBC wouldn't pay. I walked all around the streets where he walked. I passed the corner where he got his cigars every day. I spent all day, every day, in his apartment building, until they got sick of me. I then met Harold Löwenthal, who was head of the Freudian Analytical Society, and I spent a long time with him telling me about Freud, and his analytical techniques, showing me Freudian analysis. He started Freudian analysis on me, and then got me to start it on him.

I then studied in Mansfield Gardens, his London home. It wasn't a museum at that time. I paid the caretaker of the house five pounds every time I went, and I actually studied in his study. I sat at his desk in the study that was left by Anna completely as it was. I was the first person to ever do that. I spent a great many days and evenings in his study, with all his African figures on the table, just as he and then Anna, left it. While I was studying, I found letters from Jung. I found the letter where he asked Freud, if he may be called his *son*, and may he call Freud *father*. I found from the Ernest Jones biography details of how he would have to open his mouth with a clothes peg, when he had cancer of the jaw. It was the only way he could get his cigar in. I found the clothes peg, and I actually used it in the series. I went up to Anna's rooms at the top of the house, and there was a coat that said *Papa* on it – an Austrian loden coat. And it fit me like a glove. I'd already grown my beard by then, and I was wearing Freud's coat in his house. I found another tin buried amongst Anna's possessions. It also had 'Papa' written on it with an elastic band around it. I opened it, and it contained all his prosthetics from his illness. Then I had one made that would have given me exactly the same speech impediment as Freud. Apart from that, I rang up the BBC and went to their archives. They had one interview with Freud that they'd taped when he came to this country. I still have it at home to this day. I heard him speak, and that was the most extraordinary experience. After doing all this research and analysis, to hear the man speak! I remember my frustration, because as he spoke, and of course he spoke with an Austrian accent, there was an exhalation of air, because of his operations and the ill-fitting prosthetic. I could never reproduce that, because my palate is intact. I then went to an ear, nose and throat surgeon who explained to me all of Freud's operations. He explained to me the condition I would find myself in at the age of 83, because I played Freud from a young age, right the way through to 83.

I was even discovering things when I was filming. For example, we went to the Bergasse, to the steps outside. We were doing a night shoot at the time, and I was walking up the stairs to go to my apartment, and a little old lady who was living downstairs opened the door. She came out, wearing black, with silver hair, a sparrow of a little woman. She said, 'Ahhh'. She looked at me, she said, 'Freud?' And I said, 'Yes'. She saw the camera, and she watched. We had to do a retake with me going up the stairs, and she said, 'He didn't walk like that.' I said, 'How did he?' She said, 'He always ran! He was always running! I remember!'

So, playing Freud was a great, cathartic moment for me in my career, and it was also perhaps the most dangerous role I've ever played, because I really did become him. I've never become a character to quite an extent either before or after. Very dangerous. I was really brought up with a jolt when I was downstairs in my house, and I heard my mother-in-law changing my son's nappies. She was saying, 'Oh, you dirty boy. You dirty boy.' And I found myself running upstairs and shouting at her, 'Don't you ever talk to my son like that, you'll effect him for life!' It was a very, very dangerous state to get to, and in a sense, grossly indulgent.

I found that Freud fought over certain aspects of his own personality, his relationship with Wilhelm Fleiss, discovering that he was capable of bisexual feelings. And that moral Judaic background in Freud that would not let him ever indulge. So, he suffered from repression as well, and that affected his work, and his science. All that repression that only Fleiss could then release, not physically – through sex – but through his operations. That was *Freud*.

David Suchet in *The Life of Freud* (1986)

Suchet's Method

I certainly don't criticise the Method. A lot of people do. If I were to have reservations about the Method approach, it would be when actors cannot project it enough on stage and it becomes a total self-indulgence. They cease to serve the piece, and only serve themselves. I suppose that's what evolved: actors only being concerned with their own performance, and losing a generosity of spirit. Well, I can genuinely say I am not like that, because I learned very early on as an actor that the more you give to another artist, to another character, the more you receive. It's like life. There's very little difference between art and life. I will become immersed in character, but only insofar as it is serving the piece. Now, as far as Freud was concerned, it was called *Freud*, it was about Freud, it was all Freud. Certainly, in other performances, I will go into huge analytical detail. I'll use the Stanislavskian approach, but only insofar as necessary. I won't go into it to the extent that it becomes an indulgence. And one is aware when it does become an indulgence; when you become too protective in rehearsals, for example. Somebody makes a suggestion of how you might say a line, or what you might be doing, and you say: 'No, no. No I won't do it!' Now that's getting indulgent. Try everything, and keep yourself as open as possible. So, for Freud, definitely the Method. But I don't use that every time and all the time.

Hercule Poirot

I used the same approach for Poirot: as though he was a living man. I had a cause, you see, with Poirot. When I was asked to do Poirot, I didn't know anything about him, really, except the films I'd seen. I hadn't read any books. But Poirot to me was always a bit of a joke, from what I'd seen. I was taken out to lunch by Agatha Christie's daughter and husband, and they very firmly said to me, 'We don't want Poirot any more as a buffoon'. So, I had a three-year contract. I started reading every single book that Agatha Christie wrote, from *The Mysterious Affair of Styles*, right through to *Curtain*, where he dies, and started filling a notebook with characteristics.

You ask me how I make a role personal? How I make a role personal is that I always have two big columns: similarities of the character to myself, and differences. The similarities, I completely draw a line through. I never think about them again. I then concentrate on the differences, and together, that becomes my interpretation. Because where is me, and where is the character?

Because of my background, there would be quite a few similarities with Poirot. Certainly, from a visual point of view, I've always been interested in shapes, and I am very much affected by what I see. My whole being can react to what I see in quite a passionate state. So, for example, with Poirot, if I walk into any room that is untidy, I am very disturbed. I don't like shabbiness in dress. I don't like dirt. I don't like dust. I can, in fact, put a picture on a bare wall, and hit dead-centre without a problem. It's just the way I am. Of course, I picked up that Poirot would be totally anally-retentive. Thankfully, I may veer toward a retentiveness, but certainly – not clinically – to Poirot's extent, when he washes his hands, and has to put lavender water on every time. I used the anal-retentive analysis from Freud on Poirot. The results are on the screen. It doesn't make him lose his twinkle, his little fun and sense of humour. I also hope I've given Poirot a darker side as well.

What you saw over the course of the series was an actor trying to fight for his character from early on. Because when I first started, the costume and make-up designs turned Poirot into a buffoon. My first costume design was going to be check plus-fours, and hunting jackets, and moustache out to here, and Sherlock Holmes caps. I remember one particular meeting when I walked away from the production before it even started, because I wanted to wear the clothes that he was famous for: his suits, his wing collar, bow ties, and most important of all, his morning jacket and striped trousers. I was forbidden to do so, because 'the television public would find it boring and depressing'. At that meeting, I said, 'You will have to cast somebody else. If you want me to play the role, I can only approach it in the way that I as an actor would approach the role. You are now taking away my individual creativity, and you must find somebody else.'

I didn't know at that time that the Agatha Christie estate only wanted me to play the role. I didn't know the power I had. All through the first three years, I was fighting scripts that tried to make him jokey, while I was trying desperately to find the real man. Doing the short stories first – I wasn't able to bring in the complexities of the character. But gradually, as the character evolved, I made him far more internalised in his mind, and less active physically. If he did any gestures, they wouldn't just be gestures. He was doing something in his head, while he was active. And I allowed his darker side to come through. I won't explain now, what his dark thoughts were. What was it like being a man, at that time, unmarried? He was not a homosexual. He was a true bachelor.

Did he have any sexual frustrations? Was he lonely? All that, I began to build into the character. Hopefully I'm doing a Poirot movie next year. If I do continue, I hope to develop him as Agatha Christie wrote him, not just going off on my own. Her books are full of these dark moments. Poirot would brood, and would take himself off into the corner of a room, to sit and think. He didn't know why, but he became suddenly troubled as he looked at a young girl. Agatha Christie was really into all this, and yet he was turned into, what I consider, a playful buffoon. That's not what she wrote, and it's only by playing him that I realised the seriousness of that lunch where her own family turned to me and said, 'We don't want that. If we laugh at all, it is to be *with* him, and not *at* him'.

David Suchet in *Poirot* (1990)

Film acting vs. acting for the stage

Film is about individual little moments. It encapsulates the essence of a second: the glance of an eye, the blink of a lid. They're not to be rehearsed. Film is more a directors' and editors' medium. A director and editor can make a bad performance into a superb one. It has happened many, many times. I have been amazed in films that I have actually been in, where I have witnessed bad performances. And I've gone to see the film, and I'd turn to my wife and say, 'You know, that was wonderful!' There were moments with Sean Penn in *The Falcon and the Snowman*, when we were on the set, which I felt, as an actor watching him, to be quite honest, were really not good. These moments were never shown, and his performance was brilliant. There were moments of my own work that I consider to be disastrous, and can only thank the editor for removing them, and keeping the performance well-enhanced for the public, or for the story. You can't do that in the theatre. It is possible in film to enhance. And it is also possible in film, not to let the character be dominant, whereas in theatre, if you have an actor who has been allowed to dominate the stage in the character, you're stuck with it. In practise, for film, a lot of sewing up is done in the editing room to make something better.

I never, ever go to rushes. I'll tell you why I don't, and it's quite simply this: if I do something so bad in the rushes, that is really, really bad, they're going to reshoot it. If not, they can cut around it. Because, sure as hell, I've never been in the position of seeing dailies, and then saying, 'I would like to reshoot'. It's not up to me. I've never been in that privileged position, and I don't think many actors are. So, why give myself the headache and the heartache? I also don't have the vanity to do so. I don't need to see if I look good.

Playing 'the Baddie' in a big Hollywood film

I found the whole experience of making *Executive Decision* one of the worst experiences in my life. I got on famously with the other actors. But in terms of the studio system, in terms of the hierarchy, in terms of being shouted at by the first-assistant director, really being treated like a nothing, it was awful. It wasn't my world. I do care whether I make good, quality films. I do care whether I really have an active role in an important piece of film-making. And I also have to say, and admit, that film is the second greatest earner and export that America has. But the Hollywood system: the huge caravans, the small caravans, the trailers, the this, that, and the other. Really, I couldn't give a damn about all that. It doesn't interest me in any way, whatsoever.

I never think of a character as being secondary. I'm always keen on trying to avoid cliché, and in a film like *Executive Decision*, the big cliché is to play the bad guy as a bad guy. But I try to look for what's good, or what genuinely motivates badness. Therefore I tried to play him as somebody who has a definite cause in which he believes; that he'd be intellectual, and not just one of the evil *monkeys*. That sort of interpretation, being driven by a fundamentalist faith, seemed to transcend the cliché of just the bad-guy. So, that's how I fleshed him out.

I want to explore different characters in the medium of film, I want to do films so that my work can be seen globally, for different audiences, different age groups, and not for just a British audience. The only way I can really do that is to have a successful television series, which, thankfully, I have – and make films. The fact that I get evil roles, is probably just because of the way I look. With film, you take what you get. Until you're picked up for something else, as I was on *Sunday*.

American independent filmmaking: *Sunday*

The director of *Sunday* simply rang me up, and said that he'd seen nearly everything I'd done on screen, had read some articles I'd written about acting, and thought that I would be right for his role in that film. He came over to this country, and we met. Of course, I was about the size I am now, which is about 40 or so pounds lighter than I am in the film. We met, and he went away and thought about it. He rang up and said, 'Now, having met you, I'm even more convinced that you're the sort of actor I want for this role.' So, I got it.

The big understanding of the character of Oliver is that he's an outsider. The first thing I do, as myself, is to find out what it means to be an outsider. So, I spent a day and night in the homeless shelter. I got talking to people in there, met people, made notes about them. A lot of people were wonderfully kind, and generous, and talked to me about their problems. And I just said a big prayer of thanks that that was not my life. It gave me a good idea of what Oliver would be going through: lack of self-respect, the isolation, the bitterness, and constantly in memory-land. It wasn't hard to get into his psyche. I didn't have to do great textual study. More and more now, my acting is becoming instinctive, whereas it wasn't in the beginning. It was firmly rooted in research. It's almost as if my own personality needed that as a foundation, to give me a sense of security. Now, I find that I'm able to assimilate more. To be able to react to all the things going on at the same time. But things like having to be fat for the role . . . Jonathan (Nossiter, the director of *Sunday*) did not want my shape at all. And if I couldn't get my shape, then I was going to have to wear padding, and cut around the nude scenes, or do something. But, I decided to put the weight on because of what that was going to do to me psychologically. You can't be that big, without it affecting you. Without it affecting how you feel in your clothes, or affecting how other people treat you, how you perceive yourself in the world, and how you are perceived. But that was all. Really, as far as the moment-to-moment play, with Lisa Harrow, my co-star, and the script, that was actually instinctual at the moment.

Confronting Caliban: challenge and transfiguration

The part that changed my whole career in terms of my acting attitude was Caliban. I was to be directed by Clifford Williams in Stratford. I read the play, *The Tempest*, and I remembered Peter Brook's production where Caliban walked around with an arm like a fin, like a fish. When I read the play, I thought: 'What is this man? What is this monster? What is this animal?' I didn't know where to go with it. I went to my first meeting with Clifford, and he turned around and said, 'I haven't got a clue what this character is about at all, except that I was reading a book the other day and I wonder if he could be a mixture between a foetal embryo, sort of like an abortion, and a monkey, so that you'd never walk. You'd slither across the stage like a sort of foetus. And you'd roll on your back sometimes, and scratch your balls, and pretend to be a monkey.' I left that meeting absolutely in sheer, bloody panic, nodding wisely during the meeting, thinking, 'I've got to get out of this. I have really got to get out of this'. But I didn't, because I wanted to go to Stratford at that time, nice roles were on offer. And I loved Stratford. I love the Royal Shakespeare Company; it's a wonderful company. We started rehearsing, and I could hardly open my mouth. I didn't know what I was doing. How do I analyse this role? It's impossible. Getting to terms with the Shakespearean iambic pentameter was bad enough, but to do this! So, I started reading around how people played the character in the past. I read that Beerbohm-Tree as Caliban swung from trees during the play, and another actor played him as a turtle.

Time was running out, and I went into the Shakespeare Institute. I started looking at past productions, and one of the librarians came up to me and said, 'Oh, Mr Suchet! I'm so pleased you're here. I've enjoyed your work so much'. She said, 'I'm such a fan. I can't wait to see what you're going to do with Caliban.' I looked at her, and said, 'Madame, you may be in for a great disappointment. I haven't got a clue.' And it was this darling lady who put me on to it. She showed me Trinculo's speech where he first finds Caliban. She revealed that speech to me in a way that made me understand exactly what Shakespeare was writing. Very briefly, Trinculo comes on and sees this mass under a blanket and says, 'What's this?' He smells it; 'Man or fish?' He lifts the gabardine, they call it, he says, 'Legged like a man'. Then he lifts the gabardine again, and he says, 'Fins like arms. I now declare that this is no fish, but an Islander'. An Islander without a real deformity at all. Because he said 'Legged like a man, and *his fins like arms*', not '*arms like fins*'. And I suddenly clocked into the fact that here was Shakespeare writing a human character, and I did some historical research and discovered that at the same time, the Antipodes was being discovered, that Australia was being taken over, the Aborigines were being discovered. I looked, and found Elizabethan drawings sent back by people who were discovering the New World of Islanders, the natives. Never having seen a native before, with things in their mouths, and ears, 'Of course, they were deformed', I said to myself. So, Shakespeare was writing *universal* man. Plus, the anagram of *cannibal*/Caliban, plus the fact that calibone means *black*, plus the fact – I don't know how Shakespeare would have found out – that this man worshipped the moon, and Eskimos worshipped the moon. So I suddenly realised that were I ever to direct the play, it would be about colonisation. I'm interested in what Prospero was doing on the island. He set up a whole society with Ariel and Caliban. And remember, Caliban even tried to rape his daughter, which is why Shakespeare made him dress in Prospero's clothes. No, Caliban is *man*, all right. But he's also the Universal Islander that the British were taking over. Obviously, Shakespeare can't just write a play about that, so he has to make them both seek to kill – like Shylock, fighting for the outsider. Caliban seeks to kill Prospero, Shylock seeks to kill Antonio. As such, they are guilty of a design for murder. Therefore, that fits in with Elizabethan morality. But, Shakespeare was fighting and writing for the outsiders that were being oppressed.

Once I discovered that, and said to Clifford: 'This is what I want to do!', I became so excited. Then came the courage, as a young actor, to do it. There was this one song that I didn't have the courage to do in rehearsals. At the end of Caliban's first scene, there's a poem, and he sings. I wanted to do it as a native, banging my feet, and getting into a rhythm with this native song. I didn't have the courage to do it. I remember saying to my wife: 'If I don't do that I'll never know what it's like to enter into this man, this psyche. I'll never really know. I'll always be able to *perform* the character, but never *become* the character.' I remember the rehearsal very well. I walked in, and they were doing a run-through of the play. I took off my shoes, and when it came to that scene, I stopped rehearsal because there were people reading a newspaper, and I was feeling a bit inhibited. Clifford was very supportive and said, 'If you are reading a newspaper, go away'. I did the scene. I took a deep breath and I let myself go. That was the first time as an actor, that I've ever 'jumped out of the plane', as I've always said when I teach acting, without a parachute. I didn't know where I was going to land! There was no analysis involved. There was no research to do. It was to do with *courage*: of a personal moment between an actor and a character. Would we meet, or would we always stand apart? No intellect would solve it, only gut and courage. Only jumping from that plane without a 'chute. And thank God, I did it. Because from that moment on, in 1978 I think it was, my whole acting changed. I had the courage to do things with characters that I would never have done before. And it was the difficulty with Caliban that actually was the greatest metamorphosis for me as an actor. Moving into that world, but really also fighting for my playwright: Shakespeare. Fighting for my own interpretation, lacking the courage to really do it, and then jumping out of that plane. Whenever I get into trouble with characters now, it's always because of lack of courage; I'm not willing to jump! And damn it, I do it. Every time. Even at 51, even with George, in *Who's Afraid of Virginia Woolf?*, the last play I was in, I had to jump out of that plane very early on in rehearsal.

On the director/actor relationship

I think the director's job is to have an overall concept of the play, and when he's cast a play, to have a meeting with those actors – or while he's casting – and make sure that the actors agree with his interpretation. I think that is absolutely vital, and it also shows respect for the actor. If an actor knows the director's interpretation, there's always that anchor to come back to in rehearsal. So, if he thinks an actor or actress is moving away from an interpretation that is going to serve the whole, then absolutely he has the right to stop the performance from going too far. But, if an actor is bringing his own interpretation and enlightening areas by going off in a weird tangent, then the director should allow that actor the freedom to do so, and the creativity to continue until he needs, literally, 'direction', pointing him the way back to concepts that the director may have. Directing's a very recent thing, anyway. It's a 20th Century invention. Actors were the directors, actor-managers.

The director is most valuable for being your only audience. But no director that I have ever worked with has imposed their interpretation of character on me. If I felt they have, I have threatened to leave. I won't allow it. I am a creative actor. If that creativity is taken away, then I reduce myself to being a puppet, and all I do is please the director. That is not my function as an actor.

Inevitably, there are going to be clashes, moments that are going to be difficult to solve. You may work or be under someone's direction whose personality you really clash with. As is the reverse, where suddenly you get on with everybody, including the director. Although, I'm here to say on record, that nine times out of ten when that happens, the result is not so good. So, a bit of a fight is probably a jolly good thing, because it makes you absolutely sure about what you want to do. If I have an overall concept of character, that has to be talked about before I start rehearsal. If the director talks to me about his or her concept, there shouldn't be a clash over the general interpretation. There will only be clashes on individual moments. And, to be honest, over individual moments, I'm terribly easy. Whether I say a line this way at that moment, or say a line another way at another moment, is neither here nor there to me. I've got a far bigger sweep on a character, than individual, tiny moments. I know that I can say: 'Good morning' in a thousand different ways, and still be me. If you want me to say a line differently, I'll say it differently. It doesn't matter to me. If an actor or an actress says to me, 'Do you mind if I do that?' My answer will usually be, 'Do whatever you want, I will react in character'. If an actor or actress says to me, 'I don't want you to do that at that point', and it's important to me because it's a moment of revelation for a character, then I will fight, and there will be compromise. The important thing is compromise. Yes, I will compromise, but I will not compromise when it comes to overall interpretation – the reason I am there. The being, the personality of the character.

The 'jobbing' actor in Britain vs. stardom

That's what I like to think of myself. We're not treated in any way special in this country. I get far more star treatment when I go abroad. What can I say? I've got no idea, why it is, except that I think it's a very good thing. I suppose it comes from the English temperament of creating stars, and then knocking them down as well. We're famous for that. Princess Diana was an example. Never had there been such a star created by the media, and then destroyed by the media. We are very, very good at that. We are intellectually critical about our artists in this country. And, in a sense, it keeps us in our place. I never had an ambition to be a star. I never wanted to be treated as a star. I think there's a great danger in star-treatment, in believing that publicity, and it effects the way you work. I believe it was Michael Caine doing an American picture, who admitted getting seduced into this. He said on television, 'When asked to do something on film, I said "No". When asked why, I said "Because I don't think my public would like it"'. I don't want to ever *not do something* because my public may or may not like it.

The *truth* of characterisation, the honesty in dialogue, in attitude, and the truth of a given situation or emotion – the *truth* is central. But my career could stop tomorrow. I have no idea what's going to happen tomorrow at all, in terms of status, in terms of roles, in terms of how I am perceived, in terms of anything. I would hate to be a *star*. What happens when you stop twinkling? It would frighten the hell out of me. It also gives me the benefit of going back to the National or the RSC, doing the Royal Court, going out to the reps. Nobody thinks that I'm demoting myself, by going back to the theatre.

Self-reflections

I'm a very bad script reader. Obviously, from the classical point of view, you know the great plays, and what the great roles are. But when you read a new play, you can never tell whether it's going to be a good or bad play. You can tell whether the role attracts you or not. I'm usually attracted to roles that have a depth to them, that have a complication to them. I've always tended to play outsiders. And that would figure, in the subtext, with my own life, background, and bloodline. I'm Russian, French, South African, and German, yet born in Paddington, London. I'm a first-generation Englishman. I've always related to characters of outsiders: the Calibans, the Shylocks.

I see a pattern in the roles that I'm offered now. I get offered roles that require depth, physical strength, and physical power. But, I'm very fortunate in that I've just played Sid Field, Timon in *Timon of Athens*, *Oleanna*, and George in *Who's Afraid of Virginia Woolf?* These are not similar in any way! So at this present moment there is no pattern that I can find, really, except that people are using me for my ability to become different people, psychologically, vocally and physically.

If I could have something more as an actor, every day, I would pray for more courage. Because, for me, courage is everything. Courage is all. You can throw research out the window. You can throw knowledge of iambic pentameters out the window. Courage is everything. And I continually come up against a block, in every character that I play. Am I going to break through? Am I going to release the truth of that moment? Do I have the courage? You never know whether you're going to have it or not. If I had a prayer that I would pray every single night for myself, as an actor, it would be: 'Please, give me more and more everyday, *courage, courage, courage,* to enter into and display the truth'.

Janet Suzman

'I think the difference between me, and the rest of my generation of actresses here is that I have a socio-political conscience.'

Janet Suzman was born in Johannesburg, South Africa in 1939. She made her London debut for the Royal Shakespeare Company as Luciana in *The Comedy of Errors*. She continued with the RSC in *The War of the Roses*, performing the role of La Pucelle. Suzman stayed with the RSC on and off for a decade playing Rosaline in *Love's Labour's Lost*, Lulu in *The Birthday Party*, Portia in *The Merchant of Venice*, Ophelia in *Hamlet*, Katharina in *The Taming of the Shrew*, Beatrice in *Much Ado About Nothing*, Rosalind in *As You Like It*, Lavinia in *Titus Andronicus*, and Celia in *As You Like It*, culminating in her portrayal of Cleopatra in *Antony and Cleopatra*, which was also shown on television. Although she then left to work independently, she returned to the RSC to play Clytemnaestra and Helen of Troy in John Barton's decathlon, *The Greeks*. Suzman has also appeared in Athol Fugard's *Hello and Goodbye* and *Boesman and Lena*, Gorky's *Vassa*, *Hedda Gabler*, *The Good Person of Setzuan*, *Andromache*, *The Duchess of Malfi*, Ronald Harwood's *Another Time* and *The Sisters Rosensweig*. She received the Evening Standard Award for Best Actress for Masha in Jonathan Miller's production of *The Three Sisters* and for her performance in *Hello and Goodbye*. *Hedda Gabler* – which Suzman played both on television and in the West End – was chosen as the BBC's 50th Anniversary Classic Drama repeat. She has also directed *Othello* and *The Good Woman of Sharkville* for the Market Theatre in Johannesburg, *Death of a Salesman* for Theatr Clwyd, and *The Free State* (her adaptation of *The Cherry Orchard*), set in today's South Africa, at the Birmingham Rep. This production will be revived at the Barbican. She has also directed *The Snow Princess* for the Tricycle Theatre.

Film and television include: *Saint Joan*, *Macbeth*, *Twelfth Night*, *Nicholas and Alexandra*, *Mountbatten*, *Last Viceroy of India*, Dennis Potter's *The Singing Detective*, the 26 part series of Arnold Bennett's *Clayhanger* trilogy, *A Dry White Season*, Fellini's *E La Nave Va*, *A Day in the Death of Joe Egg*, *The Priest of Love*, *The Draughtsman's Contract* and *Nuns on the Run*. Suzman has published numerous books and essays on acting and theatre.

I spoke with Janet Suzman at her home in Hampstead in November, 1997.

A Cultural desert/political activism in South Africa

I don't recall a heavy theatrical scenario in my youth at all, in fact, it was a cultural desert, really. I remember one touring company, with the great Irene Worth and Paul Rogers – it was the Old Vic Company, I think, that came to South Africa once. Everything seems to be when I was about elevenish, but maybe that's only because you start remembering properly round about then. There were occasional touring companies that came to South Africa – this is before the cultural boycott, of course, long before. I remember seeing Margot Fonteyn being Odette with the Johannesburg City Ballet, and Beniamino Gigli coming to sing arias. Most of all, I remember *Annie Get Your Gun* and *Oklahoma* coming on tour. I think I went about seven times to each of them; it was such a big deal. I stood outside the stage door and gawked at the stars. I knew every word of those musicals, I still do, I remember every single lyric. I used to rush about singing the songs, but I've got a really terrible voice. My poor parents. But theatre wasn't a focus for me at all, really. As I grew up in the late '50s and went to university, it was politics that took first place, because of the situation in South Africa. Though I did have a friend who went to LAMDA who used to come back and tell me about it.

I'm Jewish, I was expected to go to university. How can you not go? It was just a given, I never even questioned it. It was a very bad time; they were bringing in something which was officially called 'The Extension of University Education Act', otherwise known by all of us as the Academic Apartheid Bill. I spent most of my three years at university – we all did – on strike, sit-ins, marches and placards; there were police on the campus. I remember one march; everybody in full academic gowns, walking peacefully, five thousand students or something, from the university to the Johannesburg City Hall, bearing placards, saying 'Knowledge is colour-blind'. It was all protest. It was a time when people were getting arrested quite a lot. Many of my dearest friends were in trouble, and I could have been in a lot of trouble. I was summoned, once, right towards the end, when I was applying for visas, by the Special Branch – we called them the 'Greys' – and I was interviewed by a certain lieutenant, and on the desk in front of him he had a thick file marked 'Janet Suzman'. So you knew that they were dogging you; they knew what parties you were going to, what meetings you went to. Worst of all, the university was rife with spies. They used to land upon poor students who were finding it difficult to eke out their rent, and bribe them to spy, to see who was going to meetings and what the talk was amongst the students, because there were strong left-wing student organisations.

The reason I came to England at the end of that time was to get out. Most people just wanted to get out. There was a huge exodus, every decade from South Africa. I have an aunt called Helen Suzman, who was an MP for a very long time, who wagged her finger in Parliament at Botha, the Prime Minister before de Klerk, and said 'You've been responsible for a brain drain that this country cannot afford', and he replied in true Botha-like fashion, 'Good riddance!' But in effect, my entire generation upped and left, got out.

I joined the University Players, so I did do student stuff. The only things I recall are three productions: one of *Julius Caesar* with the entire English faculty playing the blocks and stones of the set, insensate things, which seemed fair typecasting, and another production of *Love's Labour's Lost* on Vespas, little motorcycles, and a production of Eugene Ionesco's *The Chairs*. Theatre was just another thing to do. I wasn't homed in on it, nor did I have, from an early age, any particular desire to be an actress. It wasn't at the forefront of my thinking, ever. I thought I would be a doctor. Medicine fascinated me, it still does. I found medicine much more interesting, really. Perhaps I still do.

LAMDA: pragmatism, passion and clarity

I came to England to get out; I didn't know what I wanted to do. You know, it was like throwing dice and seeing which landed uppermost. And because I had a pal who'd gone to LAMDA, it seemed like a good thing to do. I thought 'Well, I'm curious about it, I'll find out.' I didn't know that I had a talent, but I did. I applied to Central School and RADA, and LAMDA, and I got into all three, boom, like that, which surprised me. But I suppose my getting into all three began to focus my mind, because I thought 'Well, if they're stupid enough to accept me, maybe I've got something'. I had no idea.

You're always writing applications when you're that age. Mind you, I was a postgraduate by then, I had a degree in English, so naturally, I had a great interest in English dramatic literature. I went to LAMDA because it was being run by a genius teacher called Michael MacOwan, an extraordinary man. It seemed to me the least poncy of the three schools. RADA was terribly famous, everybody knew about RADA. The Central School seemed sort of large and slightly rackety; it had a looser feel than RADA. RADA seemed terribly full of itself. At LAMDA, I liked the atmosphere instantly, and I liked the man who ran it. It wasn't over-formal and they liked postgraduates. I thought that displayed a great deal of common sense. I think LAMDA has retained the feel of pragmatism. It's a very British vocational school in that sense. It doesn't teach stylistic things, you can't say 'Oh, yes, that's a LAMDA actor', as you might be able to say about an actor coming out of the Conservatoire in Paris.

At the time I went there, there'd been a terrific change, there was a new egalitarianism, really. I think the moment people like Albert Finney – which was just pre-me – started hitting the drama schools, regional people, vocational training began to change. Because it was with the advent of the Finneys of this world, (does regional accent) who talked like that and came from up north, that the whole idea of Received Pronunciation and polite expertise began to devolve. My generation was Glenda Jackson's generation, and she too was another female regional anomaly. So by then, the ground was being prepared for this more demotic influx of people. I didn't know a time when acting was posh, and that certainly was not part of the ethos of LAMDA. Michael MacOwan's view was no-nonsense: let's understand it, let's-be-passionate-and-clear-acting. There also was a very, very important voice teacher called Iris Warren at LAMDA. It was from Iris and her teaching – she was quite a catalyser, and a tremendous character – that I really understood that an expressive voice, a free voice, an easygoing instrument of a voice, was the only tool you really need, just like a musician needs a well-tempered instrument. Certainly, in the classical field – it doesn't matter a hoot on television, or a hoot on film, or a hoot if you're doing plays with very short sentences – but if you're doing plays with very long sentences, and therefore long thoughts, and long conceits, you need a voice.

I don't think vocal training now is terrific at all. Iris Warren's chief protégée was Kristin Linklater, and she upped sticks and went off to America. So, really, North America has been the recipient of the brunt of Iris's teaching, through Kristin and people like her. There are a couple of very good ones, Patsy Rodenberg who works for the National, and Cis Berry, of course, at the RSC. They work through a kind of textual pragmatism. I've not been to a voice teacher since I left drama school.

The RSC years

I was picked up by an agent just before I left LAMDA, and things fell into my lap. I did a lightning tour of the British Isles in rep. I thought I'd cut my teeth in rep very well, thank you, in truth it was only five months. But it was a wonderful training. Then one day I was at Manchester, at the Library Theatre – a marvelous man called David Scace ran it – and used to spot newcomers on the scene and grab us; Patrick Stewart and I, were grabbed by David. He gave me Viola in *Twelfth Night*. I learnt a lot. And one afternoon I was told that various people from the RSC were in the audience. I was doing some rather silly comedy. Anyway, I was asked down to Stratford to audition, and Peter Hall was getting ready for *The Wars of the Roses*, it was '63. I was just kicking my heels in the wings after auditioning and Peter Hall came to find me, and said, 'I'd like you to play La Pucelle', and I was so bloody ignorant, I said 'Who?' And then I realised it was little Joan of Arc, in *Henry VI*.

The Wars of the Roses as a whole exercise, was very radical, and very important, a turning point. That's why Peter Hall retains his sort of *master* status, because it was, indeed, a mighty undertaking. There had been a couple of magical productions I remember – *Troilus and Cressida* and *Twelfth Night*, both with Dorothy Tutin and Ian Holm – which were ravishing, the last kick, if you like, the last flourish of a kind of magical prettiness on the stage. They were very sexy, good productions. *The War of the Roses* brought in a bleaker, tougher, state-of-the-nation viewpoint. Peter Hall and John Barton, in their rethinking of *Henry VI*, and their desire to do this history trilogy, expanded it to all seven history plays the following year, so that the cycle ran from *Richard II* through *Richard III*. That was a pretty radical rethink.

Peter Hall attempted, for the first time, to emulate the continental mode, which was to have long-term contracts for actors. The British acting system always resists the idea of signing contracts for longer than two minutes. He had the idea of keeping on a proper repertoire company, and having people do the ensemble thing of playing big parts and middling parts and small parts, all as part of your year's work. He asked for three-year contracts, so that he could have some forward thrust, which was very radical.

The intellectual thrust behind *The Wars of the Roses* was due to the advent of the *Cambridge School* of directors, inspired by Dadie Rylands, who was the influence behind it, because he'd been teaching students text at Cambridge for years. Both John Barton and Peter Hall had passed through his hands. With Peter and John, the study of verse speaking became a universitarial sort of exercise, rather than a Guthriesque, theatrical one. The directors edited, as well; they didn't get a separate literary editor to do the work. They were hands-on directors who were editing and re-wrote the plays as well. John Barton restructured the three parts of *Henry VI* into *Henry VI*, and what he called *Edward IV*. So he squashed three rambling plays down into two rather tight ones, which was a major editorial exercise. There was a terrific feeling that everybody was in the same boat; it was probably the last time that has happened, maybe the first and the last. There was a tremendous feeling of company, of camaraderie. I remember the first reading of seventy-six actors, I believe, in the rehearsal room, a gigantic company, headed, of course, by Peggy Ashcroft and Donald Sinden.

Peggy was the luminous leader of us all, playing Margaret of Anjou, and we became life-long friends from that point onwards. Her glowing integrity – because that's what it was – affected everybody. And though she was by no means a university person herself, that side

Janet Suzman in *Henry VI* (1963)

of her brain responded to it wholeheartedly. I suppose everybody has a kind of icon. Peg was iconic to me, because she had a kind of blazing honesty; if she didn't believe something she wasn't able to do it. There was something both naturalistic and spiritual about Peggy's acting, which I think is probably the best. I never saw her in many of her great early parts, of course, but I did see her playing Kate with Peter O'Toole, before Peter O'Toole had his nose done; he was wonderful. He should never have had a nose job. Wonderful, handsome, aquiline face. He had it done for *Lawrence of Arabia*. The great comedies of Shakespeare have a kind of luminousness to them. Peg had that quality. You are what you play, and whatever qualities you have as a person, are distilled, reinforced, brought out by those juvenile heroines, or heroes.

Swimming into the classics

I think if the first meat you chew is particularly full of blood and muscle, as in a classical text, then that's what you like doing, and that's what brings out the best in you. Let's put it this way: if you come to classics a little too late in life, they seem immensely hard to you. But if you swim into them, as I did, with an English degree behind me, which meant that I was attuned to textual analysis, it wasn't frightening, ever; it just seemed an everyday thing. Coming to the major parts later in life – like Daniel Day-Lewis, who did a kind of interesting, if juvenile, Hamlet at the National Theatre, and then went immediately back into films – is more difficult. He couldn't last the course. You can understand why: films are physically so bloody cushy to do. Everybody looks after you, you only do short shots, so little stamina is required. Your particular temperament has to be caught by the camera. Everything is directed towards that; every muscle in everybody's body is directed towards picking up a star's particular magic. You are enslaved with people – picker-uppers of your mug, putters-down of your chair, chauffeurs who fetch you and take you to somewhere, people who put umbrellas over your head if it's hot. Everything is bent towards making that particular personality happy so that they're able to do their work. Theatre's much more guerilla warfare; you have to look after yourself. Nobody's helping you to do anything; you're having to carve your way through a lot of the day and the night, and do it yourself. Classical acting takes it out of you, it's exhausting. Sustaining a role is exhausting, if you're not brought up to it. It's a long, hard, discipline, and you have to have terrific stamina. It's gruelling, and after a bit, you get tired of it. It's a young person's profession, in my view.

The emotional journey of the character

There's an enormous difference between reading a script that has been done dozens and dozens of times before called *Romeo and Juliet*, which is already encrusted and imbued with fame and glory, and reading a new script that has just plopped through your letterbox, a different set of Geiger counters start bleeping. In the end, essentially what you do, is read what that character is saying and how she's saying it; whether it sings to something in you, whether you could see yourself emotionally making that journey.

I've played a whole range of real characters: Florence Nightingale, Joan of Arc, Alexandra, Frieda Lawrence, Edwina Mountbatten. With real characters there's an added difficulty; you need to do some duty to their shade, because you're their mouthpiece. They can no longer speak up for themselves, so there's a certain protectiveness you feel about that dead person; you don't want to do them down. On the other hand, you want to find what it was that made them tick. Fictional characters you can transmute through your own imagination, because there's no reality to them except what you make of them. Although I was able to assume Alexandra's shape in *Nicholas and Alexandra*, and wear her clothes and her jewels, the nature of the beast was probably furthest from me.

I research out of interest, out of sheer fascination for the period. I read a lot about all of them – I looked at a lot of press photos and film footage, when I could. Sometimes you can get lucky, because it's often an image, or the turn of a head, or a gesture, that can make a character click with you. Film footage is always interesting.

I remember once I was struggling with Shaw's Joan. This came after La Pucelle, and although there's a terrific difference, they're both the same girl. I'm quite sure that a bit of Shakespeare's feisty little Protestant maniac injected itself into Shaw's Joan when I did it. You do sometimes get little bits of inspiration. Shaw has a stage direction when she signs her recantation in the trial: 'She makes her mark' is his stage direction. I was in the bath one day thinking 'What mark? What mark would she make? Could she write? Thumb print? Nah, too obvious.' Then I thought 'I know exactly what she did! A circle!' Funnily enough, there are extant records of the trial of Joan of Arc; that's what she did; she made a circle. She hated recanting, and with a cross, you have to do two strokes, you have to lift a pen, you have to do it quite carefully, and see that they cross, at the middle of each stroke. A circle is something much angrier, as a movement. So maybe it was that that drew me towards it, but it was the correct choice. When you get the feeling of the character, you start finding the right details.

Hedda Gabler

I did two Heddas. The greatest gift you can have in a long life, is to do a great part twice in your career, which used to be much more the case. I think Peggy Ashcroft did a lot of her parts twice; you always get better the second time around. An early Hedda that I did on television, before I did it on the stage, was a much more jokey, malicious, superficial creature. Teasing, almost. Quite young in some respects. The essential aspect of Hedda is that she's by no means stupid and she does have a very laconic sense of humour, and is quite a tease. The second time I played her, I delved deeper into the more driven side of her. The world is anarchic, and you're simply blown hither and yon by the winds that spring up in your life. You have no power over events. Hedda hates that. And I injected a kind of fatalism into her attitude toward things, hence the black humour. That she'd plumped for the wrong man, discovered that throughout that interminable, six-month honeymoon she went through, that all her dreams about romance and sexual passion were ashes, had come to nothing, because George Tesman wasn't that way. She didn't believe he'd be otherwise. She merely hoped. She took him because, as she says in the text, he was the last one left. She was frightened of being left on the shelf; she married him out of a kind of cowardice.

It's cowardice in many ways, that drives her. She despises that in herself. There's a lot of self-loathing in her. The horror of being taken over by her pregnancy is probably the most important thing. Ibsen never dwells on it, but he makes it clear at the beginning of the play that she is pregnant. And that is a thraldom that this woman cannot bear. I can't bear being regimented either, and there were parts of me that instinctively understood Hedda's dilemma. There was no question of an abortion for her in those days; she was going to *have* to have a baby, but a baby born of a night that she couldn't even remember. The act that made the baby was, to her, distasteful; there was nothing passionate or pleasant about it. So there she is, lumbered with something that she's going to have to love, even if she doesn't want to. And like Macbeth, she sees the days stretching before her, tomorrow and tomorrow and tomorrow. There's no doubt in my mind that from the very beginning of the play she's spoiling for trouble, and the first trouble she makes is with Auntie's hat. It accelerates from that moment on, and the final trouble she makes is shooting herself, and of course it's the final liberation, it's like *the* argument for suicide. It all happens in 48 hours.

I think she wanted to taste power. I remember coming out one night after a performance – people get very het up about plays, don't they? – and there was a young man at the stage door who said 'I can't stand it. I can't stand it that you did that to the manuscript, how could you do that?' Well, the funny side is that you might have done him a great favour; it was probably a terrible book. I have no faith that Lövborg's manuscript was *War and Peace*.

Destroying that infinitely boring manuscript about the future of the world, probably saved us from a tome worse than death. But it's such a devilish thing to do. At bottom she's a very passionate person, and when she does it, she *does* it. It's interesting that there are only two moments of her in total privacy; and one of them is the burning of the manuscript. When you see a character by herself you are required to understand more than you do when she's with other people; that's what a soliloquy is for, really. But I can quite understand this heated adolescent mind of hers that saw Lövborg as a Bacchanalian character, as a young Greek god, and now he's been turned into a creature tied to the apron strings of little Thea; he's not drinking any more, he's behaving himself like a good boy. She has a vision which is slowly being chipped away by these two – by Thea, especially – who is the instrument of sanity and care, motherliness and decency in the play. Whatever picture Hedda has of the world – and it's probably a very overheated one – you could lay at Lövborg's door. And then Lövborg reappears, and he's bland, and contained, and on the wagon. He's trying not to talk about the sort of things they used to talk about before, and he's suddenly become ordinary, and very, very bourgeois. And although Hedda's exterior is very bourgeoise; she's not. Underneath she's a rebel, and that's her tragedy.

She's unable to be her dream. Running through the play, as we know, is this terror of scandal, of gossip. This small strictured town somewhere in Scandinavia – 'What'll the neighbours think?' – is a noose around the neck. But there was no choice. Had Hedda lived in the 20th Century, she would have been quite a gal. But she was just on the cusp of women's liberation, and therefore, was doomed and damned to a life which ill-suited her, which was to be somebody's possession, somebody's wife. The only way she could see of having fun, was to have lots of footmen, and horses, and dinner parties, and at least lead a glittering social life, but by the end of Act One, as we know, Tesman is unable to provide that, and that's another dream shattered. Not only were the sexual dreams shattered with George Tesman, but the social dreams as well. Even more constricted. The only person who breezes in from the outside world, of course, is Judge Brack, and he's a slimy bastard, and she knows it. She's got very good instincts, she can smell a rat. And boy, does she smell a rat! She doesn't want to be under his thumb, he's not worthy of her. She's a free-thinking character underneath it all. She's not on a destructive course, but on an elevated one, in some ways. She certainly wouldn't describe what she does to the manuscript as destruction, she would see it as a kind of saving. Just as Othello doesn't feel he's murdering Desdemona, at the end of the play; he sees himself as a sort of mighty avenger, putting a wrong to rights. Without wanting to draw too heavy a comparison, there is that in Hedda, too.

Could you see these two utterly second-rate people, Tesman and Thea, trying to reconstitute the Bible from little fragments from the Dead Sea? I mean, it's laughable. Where's the poetry, where's the spirit? No, just these two diligent, dedicated, decent people putting fragments back together, in order to reconstitute something that doesn't even matter. Why devote your life to somebody else's work? Because Hedda knows that George Tesman is not capable of his own work, and she despises that in him. He should have written the history of the world, instead of *The Domestic Industries of Brabant in the Middle Ages*, but Tesman was unable to rise to that. Hedda condemns people's mediocrity, because she has an intimation that she herself is not mediocre, and she can't stand being doomed to the Aunt, calling her 'Auntie'; 'Please, don't make me do that'. Everything is a nail in her coffin. When she kills herself, she knows it's tawdry. But it's liberating, and what it does is cock a snook at everybody. When Judge Brack says 'But people don't do those sorts of things', indeed they don't, but she does it, which is why she laughs. She knows very well that she's putting two fingers up to society.

Fiona Shaw was an interesting Hedda. I saw it; I reviewed it, in fact, for *Kaleidoscope*, I saw it in Dublin. There's this about *Hedda Gabler*: in order to do it full justice, you have to have both Hedda and Gabler – that's why it's called that; the play's not called *Hedda*, it's called *Hedda Gabler* for a reason. The inside of Fiona's Hedda, was a neurotic, timorous creature – well, Fiona saw her as timorous. I don't believe she is, I believe she's the opposite, but that's the mark of what a great part it is, that two actresses can see it quite differently. To me, Fiona's performance was almost like turning a glove inside out. You saw the inside of Hedda, but what you didn't

Janet Suzman in *Hedda Gabler* (1977)

understand was the Gabler side of Hedda, that is, the side that sees herself as having some sort of social standing in the world, the side that makes people tremble and grovel and call her beautiful, and tread lightly on the floorboards so they don't disturb her, and be nervous of knocking on the door in case she bites their head off when they come in. That's the young Miss Gabler, who can be quite frightening to people. She frightens the maid, she frightens Aunt Juliane, she even frightens George sometimes. The only one she doesn't seem to frighten – and that disturbs her a lot – is the Judge. But that's the woman that makes Lövborg drink again, the one that makes Thea stay the night when she doesn't really want to, the one who has a certain personality and power that makes people do things they don't really want to do. She's the woman that had a reputation in the village as being so popular that nobody ever takes her out. She's the one that is danced off her feet in her early years. There are certain people in the world, whom you think are so popular, and so famous, and so beautiful, that you never ring them, because you think they don't have time for you. That's the Miss Gabler side, the general's daughter. And you have to find both. You can't play what she was before, you have to play what you see her as now, and the residue of what she was before. They're all there in the play, but the other characters in the play cannot *read* her; she makes herself inaccessible to them. If they could read her, there'd be hope, and there is none.

Nicholas and Alexandra: a Hollywood experience

Directors can sometimes cut through the shit that you're mulling over in your head, when you can't find your way. Alexandra, in *Nicholas and Alexandra*, I rather had to tussle for myself, because Alexandra was just the opposite of everything I am. She was very right-wing; she was a Lutheran; she was very blinkered; and also terribly stupid. None of which I am. But I had to find a sympathetic way into Alexandra, and of course, in the end, it was through the child, because any woman can understand, if you've got a little haemophiliac son, how utterly obsessed you are with that child. So her behaviour, whether it was towards Rasputin, or towards the Russian people, was all because she couldn't see further than the nursery. She'd had an incredibly protected upbringing; Queen Victoria was her granny, and that's all she knew. She was a very limited individual. I read a lot around her, fascinating contempo-rary stuff. A maid of hers called Anna Virubova wrote some wildly overadoring diaries. One is required to find the middle way, really. In Virubova's eyes the Empress could do no wrong; it was a real maid-to-mistress eulogy, very overprotective, so I knew that wasn't quite the case. I felt quite sorry for her; I read that ladies of St. Petersburg always used to wear very tall egret feathers on their headgear, their tiaras, so that when they bowed to Alexandra, they would tickle her nose, and put her out a bit. It was a general consensus that she was not very popular. But she seemed to be very much in love with Nicholas; I think she was a good mother to her daughters, all that seemed fine. There's always a way.

You know, to do the Russian revolution in three hours is impossible! I'd rather it had been kept a domestic drama. I think it would have been fascinating if they'd stayed inside the palace, and if the revolution was merely a distant rumble – which it was to them, they didn't know what was really happening. But of course, it was a big Hollywood movie, and so Sam Spiegel had to move out to the grand set scenes, and introduce the revolutionaries, and this and that and everything. It had to be panoramic.

Acting for stage and film

There's no essential difference, you try and reach the essential something of the character you're portraying. It's just that film is that much easier, because you can do it in little bursts. Great film acting is the ability to lose your awareness about things around you. Because on a film set, you can think of the microphones hanging above you, and the cameras looking at you, and the people twitching around the camera, and the little scurried movements of people shifting lights, and flicking props, and powdering your nose, an endless amount of things.

I remember once watching Marlon Brando. I did a film called *A Dry White Season*, and we were doing a court scene and the great Marlon Brando arrived. There was Donald Sutherland, and Susan Sarandon, me, Michael Gambon, and Ronald Pickup, and all kinds of people sitting in the courtroom waiting for the great man to appear, and he did. But what was most noticeable was – and he's obviously picked this up from way back in his career – he never looked up, he kept his eyes down. Now, if you catch somebody's eye on a film set, they're sure to come rushing over to you to see that you're all right: 'Can I get you a glass of water Mr Brando? Let me just comb your hair, Mr Brando. Your tie is a little crooked, Mr Brando. You'll be fine, Marlon.' Somebody will always come up and pay attention to you, which is the last thing you want when you wish to keep hold of your imagination. Imagination is the most important thing. And I noticed that he kept his eyes down, which meant that he was inviolate, because if you don't give people a signal, by lifting your eyes, to come towards you, they won't dare. And so he had a ring round him of concentration, and he preserved it. He made people understand 'I don't want my focus to be disturbed, so don't come near me with your brushes and combs and powder-puffs; keep away.' The secret to all acting is focus.

I suppose, what you need as a film actor is self-involvement. You need to have that blithe egotism that tells you that you are the most important thing, at that moment, on the floor. And it's just got to be exactly as searing as you feel it. And for that, you are required to have a certain blinkered self-obsession. Which is why in the end, acting to me has become less fascinating than it used to be, because I don't feel very self-obsessed, and you *have* to be. You have to really believe that what you're wearing, and what you're doing, and what you're saying, is very important. With acting at its best, though – not to remove from it a dimension which it ought to have – there's a kind of inner burn which can't be taught, and which a talented performer will have – where the detail with which you illuminate your character's life, seems preordained and infinitely natural.

Acting with Shakespeare: Suzman the author

'I once shared a scene with an actress who had to come on and deliver a long speech about the horrid things that had happened to her during the day. It was written as a comical, end-of-tetherish speech . . . . One night . . . something horrid must really have happened to her during the day, and she came on and delivered that same speech truly angry and truly frazzled. It took off and was fast and funny and full of feeling . . . . "Oh, good," thought I, "she's finally cracked it." Not so, for the next night we had reverted back to the well-worn delivery. She had effectively forgotten what emotion had powered the speech the night before.'*

That night, when something happened to her, she'd been hassled or been delayed in a traffic jam, the anger of the day fed into the scene, so there was a kind of lick to it, because her adrenalin was running, that made it work for the first time. She didn't come off the stage and say, 'Why did that work? Oh, I know, it's because I was talking quicker. Why was I talking quicker? I was talking quicker because I was angry. Why was I angry? Because this thing happened to me.' And when you're angry and adrenalin runs, you think more quickly, it's perfectly natural, it's what people do. She hadn't stopped to ask herself the question. She was uncurious, put it that way. I think the chief thing you need as an actor is curiosity.

* Janet Suzman, *Acting With Shakespeare: Three Comedies*. Applause, 1996, p. 35.

'I wonder what it was that I did that made it work?' Then you have to really work it out and say 'Yeah, I see'. Then later on you can get so good at it you don't have to think about that any more, it'll just come to you, like a carpenter's hands know how to hold a hammer, and know where to butt a nail. Your body begins to take over. But the initial working out, has got to be a curious self-questioning: 'Why, when I did that, did it seem easier, better, more natural, to flow more? And when I do this, I get bogged down, my sense of timing goes, it doesn't feel so good, I feel I'm *acting*, it feels effortful.'

You have to ask yourself what is the difference between the two. If a daily event, something that happened to you on your way to the theatre, or on the way to the rehearsal, triggered something, you have to say to yourself 'Oh, that's what it was! I got mad at that traffic light, because x happened, or y happened, and it fed into me, and that's why I was able to play that scene with a certain feeling of mmph'. So, I think – curiosity. Uncurious artists are quite tedious, really, because they're not asking themselves questions.

That's what rehearsals are for. Rehearsals are not to get it right straightaway, they're to do it wrong and then find another way of doing it, and see which is the better way, which serves the play better and serves the character better. And a lot of actors don't use rehearsals in a curious way. You've got to be curious: 'Why did I do that so well?' or 'Why did I do that so badly, and what do I mean by well and badly?' Badly means I was acting a lot, I was trying to make you think I was doing it well. Really good acting is the opposite, it makes you think it's dead easy.

If people are finding language in a speech difficult – paraphrase it; it is actually sometimes a key. Ian McKellen taught me that you can often talk your way through, out loud. It's always through the mental links between one thought and another, that an actor needs to find his way in order to achieve the consistency of the journey. After all, when you're following a route map, and it says 'Turn left here', or 'Turn right here', your feet don't leave the ground. You might walk in a circle for a bit as you decide whether to take the right-hand fork or the left-hand fork, but you don't actually leave the ground as you make that decision. And similarly, in acting, you have to find your pathway. You can't just fly off it and then land on another daisy, you have to keep walking. And it's those links which I think you can talk out to yourself, especially with rather complex language, in order to find the thought-route for yourself. I can be a pain in the ass. I very much like discussion during rehearsal. If I'm not clear what I'm doing, I like to talk it out, see what I am doing, and that can be quite irritating to people, I think, but too bad. When I know what I'm doing, I'm quiet as a mouse.

Of course not everything is plain sailing. You can be acting with people who you largely dislike, which is a trial, it's much nicer to act with people you get on with. But it doesn't always bring out the best acting. Friction needn't necessarily destroy a performance. There can be something quite sparky on stage between two people who intensely dislike each other, so this can be very good. I used to have a very pleasant – because I like him a lot – but quite tempestuous relationship with Alan Howard when we did *Much Ado*; sometimes he used to annoy the hell out of me, although I admired him as an actor. We had quite a jokey relationship. Sometimes a little barbed humour here and there is a very useful thing. It served the play well.

The job of the director

When you're cast, it's the director pointing a finger at you and saying 'I want your personality for this creature', so it's rather rare that a director will admit he's made the wrong choice. You have to make the most of the choice you've made. You will it, you bend over backwards to make it work for that person. It's the director's burden more than the actor's burden in many ways, although you can make mistakes, bad mistakes. I can't think of a part I've acted where I've been at complete loggerheads with a director. You take it moment by moment and work it through. The thing is to always find consistency. There's an overall consistency to the character that you have to map out, and be able to justify. If a director says to you 'Why are you doing that there? I don't believe it.' The actor must be able to justify it and say 'Look, I'm doing this because at this particular moment, I think this is what she feels, and so this is what I feel she must be doing at this point.' Either he buys that or he doesn't.

Sometimes a director doesn't have an overall view; he's waiting for the actor to unravel it. I did *Three Sisters* with Jonathan Miller, who's utterly adorable to work with, and brilliant, but doesn't ever say 'This is what I think the character is like, and should do'. He waits with a sort of benign amusement to see what you might come up with. There was a point when Masha declares, in a roundabout way, how much she loves Vershinin, and I really wasn't clear how to do it. I was being rather dramatic and romantic about it. Somebody did something stupid in rehearsal, and we all got the giggles, all three of us, Olga, Irina, and Masha. I kept on trying to do my speech, and we all agreed, as one, that's the way to do it! The difficulty then was to recreate that laughter every time. Masha brings out her feelings for Vershinin, because laughter opened her up. The more she spoke, the sillier it sounded, and the more she giggled, the more hysterical they all got. It played wonderfully. I'm very prone to opposites, I'm very prone to exploring the unobvious way to do something. It seems on the surface to be one way, and yet there's always another way that you can find. That was a particularly happy discovery. If Jonathan Miller had been an improvisatory sort of director, he might have set up the scenario, and we might have arrived at the same conclusion, but it just happened by accident. Improvisation is not best-loved here, I would say. But after all it is only the means to unlock a tricky moment.

Visual imagination and the text

Increasingly, if you go to the large subsidised companies and you don't see something gorgeous on the stage, you feel a bit cheated for your money. That's because everybody is visually very aware, and you've got to present something which delights the eye. The difficulty with that is finding the balance, because if you've got a very complicated play, and a complicated set as well, one is liable to subsume the other. Always, good design is a balance. Really gorgeous stage design will explain and elucidate the play for you.

But, I can sort of understand; people don't want to be bored when they go to the theatre, and going to the theatre is very onerous. You have to find parking, you have to buy the ticket, you make an *effort* to be present. And you've made that effort, in the particularly lazy age we live in. It's lazy only because people want the minimum of effort to get the maximum of every-thing, which is why e-mail has got so popular – press a button and you get a letter. It saves you stamping it, licking the envelope, addressing it, and posting it! Several actions are cut out. So, going to the theatre is a whole big deal, and the last thing you want to do, and the most important thing you have to do when you're there, is concentrate. I'm always looking at the audience rather than the stage, to see how the audience is. That tells you about the play.

But I feel, '*Quot hominae tot sententiae*', not to be too sententious, that means: 'There are as many opinions as there are people', and theatre should cater to everything, shouldn't it? I took my kid, when he was much littler, to see *Starlight Express*, and he had a lovely time, so I climbed into his eyes, and watched it with a kid's eyes, and it was just fine at that age. That's not a grown-up experience, no, of course it isn't, it's for kids.

In the end, theatre's a language medium, isn't it? Think of the day that Stanislavsky received *The Seagull*, by Anton Chekhov. Completely undoable, but what a strange, weird and wonderful play. So, everybody hopes the script that they open is going to make them go 'Oh, wow, that's fresh, that's new, that's original, that's full of life and imagination'. When people talk about text, that's what they mean. The marks they see on the page are saying some-thing original, lively, human, passionate, provocative. It's got blood in its veins. Good playwrights know how to write dialogue, and write scenes between characters that have some kind of life and conflict. That's what people mean by text. Don't let's just have sets that do miraculous things. Straight theatre is not dancing, so therefore you can't rely entirely on bodies, and it's not singing, so you can't rely entirely on voices, so let's rely on dialogue. Thoughts, ideas.

The theatre is a broad church. It all depends on the performer. So a text is nothing without actors to interpret it. The greater the play, the greater the actors who must interpret it, that's the measure of everything. The issue comes down to talent. We interpret in a million ways, but each person who reinterprets, brings their own talent to it. Going back to *The Wars of the Roses* for a moment, not everybody in Peter Hall's company was a genius, by any means. Only about four of those actors were stunningly talented as individual artists, and the rest were journeyman actors: damn hard-working, good actors. But there is definitely something about the whole being greater than the sum of its parts, in a well-directed panorama. Peter's talent made it work.

But that's the great thing about films: the visual high. That's why I enjoyed working with Peter Greenaway so much on *The Draughtsman's Contract*, because he's visually so adept; he knew exactly what pictures he wanted to make, so I was rather enthralled by his visual sense. When he was setting up a shot, there should be one orange just *there*, and the rest should be white and black, so one was admiring a painter painting on celluloid. I knew that he was painting pictures with every frame, and I thought that was tremendous. He's a real original.

I had a whole week to myself with Fellini when I did *E La Nave Va*. We filmed all that silly stuff of the diva, long before the film was actually up and running, because he wanted to insert these scenes into his movie. A lot of the scenes were terribly complex, but he was just such an *enabler*. He had such a *joie de vivre*, such a wonderful sense of humour, such an expertise as a filmmaker, that you felt you were just floating, really. He was amusing and easygoing, and such a *bon viveur*; we used to eat out every night in this fabulous restaurant, he loved his food.

There was one scene, I remember, where people had to get up and make after-dinner speeches. There were all sorts of nationalities of actors there, and some of them couldn't speak Italian, and he said 'It doesn't matter, count', so they're going (counts in Italian), and he would just dub it, he would put the speech on afterwards, he didn't care. The Italians think nothing of that. He wanted the atmosphere, the feel. I just thought he was great. A real sensualist, and such an instinctive genius. That visual sense is just thrilling.

Theatre for the real thing

We get to play a wide range of roles here. American actors, because there's a huge geographical separation between Los Angeles and New York, need to typecast themselves a bit more. They need to be known as doing 'this' sort of a part. If Malkovich had spent his youth here, and maybe a season at Stratford, he would have been asked to play yokels, and young lovers, and buffoons, and all sorts of things, in order to stretch himself. And an actor's working career, at its best, is one where you're asked to play unlikely parts for yourself. I think that opportunity isn't as open to American actors; they're asked to play the type they seem to be, straight off, and they don't get the opportunity to play a wide variety of roles.

Young actors don't have that opportunity any more. It's television for fame, films for money, and theatre for the real thing. But theatre is *hard*. And you have to be devoted, and you have to spend so much of your time doing it. Just think, if I was in a play now, I'd have to say 'Excuse me, I've got to go now', and just at the time when you think 'Oh, that's nice, I'll have a tot of whisky, put my feet up, go to see somebody else working, whatever', you have to run off to work. It's very demanding. Television's not too demanding, for all those reasons that I've gone on about. But in theatre, you've got only yourself to deal with. You sitting in the dressing room, you putting your make-up on, you stepping out onto the stage, and you standing in front of the audience, making them believe you're somebody else.

Changing direction

I confess to a slight change of attitude in the '80s, when I'd had a child, and I found that, for the first time in my life, somebody else was infinitely more important than I was. In the '80s, and consequently in the '90s – now, when I'm a director more than an actor – that's a natural progression, I suppose – I found myself less interested in acting. I became less interested because, as I say, I wasn't taking myself as seriously as I did before. You have to have that trust in yourself and in your instincts, which makes you able to plunge in, so the water closes over your head. I found myself very happy to do that at a certain stage in my life, and then I simply began to grow out of it. There are not that many absolutely riveting parts, as you get older, as an actress, and that is the truth of the matter. Therefore, your passion for the art – it is an art – gets depleted, I suppose.

I've got a different strand to my life, and that has been my obsession with South Africa, and that drew me off that particular acting stove at the end of the '80s. I became, and have become, infinitely more interested in what I could do in that respect than in pursuing my own star on the stage. There's some element in me that began to be more fascinated with directing, in other words, thinking up a project, and making it happen.

I'm been completely enthralled by the various things that I've done as a director. I find it thrilling. I realise also that it's another career; you have to learn to be a director, you can't just *be* a director. So, I had to start all over again. I left one profession behind, in a sense, and started another. When I look back, I can divide my life into the '70s, the '80s, and the '90s. In the '70s, I had the luck to play every part that I ever wanted to play, really, that I was the right age for. In the '80s I got much taken up with my child, and everything else seemed a little peripheral. Towards the end of the '80s, when he was about six or seven, I got this strange tug back to South Africa, the land of my birth – and the land, in the end, that fashioned me. I think the difference between me, and the rest of my generation of actresses here is that I have a socio-political conscience, and it was what was happening to South Africa, that began to take precedence over just doing a *play*. I have been, up to now, the sort of person that needs to find, in a play, a wider social context; I find it difficult to do a play just for the sake of doing a play. The last play I did in the West End was *The Sisters Rosensweig*, which I quite enjoyed, but there was something intellectually, that I was restless with. I was getting into the theatre and doing this quite sparky sort of New York comedy every night, but I was finding that I got impatient with it. And really, it was at that point that I decided 'No, no, you can't just do plays any more'. I need to have all the bits of me involved, and so that's what happened.

Penelope Wilton

'As you get older, you essentially try to do less – it goes deeper, and it becomes more fermented. That's what you're trying to do.'

Penelope Wilton was born in Scarborough, England in 1947. Her varied work in theatre includes her debut in Jonathan Miller's *King Lear* at the Nottingham Playhouse. Wilton's first experience on the boards in London was in *The Philanthropist* at the Royal Court, followed by *West of Suez*. She has since appeared in *The Cherry Orchard, The Seagull, Uncle Vanya, Measure for Measure, All's Well That Ends Well* and *The Norman Conquests*. At the National Theatre, Wilton has played in *The Philanderer, Betrayal, Sisterly Feelings, Major Barbara, The Secret Rapture, Piano* and Pinter's *Landscape*. Her performances at the National in *Man and Superman* and *Much Ado About Nothing* garnered the Drama Magazine Award. For the Pinter Festival at the Gate Theatre in Dublin, Wilton performed *Landscape, Moonlight* and *A Kind of Alaska*, for which she won the Irish Theatre Award for Best Actress. Wilton's performance in this award winning role was reprised at the Donmar Warehouse. She has also acted in *Vita and Virginia*, at the Chichester Festival and in London, *The Cherry Orchard* at Stratford and at the Albery in London, and *Long Day's Journey Into Night*, which originated at the Theatre Royal, Plymouth, and transferred to the Young Vic. Wilton has appeared in Karel Reisz's production of *The Deep Blue Sea*, for which she won the Critics Circle Award, and David Hare's production of *Heartbreak House*, both at the Almeida.

The actress' television work for the BBC includes *Mrs Warren's Profession, The Song of Songs, The Pearcross Girls, Othello, King Lear, The Widowing of Mrs Holroyd, Country, The Norman Conquests, Ever Decreasing Circles, Landscape* and *This Could Be the Last Time*, as well as the series *The Borrowers*. For Channel Four, Wilton has appeared in *Madly in Love* and *Alice Through the Looking Glass*. Amongst her films are *Clockwise, Cry Freedom, The Secret Rapture, Carrington* and *Tom's Midnight Garden*.

I spoke with Penelope Wilton in her dressing room at the Albery Theatre, where she was performing in *The Cherry Orchard*, in December, 1996.

Born into an acting family

I was born in the north of England, in Scarborough, a little town on the northeast coast. I came to London when I was very young, because my father was working down here, so the family moved. I was born in 1947. He was in the war, and was training to be a barrister before the war. After the war, to finish his training, he came down to London. So I've lived in London most of my life, apart from a couple of sojourns when we've gone to the country.

My mother was an actress before she married, and then just after she married, the war came, and she stayed at home looking after my older sister. But her sister was an actress, and her brother was an actor – the influence of the theatre was all on my mother's side of the family. There were actors in the family who were always working – or not working, as the case was. Then they all married actors, and so that's where the influence of the theatre came from. My father's family had nothing to do with it. We went to films quite a bit; we went to the theatre more. We went to the cinema, but I don't suppose any more than any other kids. The cinema wasn't so big over here as it was in the States. As I grew up I went to the theatre much more. From the age of about 14 onwards, I went quite regularly to the theatre in London. When I was 16 or 17 we used to go up to Stratford and see plays; I had an uncle who was in the company for a while. So I saw quite a lot of theatre when I was young.

Support for a young actress

My idols were the usual ones like Laurence Olivier and Ralph Richardson. And then I worked with Ralph Richardson when I was 23 in a play called *West of Suez*, at the Royal Court. It was the first thing I did when I left repertory in the provinces. I finished drama school when I was 20, and then I went into rep – they had companies in those days. I was in rep for two years, and we did three weeks of rep, a new play every three weeks. When I left there, I went to the Royal Court, which was then run by Bill (William) Gaskill – this was in the late '60s. The third play I did there was *West of Suez*, which was one of John Osborne's later plays. We started at the Royal Court, then we went on a little tour, and finally came into town with it.

It was wonderful to work with Ralph Richardson. There were a lot of ladies, a lot that were still quite young, like Judi Dench, and Maggie Smith, who I thought were wonderful. And of course Peggy Ashcroft. I saw all those people on the stage. Who else was there? Irene Worth, who I also worked with when I was about 24, 25. We did *The Seagull* together. I was Masha, the one who's always in black. Irene taught me a lot. I was very lucky to work with some great women. I worked with Coral Browne in a play called *Mrs Warren's Profession* by Shaw, when I was very young. And then I worked with Jill Bennett, also in *West of Suez*, and who was married then to John Osborne. As I got a bit older I worked with Janet Suzman. All the older – I mean approximately older – women I've worked with were wonderfully helpful to me as a young actress. The men were too, but particularly the women. I enjoyed working with them immensely. Irene and Coral were particularly sweet to me as a young actress.

The Drama Centre experience: a hothouse environment

I had first trained at the Drama Centre, which was very influenced by the American Method. We had a wonderful teacher called Doreen Cannon, who taught me, and who, sadly has died. She had trained with Uta Hagen, I think. But there was no one method, I mean, they used all sorts of different ways of teaching there. The man who ran the school when I was there was a wonderful man called John Blatchley, who has now died, and he had been a teacher at the Old Vic school, with Michel St-Denis and Glen Byam Shaw. I suppose the Drama Centre followed that tradition of theatre, which was not just purely English-based, it was rather European and American. Of course, Yat Malmgren, who was the principal before Christopher Fettes, is Swedish, and he brought his Rudolf Laban method of training to the school. It was a very cosmopolitan, widely-based training.

I'd auditioned for a number of schools; I auditioned for LAMDA, and for the Royal Academy, and the Drama Centre, and the Douglas. I liked John Blatchley very much when I had my audition, and also they offered me a place! They seemed to think that I would fit in because they ran very much as a group thing, everything was done in a group. You started off at the beginning of your first year – the training went on for three years – with a group of about thirty, and the group was everything, and as the years went on, that group got smaller. People either left because they felt they didn't want to stay, or the school didn't feel that they could offer them anything. By the end, there were only about twelve of us, in the third year. It was a very rigorous training, but an extremely good one.

I must say I think there *is* a lot of talk about stripping down the student's ego and that sort of thing, and a lot of the ex-students don't help, because they sometimes feel it's the biggest thing that's ever happened to them. When you're 18 or 19, and you go into a very hothouse environment, one's very impressionable at that age, I suppose it seems rather stringent and tricky. You have to be there on time: you start at nine, and you're there at nine, and if you go on being late, then you're out; it's very strict. That is, I think, an extremely good training, especially for an actor, because nothing happens until you arrive.

I'm 49 now; I was 20 when I left. But when I was there, I didn't think it stripped one of one's ego. It got rid of all those silly ideas that people have about acting, which is based on things that suit them, instead of you suiting the play. It seemed to put the emphasis in the right place. You hear a lot of people saying 'The part suits me', well, what about the part? That's written by Chekhov. I'm lucky enough to be playing Madame Ranevskaya at the moment, but it was a genius who wrote the part, so I think the boot should be on the other foot.

I didn't find the training at the Drama Centre went against being faithful to the text at all. On the contrary, I think the play was all, the play and the group. The play is more important than the individual, and that doesn't suit everybody, because a lot of people want to be an overnight success. The Drama Centre doesn't equip you particularly well to show off, which a lot of people like to do in theatre. It's eye-catching, you can do something quick and surface which can get you a job. The Drama Centre is a more in-depth thing, which teaches you to actually notice things that actors have to notice. A painter will have to know about colours, and be aware, and the actor has to have a similar vocabulary, which is to do with what he notices, and what he keeps. It's all to do with opening your eyes to what's around you, and being aware of your emotions and how you can use them.

I thought it was a very good, serious training, a bit like going to university. You had a reading list, and you did plays that you don't normally do in other schools. We did a lot of European plays by writers that aren't really used. Karl Sternheim, plays that came out of German Expressionism, and we did American plays. We didn't really touch Shakespeare, because I think it was felt that we weren't equipped to do it at that age. We did all sorts of interesting works by different people. It was a wonderful overall education, which is education about life, and that is what actors really need. You have to broaden your horizons, really.

We had a number of different classes. First of all, we had a class called an 'acting class' where we did memory exercises, and improvisation classes. We had improvisation: 'as if', 'what if' you were in situations, to build up the role. Then you would write a biography of your character. There was a great deal of talk of objectives in the play, in the act, in the scene, you were playing. You had an objective to achieve on the stage, and what action did you use to achieve this objective, and what activities you used to get to the action, to get to the objective? You could break down your script in objectives, which is actually 'Why are you there?', those questions: Why? Where? What for? How? All those things. So there is a through-line in what you are doing.

You don't always have to use that; that's good when you're studying and starting. Sometimes you know immediately and instinctively what to do, but if you have a problem, I think it's a very good thing to fall back on, and say 'What actually am I doing in this scene?' Most plays are stories, you start as somebody and you end up as somebody else, normally, but you've had some experience. In this play, *The Cherry Orchard*, my character starts off as one person and a great deal happens to her over the course of two and a half hours on the stage, and the audience sees that story unfolding. You are telling stories, as an actor.

I don't use those exercises so much now, because I have a more overall view of something, and also one gets used to it. If I have a problem in a scene, as to not knowing where it's going – that normally means that we're playing it wrong – then I will go back to the text. I am very text-orientated, but that's because I'm English. We're brought up with text; text is very important, and the speaking of text is very important. I happen to think that that's all the theatre has. Every other medium can do everything else much better, apart from, of course, musicals, that's different. Any film you see now can do better special effects than anything that can happen in the theatre. The magic of the theatre is the words, and the stories we tell. That is a living thing, and it has to be kept alive. The words are our greatest asset, and what we do with them, of course. But they are an alive thing that won't change. People can come and go and do terrible productions.

Shakespeare is the greatest living dramatist, he still lives on, he's not dead. He says as much today about the human situation as he ever did, and that's genius and greatness. I think the same of Chekhov, and I think the world of all of his plays, this one in particular because I'm doing it at the moment. It's all to do with relationships, and how people cope with the yearnings, and the wants, and the loss, and the things that happen in everyone's lives.

The Cherry Orchard

Madame Ranevskaya's journey is very complicated. Her name, Luba, means light, and I don't think Chekhov chose that by mistake. She is light. When she comes into a room, people like to be with her. She makes things happen. When she's not there, nothing happens, it's dead. I think she is a selfish woman, but she's not selfish insofar as she's cruelly selfish, she's selfish because she's a survivor. She adores her children, but the most important person in the play, to her, is her lover in Paris, whom she's obsessed by. And I think that's a very sexual relationship, so those telegrams that keep coming, churn her up. She's left because he's behaved appallingly; he's left her for another woman, gone through all her money, she's got nothing left, and she comes home. But she does come from a period of time where people of her class were hopeless. She's never had to do a thing in her life, there's been an enormous estate, they've gone through the money, she and her brother. She married the wrong person; she's ruled by her heart; she didn't marry an aristocrat as she was supposed to, in the world she comes from. She married for love; he turned out to be a drunk, then she fell in love with someone else, and she went away, and he followed her. She went away because her son died, he was drowned; she has had enormous tragedy in her life. A son drowning at 7 is the most terrible thing. She lives for the moment, she lives life to the full.

Penelope Wilton and Alec McCowen in
The Cherry Orchard (1996)

I think that the character of Madame Ranevskaya, the Russians knew about. As with *War and Peace*, there's this aristocratic woman who follows her heart, and they're always looked on by the society from which they come as being terrible, but actually they're rather impulsive, very warm people, who love life. If life is terrible, let's throw a party. The sort of people that people like to read about in *Hello* magazine; people live vicariously through them; they see them, and they think, 'Oh, isn't it terrible, she's had this child when she wasn't married, or she's gone off with her lover'. I think he's written her very, very clearly. And she's a mother, a very loving mother. If things had been better in Paris, I think she'd have sent for Anya. But if you're going around Europe with a lover that's behaving appallingly, you can't manage to have a ten-year-old child with you. Her little boy had died, and I think she was grief-stricken and wanted to get out.

I'm afraid of what happens to her, after the play is over. I mean, she is entirely selfish, and she takes the money that the great-aunt sent from Yaroslava, which was about 15,000 roubles, and goes to Paris, and I think she'll stay somewhere and her lover will come back to her, and as soon as the money goes, he'll push off again. This is me, the actress speaking.

Madame Ranevskaya doesn't look about tomorrow, or next week, she wants to get back to him more than anything. But I think, as the actress, what will happen to her is that he will go through the money and leave her again, and she'll end up in one of those cosmopolitan cafés telling people that she once had a big estate in Russia, and people will say 'Ah', and she'll have a bed-sitting room, and go to the Russian Orthodox church, and be known as an eccentric.

I think one has to understand the relationship that Russian aristocracy had with servants. It's not like an English relationship. We had servants, but it was based on class in a way that I don't think was the same in Russia. The English class system is much more snobbish – you don't talk to servants. I don't think that was entirely the case in Russia, it was much more a family thing, much more patriarchal, you looked after everybody. I think the relationship with Lopakhin, for example, is one partly of necessity and partly because she's not a snob. She's had a much more worldly view of life, and she likes people. I don't think it's a complicated relationship. She admires him, and also he's a source of money! And he might marry Varya. When we were rehearsing this play, it was interesting to work out who you actually spoke to in the play, and who you didn't. I never once address Charlotte, or mention her name. I never once mention Epihodov's name, but I think I speak to everybody else. If you put into a room all those actors, and say 'Go and stand next to whom you stand by', they all talk to me, except for Epihodov and Charlotte. It's interesting; she has a relationship with nearly everybody.

Another thing about Ranevskaya is her grief over the loss of her little boy. I don't think you get over grief. You think about it less, but when you're met with it again, I don't think you ever quite manage it. That's been my experience. My mother died very sadly of cancer, very badly, and I don't ever get over that. If I allowed myself to think about it, it would upset me as much now as it ever did. As time passes you think about it less. My sister gave me a photograph – of my mother and my father, who are both dead now – just the other day, of them laughing, and I immediately burst into tears, because it's just so: 'They're not there'. And that's the same thing in *The Cherry Orchard*, Trofimov catches her at a very, very vulnerable moment. She's very tired, it's two o'clock in the morning; seeing everybody again, she hasn't seen anyone for five years, and then this person from the past walks in – that's where Chekhov is brilliant, to bring him in at that moment – and I think it's too much. 'Why was he drowned, why? Why was it my son?' That's the question people always ask when something terrible happens. It's a mixture of enormous sadness and anger. I think that bond with Trofimov is based on the fact that he was my son's tutor, he was the nearest thing to my little boy. I can only remember thinking 'What would I feel if I were suddenly reminded of my little boy's death?' You don't see a person from your past for a long time, and then suddenly, there is the person who was as close to your little boy as you were, and she nearly collapses. It's a movement that came about in rehearsal, and that's what we'd decided to do. It doesn't change. Sometimes it's better than other times, because it's not easy to act that sort of thing every night. I just try and get better. You're never, and this is not being falsely modest, you're never really pleased. I mean there are a few times when you're really delighted. As you get older, you essentially try to do less, and it goes deeper, and it becomes more fermented. That's what you try to do.

Chekhov in particular, is the most difficult playwright I've ever done. I did *Long Day's*

Journey Into Night in the summer, and that's very, very hard as well, but it's hard in another way. But at least O'Neill writes it all; they talk all the time, and in Chekhov they don't. O'Neill is also in a language that I understand. This is in translation, an adaptation, so I have to guess, even with a very good adaptation, which I think this one is, because it cuts out a lot of the silly talk that some translators make people say. Some things are untranslatable that Russians would say; we don't have a word for it here, or we don't have a sentence. There's a sort of flavour that you know is missing. It's quite tricky, doing translation. You just try and get as near to the feeling as you possibly can, or what you think the feeling is.

Things go down in history, like painting. When people did paintings of actors in the early 19th Century and 18th Century, playing parts, they were portrayed very romantically and very egotistically. People used to act in a sort of grand way, because that was the style and the fashion, and I think there are certain traditions about certain parts that have developed. Madame Ranevskaya and Mary Tyrone are people often played by grand dames of the theatre, often rather older than they should be for the part, and they're played on that person's personality, so people see 'whoever', and they give 'their' Madame Ranevskaya, or 'their' Mary Tyrone. In a way I am doing that, but I try to bring to it more than just being me, because I don't think I'm that interesting – but they are fascinating. I have to try and get in there a bit.

Long Day's Journey Into Night

Mary Tyrone is played as a little thing who's on morphine. I think if she wasn't on the morphine, she would be a very nice, ordinary woman. She's married into a family she couldn't cope with, which was this acting family. She doesn't have doilies on plates, and have people come round, and a nice home. She's not complicated, but of course she's been dragged round the country and then got caught on the morphine, and married to a man with an enormous ego. Her escape is in the morphine, because she can't cope with the rows and the drinking. I think if she'd married somebody else, she'd have had ladies come round for tea, and had a nice house, and had a normal existence, and said 'Oh, have you seen, so-and-so's got a new car', and been a very pretty, small-town lady, and had quite a nice life. But the fact is that she hasn't. In the beginning of the play, when she's off the morphine – for a very, very small period of time – I think you see her at her best. She adored her husband, and he adored her. If you don't see that moment, then I don't think the rest works. I think with Madame Ranevskaya, you have to see her joy and silliness, and her vanity, otherwise you can't feel for her when it's all gone. That's what I mean when I say these people have journeys.

If you read the script, O'Neill writes: 'angrily', 'with fury'; his stage directions are very, very specific. I tried to do what he said; you can't just do it for nothing, you can't just be angry for no reason, so there must be a reason why he wrote 'angrily'. I think plays are a bit like detective work, you have to go through it to find out what they mean. These were O'Neill's stage directions, it's not something that somebody else who has played the part has written down in French's acting edition, it was his original text. And the word 'winsome', and 'melancholic' and 'vague', and 'passive', all those things that I'm told to play, none of those words are used in connection with her. She turns. When she's not on the morphine, she will pacify people; when she's on the morphine – until she's taken too much, of course, which turns her into a zombie by the end – it gives her a sort of Dutch courage like drink gives other people. It loosens her tongue, she says all the things she wants to say. It makes her furious, and she keeps repeating it.

O'Neill does write it all down; he says her hands are never still, they never cease to move all the time. She is described as a rather handsome woman, and quite robust. Her face is very, very pale and doesn't really go with the rest of her. But her hands move constantly. And of course she's embarrassed by this. I had to wear little gloves because I don't have arthritis. I thought 'How am I going to do this, because it's such a giveaway', I couldn't hold my hands like that all the time (contorts hands arthritically), it's so restrictive, and so I thought, 'If I was a very vain woman . . .', which I think she is, she was once a pretty woman, and all pretty women like to keep their looks. Women on the whole hide the things they're not good at. If you have a big bottom you wear a long jumper, if you have a bad neck you wear a polo neck, if you have thin hair you wear a wig, or whatever. I thought, 'Well, if she had arthritis she would wear little mittens so you wouldn't see it.' Which of course worked quite well theatrically, because you're rather drawn to these white hands, but you didn't know quite what was wrong with them. I just thought of that. But when she's taken the morphine, for a while, until she needs another fix, everything calms down. Her hands don't move so much, and she's able to talk rather simply. Apart from having a rather dry mouth, which apparently happens, I think that's when she feels normal, when she's on the drugs. But before that, you see, it's terrible, because she can't ever rest. It's the most terrible unrest; it's so exhausting for her.

I did think about her addiction, but I didn't think about it in the modern way. We all rush off to counsellors now when anything's wrong, or say it's somebody else's fault. It's partly her fault that she's on morphine. It's not all the family's fault, and part of her knows that. It's an escape. They all escape; the others escape through drink, she escapes through a drug. She can't face the possibility that her son may die, which is what she thinks is going to happen, and that's what pushes her back onto the morphine. They play happy family at the beginning, and they're all trying so hard. It's the most heartrending play, because they all want her to succeed; it's terribly sad. It means so much to them. It means that Edmund will have a proper mother to look after him, instead of pretending that there's nothing wrong with him. It means that Jamie would have someone who could stop him from getting addicted again, because if she was strong enough, he would be strong enough to get off the booze. And the father would have his wife back; this young beautiful girl he fell in love with. They've got so much invested in her keeping up.

Long Day's Journey is a particular play, because it's such a personal autobiographical piece about his family. I think Chekhov comes at things from very different directions, and he's extremely funny. He's satirical; he's not cynical. But he is very amused by the human condition, where O'Neill is more hurt and damaged by it. But I think Chekhov, being a doctor, saw everything, and he understood, and didn't blame, and was very warm about the human condition. He talks about all sorts of things in his plays – in *Uncle Vanya*, which was many years ahead of its time – about conservation and revolution, things that we are familiar with now. How he had the foresight to see all of these things before they happened or were important! And his characters are imbued with very real physical characteristics – Pishchik keeps having to have a glass of water. Chekhov, as a doctor, knew that when someone got out of breath and needed water, got overexcited, that his blood pressure was up and he had to cool down all the time. Pishchik had that very red face: Chekhov knew about somebody who'd had a heart attack, who has bad blood pressure problems, and has terrible worries about money and laughs all the time. It's tragic if you think about it. If you had psychologists now, they'd put him on Valium or whatever, but in those days, you didn't, you just worried – which is what caused the heart attack, probably. I think Chekhov is more ambiguous, insofar as he plays his cards much closer to his chest than O'Neill. I think O'Neill, particularly in *Long Day's Journey* – which is the only one that I'm familiar with, I've seen others, but I've never done any others – is able to vocalise clearly in words what he wants to say. I think that Chekhov is much more of an impressionist, and he doesn't always say, but infers things. Isn't it interesting the way Gaev is the only one who smells things: 'I smell chicken', 'Go away, you smell of chicken', 'Who's wearing patchouli?' All those little things are something partly of class: she and her brother are the only ones who hear the music. Lophakin says 'I didn't hear anything.' They live in another world, those two. If you just read it in the script, he says 'Oh, you smell of chicken'. Nobody else says anyone smells of chicken. It's used to be rather rude about Yasha, and the patchouli is supposed to be rather rude about Lopakhin, but he uses oblique ways of describing things. It can be thought of as being Gaev's sweet old eccentric ways, but it's also saying something about the class, and the awareness of things; they've had time to be aware, they're not working in fields. Their lives have been led in nurseries with manservants, who even at 60, are still dressing them in the morning. It's such a rarified atmosphere that they've lived in, and those are little pointers. If you're a detective – which you have to be in acting – you can find them, and pick them out. I'm not saying that the audience is going to go 'Wow', but they all add to the texture of this sort of tapestry, or patchwork that you're building up, that go into making him who he is, and her who she is. I think his canvas also is probably a bit bigger than O'Neill's.

Emotional wisdom

I've had some fascinating journeys with some of these women that I've played. You notice how people will fool themselves, like Mary Tyrone, but we all do that. Not to her degree, of course, but we all pretend things. What we don't want to face, we don't face, we'll find some other way. Even the most honest person will have things they don't want to address, at the time. And I find I've done that. I hope also that I bring things of my own to a role. I can recognise a lot of the emotions that go on, because all these people are living beings, flawed human beings like all of us, who have these enormous emotions going around in them. The lucky thing is, I'm allowed to get up and be them, let all that out – whether it's humour or tragedy. And you learn something because people say very wise things in plays, even if they're not very wise people. The relationships of people are very fascinating, how people cope with situations.

Sometimes, when I start working on a part, I say 'Well, it's "as if" this had happened'. Like the loss I was talking about. I had lost a baby before Alice, my daughter, was born, and one doesn't get over these things. Of course one gets over them, but you don't forget. There are certain times, terribly bleak times, when you've felt such pain, because you've let people down. I think that's part of Madame Ranevskaya, that she wasn't there. You never forgive yourself. 'I never wanted to look at this river again, I never wanted to see it' – why wasn't she there? 'Why? If only I hadn't gone out that day, if only he hadn't been left alone', if only . . . . All those 'if onlys' one uses.

But I don't get terribly affected by parts, emotionally. I've been in plays which have depressed me. I did *The Deep Blue Sea*, by Terrence Rattigan, and I found that, after a while, very, very depressing, mainly because you have to think these sad things every night – you're committing suicide, your lover's leaving you – and draw that emotion out of you, and it gets very tiring. But I leave things alone at the end of the day. I've got too much to get at Sainsbury's. Life takes over.

The community of theatre: 'we're all in it together'

I've found directors to be very helpful; I like them very much. I can only think of one who I didn't get on with. There have been better ones. The ones that I've worked with have had their strengths, and some have had weaknesses in staging or whatever, but on the whole, I've found the directors I've worked with have wanted to serve the play more than them-selves, which seems to me to be the most important thing. We're all in it together.

If there is a problem, I think it's best to have it out. There must be a reason why. I think one should go halfway along the road. Sometimes a director will say to me 'I'd like this scene played like this'. Well, I'll do it like that, and he's usually the first one to say 'No, that's not right', so we'll try something else. I haven't found great difficulties; I might have been lucky. I think it's very rare to find people one doesn't get on with, unless they're very untalented. When they're untalented, they stick in their way, and there's no one way to do anything. You can usually find a way which is best for the play, not best for you. I think you have to think about the play, and that mostly solves the problems. Go through the lines! There's nothing else you can do. Creativity doesn't just happen like that.

I don't think you do anything by yourself in the theatre, it all comes off the other actors. You work together, so when Paul Rhys and I worked together in *Long Day's Journey*, I was playing his mother and he was playing my son, we sparked together, we did the scene together. It's a very communal thing, acting. You think about characters by yourself, and you bring a lot of ideas, but scenes only work like playing a game of tennis: you have to play with somebody who's going to return the ball, and once you've got that going, then it starts to happen. But it all depends on how the other person is going to react to what I do. You can't do it by yourself.

I notice some young actors now – I don't know if it's their training – seem to pull focus sometimes, in an annoying way. You think 'This scene isn't about you. This scene is about whatever we're trying to do in the scene. If you do this, the audience will not listen to the story, which will make the next scene very difficult to do. It will be like a curtain coming down and we'll spend the next five minutes trying to get the curtain up, to get on with the story.' You must tell the story, and everything goes towards that. If there's a very big scene happening, and someone's picking their nose in the corner, and the audience finds that amusing, that is not helpful, so don't do it. You've got to all be in the same play.

The Secret Rapture: reprising a stage role on film

There's a big difference between acting for the theatre and for film, because if you're in film, you're not in charge. In the theatre, you tell people where to look as an actor, because you start at the beginning, and you end up two and a half hours later at the end of the play. But on film, it's up to the director who puts the dynamics into a film because he's editing it. So you see what he wants to see. If he's a good film director he will get the timing, the energy and the dynamics of a scene. It's he who knows where to cut a scene so that the next scene will start with the dynamic to keep the story going.

Penelope Wilton in *The Secret Rapture* (1993)

You work in much smaller bits, so that's quite tricky. The nice thing about it is that you can do very subtle things, very close up, and you only have to do it once, you don't have to keep repeating it; it's very exciting. You build a scene up over a day, or a morning or whatever, and then you play it, and then you don't have to do it again. Theatre's hard because of the repetition; you have to make that fresh every night, and that's very difficult. But actually, if you do a lot of theatre, each time you do it, you learn something about keeping up the momentum. Over a period of time, it can be wonderful, because the audience won't notice it, but you change it, try and get better. But repetition is hard, and you have to do it. If it goes on for a long time, it can be a nightmare.

In *The Secret Rapture*, I think my part was more emotional in the film, and the film was much darker. In the play, Marion's very funny. She doesn't think she's funny, but she is, because it was written at the time when Margaret Thatcher was Prime Minister, and those are the sort of values that were around at that time. People recognised her as that sort of young, up-and-coming Tory, who was going to change things. Unsentimental, 'there is no society'; the politics were very English. Of course that wouldn't translate into film, and also it wouldn't translate into film five years later, because John Major was then in charge, and the whole climate had changed. So it was very much of the moment, the character or Marion. The other character, Isobel, had a rather wider and a longer shelf-life, but Marion didn't, so it had to become more about her relationship with her sister. In the stage play, although it was very importantly about her relationship with her sister, it was also about all these other influences which were around, and pervading society at the time. I did know about her from acting in the play, but it became a much more personal thing in the film.

I think she loved Isobel, as you do love your sister, but I don't think she liked her, and I think she was terribly jealous of her, of that free-spirit in people. In Marion's speech, she says, 'Those do-gooders, these people, they can jolly well get a job. If you don't benefit, that's not good enough. Get on your bike', as Norman Tebbit said, and get a job, go where the work is. And also, she had a career, and life had to be sorted. The family was in one compartment, and I think she was terribly, fantastically jealous of Isobel who seemed to drift through life. Everyone liked Isobel, whereas Marion was older and had a less attractive personality. I think she wasn't favoured, Isobel was favoured. She was the pretty little one, and I think Marion was the tall, thin little thing who people didn't warm to. She was dark and thin and cross.

Stage acting: 'a rough thing to do'

Actors are inclined to say they like to be treated like folks; a lot of them say that, but I don't think they really think it! I think they quite like to be recognised: 'Oh yes, here I am'. I think the reality is – and I'm just an actress, and a stage actress to boot, I don't make a lot of films – that acting is a much more down-to-earth thing to do than people make out. You have to be quite strong physically; you have to have stamina; you have to be quite brave, because you can be knocked down like that (snaps fingers) by a lot of critics, if they don't like what you're doing. You spit in people's faces on stage, and you shout every evening at half-past seven. You have to fill a theatre, you have to wear big make-up. There's nothing *pretty* about it. If something goes wrong you have to get out of it. You turn to an actor who might look wonderful from the front, and there's sweat pouring off his face because it's boiling hot, or your wig's hurting. It's a pretty rough thing to do, actually, and it's very hard work. Every evening except Sunday and two matinées, you do this play. You don't get paid a lot of money. And you still have to go to Sainsbury's. You don't have much of chance to get big-headed. But then I'm not a film star; film stars have a lot of people working for them, and they're building an image of this person that is just like anyone else, less intelligent, often. Some of them are very intelligent, I'm sure, but they're out selling themselves. I'm not out selling me, I'm out selling *The Cherry Orchard*, hopefully, or *Long Day's Journey Into Night*. I'm not too interested in people knowing me personally, because then they'll never believe in you on the stage; they'll think 'Oh, that's Penelope Wilton'. I'd like them to think, 'Oh, that was Madame Ranevskaya', or 'That was Mary Tyrone'. I'd like them to see that person and not know what I had for breakfast. Because if you know too much about a person, there's nothing secret about them.

The only trouble is that now we're in a world where you have to publicise everything, so you have to be interviewed and have your photograph around, so people can know that the play is on. But it's awfully tiring, and it's a side that you have to do, just so people will come see the play, because that's what you want. I don't think I'm being modest, I'm just saying what most actors are like. I mean, I love it when people like a play, when I get letters saying 'I love it!', because it means that I have moved somebody. But I don't particularly like the other side that much, I don't have time for it, really. And also, as you get older, you realise that it's very time-consuming.

Americans act from the guts, the British from the head

I don't think it's an entirely false dichotomy; there is some truth in it. I think because historically we have dealt a great deal with the spoken word, and theatre has, it would be fair to say, played a larger part in our lives, perhaps as films have in the American actors' repertoire. But I think we are more used to using words probably because we had to do it, and most English actors spend certainly quite a lot of their time in the theatre doing the classics, which I don't think is the case with American actors.

It's also to do with our repertoire, which doesn't have a lot of Millers and O'Neills in it, and other great American writers. We have a great deal of comedy, and Shakespeare, and people who require a different way of playing. I also think it's got something to do with how we are as people. I think Americans aren't embarrassed, or find it easier to express themselves more straightforwardly, and I think we go on a more circuitous route. I don't know why that is, but it just happens to be how we are. That isn't to say that there aren't fantastically gutsy actors here, and I hope, given the role, you could play it.

Photograph Credits

The publishers wish to acknowledge the following for permission to use stills:

Copyright © BBC for *Duchess of Malfi, 102 Boulevard Haussmann, Absolute Hell, Marie Curie, Portrait of a Marriage, Hedda Gabler, Freud, House of Cards* and *Yes Minister*
Alex Bailey for *The Madness of King George*
Shiela Burnett for photograph of Jane Lapotaire
Channel Four for *The Secret Rapture*
Clive Coote for photograph of Ian Richardson
Copyright 1997 Danjaq, LLC & United Artists Corp for photograph of Judi Dench
Zoë Dominic for *As You Like It* and *Hedda Gabler* (Janet Suzman)
Jake Fitz-Jones for photograph of Antony Sher
Brenda Fricker and Joan O'Hara in the Gate Theatre's production of *The Weeping of Angels* by Joseph O'Connor - photograph by Tom Lawlor
Hugh Glendinning for photograph of Simon Callow
Granada Television Limited for *My Left Foot*
Sasha Gusov for photograph of Penelope Wilton
John Haynes for *A Delicate Balance*
© Neil Libbert/Network for *Electra* and *Stanley*
LWT for *Poirot*
Alastair Muir for *A Doll's House*
Fatimah Namdar for photograph of Brenda Fricker
Miranda Richardson and Willem Dafoe in *Tom & Viv* © Samuelson Productions Ltd 1994
Ronald Grant Archive for *Angel*
Shakespeare Centre Library, Stratford-upon-Avon for *Macbeth*, The Other Place (1976), *The Cherry Orchard*, Swan Theatre (1996), *Henry VIII*, Swan Theatre (1996), *Cyrano De Bergerac*, Swan Theatre (1997), all Royal Shakespeare Company Productions.
Trustees of the National Library of Scotland for *Orlando*

The Publisher has made every effort to contact the copyright holders of the photographs used in this book. In some cases this has not proved possible and the Publisher apologises to any copyright holder whose work has been used without specific permission.

Index